Karl Barth's Doctrine of Holy Scripture

Karl Barth's Doctrine of Holy Scripture

by
Klaas Runia
*Vice-Principal and Professor of Theology,
Reformed Theological College,
Geelong, Victoria, Australia*

Wipf & Stock
PUBLISHERS
Eugene, Oregon

Wipf and Stock Publishers
199 W 8th Ave, Suite 3
Eugene, OR 97401

Karl Barth's Doctrine of Holy Scripture
By Runia, Klaas
Copyright©1962 by Runia, Klaas
ISBN 13: 978-1-5326-6370-3
Publication date 7/27/2018
Previously published by Wm. B. Eerdmans, 1962

FOREWORD

No matter how we assess it, the *Church Dogmatics* of Karl Barth is one of the greatest forces in the modern theological world. In its vastness and variety, its comprehensiveness and detail, it constitutes a challenge to every school. Nor is it to be met by caricature or sweeping generalization. The individual themes demand searching analysis and appraisal at the exegetical, historical, and dogmatic levels at which Barth himself develops them. Only on the basis of detailed treatment can there be ultimate understanding and assessment of the whole.

It is because Dr. Runia tackles this preliminary problem that his present work is so significant. He does not add to the list of general books. Choosing a critical and sensitive area, he devotes himself to the concentrated task of presenting the Barthian teaching on inspiration in its normative form. In the course of his analysis he examines the proposed biblical basis of Barth's statement and brings it into lively interaction with the Reformation tradition which Barth believes that he represents. By means of a thorough inquiry into the single point, Dr. Runia thus gives us a far more informative, stimulating, and authoritative criticism than is possible in more comprehensive studies.

The result is a valuable work which deserves to be widely studied and which should serve as a model for similar investigations into the many detailed themes of the *Dogmatics*. It is characterized by an honesty and relevance which gives it more than a narrowly academic interest. The real problems are faced, and it is candidly seen that there may be deficiencies in even the most orthodox of statements. Yet the great verities of the traditional doctrine emerge the clearer and stronger for this powerful discussion, and in such a way that they may again make their salutary impact on a wider theological front.

—G. W. Bromiley

PREFACE

Hardly any Christian doctrine is discussed so much today as the doctrine of Holy Scripture. Innumerable books are published about it, and official discussions in many Churches are concerned with it. We think, e.g., of the report "The Holy Bible: Its Authority and Message," which was presented to the Lambeth Conference of 1958;[1] of the Statement on Scripture adopted at the 1958 Synodical Conference Convention of the Lutheran Church in America (Missouri Synod);[2] and of the discussion now going on in the Christian Reformed Church (U.S.A. and Canada).[3] There is, moreover, discussion on the ecumenical level: the Fourth Reformed Ecumenical Synod (Potchefstroom, South Africa, 1958), e.g., discussed the problem at length,[4] and at the National Conference of Australian Churches (Melbourne, 1960), one of the major committees studied the authority of the Word of God, primarily as that Word is mediated in Holy Scripture.[5]

We may add that the doctrine of Karl Barth plays a great part, whether positively or negatively, in all of these discussions and reports. So great is his stature that no one can deal with the problem of Holy Scripture without considering Barth's view and defining his own position over against it.[6] Indeed, many aspects of Barth's view have come to be generally accepted as beyond criticism. We refer, e.g., to his teaching that there

---

1. *The Lambeth Conference, 1958*, Part II, pp. 1-18.
2. Cf. *The Lutheran Witness*, Feb. 24, 1959.
3. Cf. *Acts of Synod, 1959*, pp. 62f., 73, 87f. and *Acts 1961*, pp. 253ff.
4. *Acts of the Fourth Ecumenical Synod of Potchefstroom*, August 6-13, 1958, pp. 33-56.
5. *We Were Brought Together, Report of the National Conference of Australian Churches, 1960*, pp. 15ff.
6. It is one of the defects of that excellent book by J. I. Packer, *Fundamentalism and the Word of God*, 1958, that it hardly touches the Barthian view. Only on p. 159 is it mentioned in passing.

is an indirect identity between the Bible and the Word of God, that the Bible is a fallible human book subject to higher criticism, and that the Bible becomes the Word of God in the act of revelation.

Such uncritical acceptance is itself a good reason to devote a special study to Barth's doctrine of Holy Scripture, even though the latter was published over twenty years ago.[7] At the same time we must admit that such a study is a difficult task. Barth's thought is, on the one hand, wide-ranging and deep, and on the other hand, sensitive to nuances and details. Frequently he expresses himself paradoxically, in the dialectical mode. Hence it is no wonder that Barth is so often misinterpreted. To guard against this danger we will quote his own words extensively, so that the reader may hear Barth himself.

Another feature of the present study is its heavy reliance upon Reformed theological literature in the Dutch language. The reason is twofold: first, the Dutch Reformed tradition is the author's own; and second, this book represents an attempt by one who now stands at the juncture of different traditions to use that position advantageously. The correlation and cross-fertilization of theological traditions is not only desirable, it is a duty not to be neglected.

Finally, I wish to express my appreciation for all the work done by my colleague, the Rev. Alexander Barkley, M.A., Principal of the Reformed Theological College, Geelong, Victoria, Australia. He read the whole manuscript carefully and suggested many valuable stylistic improvements. The two foregoing sentences are probably the only ones he has not read before the publishing of this book!

—KLAAS RUNIA

7. *C.D.* I, 1 was first published in 1932, and *C.D.* I, 2 in 1938. (Hereafter *C.D.* will refer to Barth's *Church Dogmatics* in English translation, and *K.D.* to *Kirchliche Dogmatik* in the original German).

CONTENTS

Foreword by G. W. Bromiley   v

Preface   vii

1 The Starting Point   1
2 Scripture as a Witness to Divine Revelation   18
3 The Humanity and Fallibility of the Bible   57
4 "Proofs" of the Fallibility of the Bible   81
5 The Bible as the Word of God   116
6 Inspiration or Theopneustia   137
7 The Authority of the Bible   169
8 Basic Motifs   189

Karl Barth's Doctrine of Holy Scripture

CHAPTER I

THE STARTING POINT

From the early years of his ministry in one of the country-parishes of Switzerland, Karl Barth was captivated by the problem of Scripture. Nor was this problem merely a theoretical one. As a young minister in Safenwil (1911-1921) Barth had to preach twice every Sunday, and thus these questions forced themselves upon his mind time and again: What is preaching? What does it mean to proclaim the Word of God? What is God's Word itself? How can the preacher, himself a human being, bring this Word of God to others?

In a 1922 lecture on "The Need and Promise of Christian Preaching" Barth himself says that his theology

> did not come into being as the result of any desire of ours to form a school or to devise a system; it arose simply out of what we felt to be the 'need and promise of Christian Preaching'. . . . For twelve years I was a minister as all of you are. I *had* my theology. It was not really mine, to be sure, but that of my unforgotten teacher Wilhelm Herrmann, grafted upon the principles which I had learned, less consciously, in my native home — the principles of those Reformed Churches which today I represent. . . . Once in the ministry, I found myself growing away from these theological habits of thought and being forced back at every point more and more upon the specific *minister's* problem, the sermon.[1]

To find the answer to this burning problem of the sermon Barth (and many of his friends, such as Eduard Thurneysen,

---

1. Karl Barth, *The Word of God and the Word of Man*, 1957, p. 100. Cf. Ed. Thurneysen in the Introduction to the correspondence between Barth and himself in those early years, in *Antwort*, Karl Barth zum siebstigen Geburtstag am 10 May, 1956, 832ff. "Aus der Predigtarbeit ist sie [Barth's theology] gewachsen, und der Verkuendigung der Kirche dient sie."

Emil Brunner, Friedrich Gogarten and others) began to study the Bible anew. For only the Bible could give this answer. In joyful recollection Thurneysen later on wrote:

> We read the Bible in a new way. We read it more respectfully, more as an eternal Word addressed to us and to our time. We criticized it less. We read it with the eyes of shipwrecked people, whose all had gone overboard. The Bible appeared in a new light. Beyond all interpretations, its genuine word began to speak again; the word of forgiveness, the Gospel of the coming Kingdom.[2]

To understand these words and the attitude underlying them we must recall the time in which these young men had to perform their ministry. It was during the dark years of World War I, and the almost-even-darker postwar years. Suddenly men were confronted with the complete bankruptcy of the prewar optimistic idealism. How could one preach to people living in such a disillusioned world?

Barth and his friends had been trained in the Liberal theology. Could it still help them? The answer was a clear and plain No. In their new study of the Bible they discovered that the message of liberalism was quite different from the scriptural preaching. Liberalism not only was characterized by the same discredited idealism, but, far worse, it appeared to have a wholly incorrect and distorted conception of God and His revelation. In liberalism God and man were practically on the same level. God's immanence received all the emphasis, at the cost of His transcendence. As a result revelation was no longer revelation of God and by God, but nothing else than man's discovery of God, man's idea about God. The Christian faith was completely detached from its basis and center, namely, God's free and sovereign revelation in Jesus Christ. The theocentric starting point was exchanged for the anthropocentric, and God's self-revelation was entirely subjectivized into a human notion about God. From their new discovery of God's revelation Barth and his friends could only speak a heartfelt No to liberal theology. Later on in the preface of the first volume of his *Church Dogmatics*, Barth declares emphatically that in any thinkable re-adoption or continuation of the Schleiermacher-Ritschl-Herrmann approach he can see only

---

2. Quoted by John McConnachie, *The Barthian Theology and the Man of Today*, 1933, p. 94.

the plain destruction of Protestant theology and the Protestant Church. "I can only say No here."³

But what, then, about Orthodoxy? Could orthodoxy be the solution? Could it provide the help and understanding which they needed so badly? Here again the No had to be sounded. It is true that orthodoxy had preserved many scriptural truths lost sight of by liberalism, but it was exactly at this point that the knife of criticism had to begin its work. In orthodoxy the divine revelation had been frozen into a system of truths which man could *have*. Again man considered himself able to control God and to dispose of His revelation. Moreover, the authority of the living, sovereign, revealing God was identified with the authority of a book, and again God's revelation became a human possession. To say it in Barth's own words:

> The weakness of orthodoxy is not the supernatural element in the Bible; on the contrary, in that lies its strength. It is rather the fact that orthodoxy has a way of regarding some objective description of an element, such as the word "God," as if it were the element itself.⁴

Barth saw, and still sees, this weakness of orthodoxy coming particularly to the fore in the doctrine of verbal inspiration. Here man again has imprisoned God and thinks that he can control God's revelation, completely forgetting that God's revelation is God Himself, God in His act of revelation, and that therefore God's revelation can never be "caught" by man or brought under human control.

Against the background of these considerations Barth saw as *the* great task for the present and future to think through again the category of revelation. Was not the great defect of both liberalism and orthodoxy the same? Did not each, in its own way, fail to perceive what revelation is? In both cases the corruption was such that a mere reconstruction on the old foundations would not do. The only cure for theology and thus for the Church and her proclamation would be a complete and thorough rethinking of what divine revelation really is.

* * *

To this task Barth has devoted many years. Throughout all his earlier works we see him struggling with this gigantic task. The maturest results of this "rethinking" we find in the

---

3. *C.D.*, I, 1, x.
4. *Ibid.*

two parts of the first volume of his *Church Dogmatics,* entitled "The Doctrine of the Word of God" and published respectively in 1932 and 1938. Both parts are largely[5] dedicated to the question of the Word of God, and that in its threefold form.[6] First (not chronologicallq, but as it comes to us), there is the *Word of God as preached;* second, there is the *written Word of God;* third (but logically first), there is the *Revealed Word of God in Jesus Christ,* the incarnate Son of God. This distinction does not mean, of course, that there are several Words of God.

> It is one and the same, whether we regard it as revelation, as the Bible, or as proclamation. There is no distinction of degree or value between these three forms. For so far as proclamation really rests upon recollection of the revelation attested in the Bible and is therefore the obedient repetition of the Biblical witness, it is no less the Word of God than the Bible. And so far as the Bible really attests revelation, it is no less the Word of God then revelation itself.[7]

But however great the inseparable unity is, yet there is room for distinction. The revelation in Jesus Christ is not the Bible

---

5. We deliberately say "largely." In the first part Barth also deals, for example, with the doctrine of the Trinity, the incarnation, and the outpouring of the Holy Spirit. According to Barth we must begin with these doctrines, for we can speak of Holy Scripture only when we know Him who revealed Himself in it. As a matter of fact, as soon as we put to the Bible the question about revelation, we immediately meet with the problem of the doctrine of the Trinity. For "when we ask, Who is the self-revealing God, the Bible answers us in such a way that we are impelled to consider the Three-in-oneness of God." (I, 1, 348). For the Bible says: *God* reveals Himself, God reveals *through Himself,* God reveals *Himself.*

6. We find this distinction already in Barth's early works. For example, in his article in *Zwischen der Zeiten,* 1925, entitled "Das Schriftprinzip der reformierten Kirche" (The Scriptural Principle of the Reformed Church) p. 228. "Between the Word of God, that there and then became flesh, and the Word of God that today and here has to be preached and heard, stands (not to be separated from it, but only to be distinguished) the Word of God as Holy Scripture, the bridge over the abyss of time, the bridge by which we, who are not apostles and prophets, are made partakers of and simultaneous with the revelation." Later on this distinction was taken up again and worked out in *Die Christliche Dogmatik* of 1927 (pp. 37-46). In the first volume of the *Church Dogmatics* of 1932 it obtained its final form. (E.T. pp. 98-140). A very good analysis of this threefold distinction with its implications is given by John K. S. Reid, *The Authority of Scripture,* A Study of the Reformation and Post-Reformation Understanding of the Bible, 1957, pp. 194ff.

7. *C.D.,* I, 1, 136.

and the proclamation of the Church is not the Bible. It is even impossible to reverse the order. "The first one, revelation [in Jesus Christ], is the form which establishes the other two." But immediately it must be added: "It [the revelation in Jesus Christ] itself never meets us anywhere in abstract form, our knowledge of it is only indirect, arising out of Scripture or in proclamation."[8]

On the ground of this distinction it is therefore possible for us to focus our special attention in this book upon the second of the three forms, which is the indispensable link between the other two, namely, the *written Word of God,* Holy Scripture. At the same time, however, we will remember the unity and so will discuss Barth's view of Scripture in continuous reference particularly to the basic form of the Word of God, namely, the Revealed Word in Jesus Christ.

* * *

What now is Barth's *starting point* in the doctrine of Holy Scripture? It is simply this: our view concerning Holy Scripture is a *matter of faith.* It cannot be proved on scientific or any other grounds. It is only a matter of obedient listening to what the Bible itself says about itself. And this holds true of both aspects under which, according to Barth, the Bible must be discussed, namely, Holy Scripture as a Witness of Divine Revelation, and Holy Scripture as the Word of God.

How important this starting point is to Barth, clearly appears from the fact that he begins and ends his exposition of the doctrine of Holy Scripture with this thesis.

* * *

He immediately *begins* with it.

In the quest for the essential character of the Bible we can only obey the witness of the Bible itself. Only and exactly in this obedience we know that the Bible is the normative Word of God.

We cannot appeal to any authority outside the Scriptures. We cannot appeal, for example, to the mind of man as was done by Rationalism, or to the religious consciousness of man as Schleiermacher and his followers did, or to the results of human scientific or historical investigation as nineteenth-century criticism asserted. Against all these attempts Barth de-

8. *Ibid.*

clares: "The Lordship of the Triune God proves itself to be a *fact* in our obedient listening to the witness of the Bible."[9] It can also be said in a different way: The doctrine of Holy Scripture is a *confession*. Such a confession is necessary because we are permanently questioned concerning our attitude towards Scripture from three sides. First, by Holy Scripture itself, which always wants us to know what we are doing when we obey it. Second, by other men, who propose that we should take up some other attitude, and sincerely or insincerely want to know whether we are aware of the meaning or consequences of what we are doing. And third, by ourselves, inasmuch as obedience and disobedience are constantly at war with each other especially in ourselves.[10]

Here, of course, the question arises immediately whether all of this is not reasoning in a circle. Is it not a weak, even an impossible and untenable position to say: We believe the Bible on the ground of the testimony of the Bible itself? At least from one side the answer is an accusing Yes. The Church of Rome charges the Reformation with reasoning in a circle here and then proudly points us to its own solution. It is the Church which declares authoritatively that the Bible is the Word of God, and this declaration provides the believers with the necessary ground for their personal acceptance of the Bible as the Word of God. This does not mean that according to Rome the Bible derives its authority from the Church. Even Rome holds that the authority of the Bible is of divine origin and nature. But this authority can be acknowledged and accepted only on the ground of the Church's Spirit-guided declaration and affirmation.

Barth, however, is not in the least impressed by the Roman Catholic charge, nor does he consider its solution to be valid. On the contrary, he sounds a definite No against Rome, and maintains vigorously that only Scripture itself, that is, God Himself can give us the answer here. Because Scripture is the Word of God, there is no higher authority from which it can obtain its authority. If this were so, the Bible would not be God's Word. For there is no higher authority than God Himself. Therefore only Scripture itself can give the answer, and

---

9. *C.D.*, I, 2, 458.
10. *Ibid.*, 461.

it does so, for "the Bible in fact answers our question about revelation, bringing us before the Triune God."[11]

Barth also *ends* his discussion of the doctrine of Holy Scripture by citing faith as the only possible starting point. He first stresses that this must not be understood in the sense that our faith *makes* the Bible the Word of God. That would mean again that man dominates and controls the revelation and that revelation is subjectivized. No, revelation is not a subjective fact — though it certainly has a bearing on the subject, that is, the reader or listener — but an objective fact. It is an act of God. And then Barth repeats once more: We can accept this only in faith and obedience to the Bible itself.

> The statement that the Bible is the Word of God is an *analytical* statement, a statement which is grounded only in its repetition, description and interpretation, and not in its derivation from any major proposition.[12]

In a lecture on the Authority and Significance of the Bible, held at the Ecumenical Institute at Bossey (Switzerland) in 1946,[13] Barth has elucidated this term "analytical statement" by the following simple example. When you ask a boy: Why do you call among all women this one your mother?, his only answer is: Because, of course, she *is* my mother. That is the *fact* upon which he proceeds. In the same way all our statements about the Bible can only be explanations of the fact that the Bible is the Word of God. "The Bible must be known as the Word of *God,* if it is to be *known* as the Word of God."

In this same connection Barth himself takes up the phrase "logical circle" as the apt expression of the Protestant view.

> The doctrine of Holy Scripture in the Evangelical Church is that this logical circle is the circle of self-asserting, self-attesting truth, into which it is equally impossible to enter as it is to emerge from it: The circle of our freedom, which as such is also the circle of our captivity.[14]

So it was said already by the sixteenth-century Reformation against Rome with its appeal to the authority of the Church. Calvin, for example, wrote in his *Institutes* that we might as well ask where we can base the distinction of light from dark-

---

11. *Ibid.,* 462.
12. *Ibid.,* 535.
13. Published in the Dutch magazine *In de Waagschaal,* II, 38ff.
14. *C.D.,* I, 2, 535.

ness, of white from black, of sweet from sour,[15] while the Second Helvetic Confession of 1562 said in Art. 1:

> We believe and confess the canonical Scriptures of the holy prophets and apostles of both Testaments to be the true Word of God, and to have *sufficient authority of themselves, not of men.* For God Himself spake (*Deus ipse locutus est*) to the fathers, prophets and apostles and still speaks (*loquitur adhuc*) to us through the Holy Scriptures.[16]

* * *

We cannot but express our hearty agreement with this starting point of Barth. It is not only in full harmony with the view of the Reformation, but also with the *clear teaching of the Bible about itself.* Nowhere does the Bible appeal to any external authority in order to vindicate its own authority, but it appeals directly to God Himself and presents itself as the Word of God. As Calvin says:

> The prophets and apostles boast not their own acuteness, or any qualities which win credit to speakers, nor do they dwell on reasons; but they appeal to the sacred name of God, in order that the whole world may be compelled to submission.[17]

The beginning and the end of all their speaking is: "Thus says the Lord."[18] Here is no room for any argument. Here man can only obey or revolt.

If the Bible is the Word of God, it can only provide its own proof. There is in this world no higher authority from which the Bible can derive its authority. It is in a class by itself and cannot be included in any sequence of authorities, of which it would be a part and with which it could be compared. The only attitude possible is that of reverent obedience and acceptance. "Deus ipse locutus est et loquitur adhuc." God Himself spoke and still speaks.

We can make this clear, for instance, by the example of archaeology. It cannot be denied that archaeology is very important for the study of the Bible. Recent discoveries have very strongly supported its truthfulness, as the famous archaeologist William F. Albright has recently written:

---

15. Calvin, *Instit.*, I, vii, 2.
16. Translation from P. Schaff, *The Creeds of Christendom*, III, 831.
17. Calvin, *Instit.*, I, vii, 4.
18. According to Dr. James H. Brookes this phrase or its equivalent is used 2,000 times by the writers of the Old Testament. Cf. Charles L. Feinberg, *The Fundamentals for Today*, 1958, I, 132.

Thanks to modern research we now recognize its [the Old Testament's] substantial historicity. The narratives of the patriarchs, of Moses and the exodus, of the conquest of Canaan, of the judges, the monarchy, the exile and restoration, have all been confirmed and illustrated to an extent that I should have thought impossible forty years ago. . . . The background of Moses and his contributions to religion and law take definite form in the light of our present knowledge. . . . The prophets of Israel are now better understood; they stand out more brilliantly than ever. The critical school associated with the name of Julius Wellhausen recognized their outstanding significance as social and ethical reformers, but failed to grasp two vitally important principles: the place of the covenant and related concepts in prophetic thinking, and the vital role of insight into the future.[19]

It is obvious that these conclusions of Prof. Albright are of the greatest importance for our view of the Bible. In clear words it is stated here that the facts as recorded by the Bible are true — which indeed is an indispensable condition for our belief in the Bible as the Word of God. Yet we should not overestimate the value and significance of such conclusions. For when we ask the question: Has it been proved now that the Bible is the *Word of God?*, we must say no. Archaeology can only prove that the facts are correctly recorded by the Bible. But the Bible is far more than a record of facts. It is primarily a very specific interpretation of the facts recorded. It is not mere historiography, to be compared, for example, with the records given by a Herodotus or a Thucydides, but it is historiography of a very special sort: it is prophetic historiography. This holds of both the Old and the New Testament. As to the Old Testament, we need only point to the fact that the Jews themselves counted the books which we call "historical" among the "nebiim," the prophetic literature. As to the New Testament, the Gospels, for example, do not give us a mere enumeration of the facts of Christ's life, but they describe His preaching and miracles, His suffering and death in the light of the resurrection. This latter fact is, as it were, the prism through which the essential nature of this entire life is discovered and revealed. In itself this life is ambiguous and liable to various interpretations — as history clearly proves! That we accept this man Jesus of Nazareth as the Divine Re-

---

19. William F. Albright, "Return to Biblical Theology," *The Christian Century*, Nov. 19, 1958.

deemer, whose death was the satisfaction for our sins, and whose resurrection was the conquest of death, is only because we accept the interpretation given by the biblical writers as the divine interpretation.

It is perfectly evident that this interpretative dimension of the Bible, which constitutes its essential nature as the Word of God, falls completely outside the scope of archaeology or any other science. It is the Bible itself as the Word of God which imposes its truth upon us. And the only task left for archaeology is that of confirming the historical reality of the facts which lie at the basis of the scriptural message.[20]

With Barth we cannot emphasize enough that the divine revelation can only prove itself, and for that reason we have to renounce all human proofs. The authority of the Bible rests in itself. Rightly Bavinck says:

> Holy Scripture is "autopistos" [i.e., it brings out faith in itself] and therefore is the last ground of faith. The question: Why do you believe in Scripture?, can only be answered in this way: Because it is the Word of God. But if then it is asked: Why do you believe that Holy Scripture is the Word of God?, the Christian has no further answer.[21]

Whoever wishes to call this a "logical circle" may freely do so. With good reason Barth is not at all afraid of this charge. He even openly admits that this is the only possibility. In the last volume of his *Church Dogmatics,* in which he deals with the prophetic office of the Mediator, he says the same with regard to the doctrine of Christ:

> We reasoned as follows: The statement of the prophecy of the life of Jesus Christ holds true, because and while it is the statement of the life of Jesus Christ! Therefore a petitio principii? A circular argument? Yes, indeed. . . . Honny soit, qui mal y pense! Only the fools will say in their heart that this is a cir-

---

20. Cf. André Parrot, *Discovering Buried Worlds* (SCM Press, 1955), p. 111, where Professor Parrot recognizes this point of view, although does not himself agree with it: "'Archaeology, while perhaps confirming certain historical facts, has been unable to do more than that. Above all, it has never proved that in those facts God was really and truly revealing Himself.'" This was the reaction — and rightly so! — against Sir Charles Marston's book on archaeological discoveries, published in 1935 under the title *The Bible Is True.* The same criticism holds against Werner Keller's *The Bible as History,* 1956.

21. H. Bavinck, *Gereformeerde Dogmatiek,* 1928, I, 559.

cular argument. As if there would not and should not be a circular argument in this matter!²²

The Christian faith and Christian theology need not be ashamed of this charge of a "logical circle." On the contrary! It is the very condition of their existence. As soon as they abandon it, they will not be any more *Christian* faith and *Christian* theology. Precisely this offense, this "skandalon" is the proof of their genuineness.

All attempts to explain this circle away, however well-intended they may be, actually mean an undermining of the basis. Unfortunately Reformed theology, too, has sometimes been guilty of this. In particular, during the last century and the first decades of this century many attempts have been made to remove this so-called offense. So, for example, Berkhof in the *Introductory Volume to Systematic Theology* argues as follows in defense of the doctrine of inspiration:

> It is possible, for the sake of argument, to start off with the assumption that the books of the Bible are purely human productions, which, however, as the productions of eye-and-ear-witnesses, which are known as men of high moral standing, can be regarded as entirely trustworthy. Then it can be shown that according to these books, Christ and the apostles held the strictest view of the inspiration of the Old Testament. From that point it is quite possible to reach the conclusion that the Old Testament necessarily required a complement such as is found in the New Testament. And on the basis of this it can be said that therefore the whole Bible must be regarded as an inspired book. By reasoning in that fashion the circle is avoided.²³

According to Berkhof this same line of argument was used by other Reformed theologians, such as Bannerman, Patton, Warfield, and Van Oosterzee. Undoubtedly there were good intentions behind this apologetic attitude. It was the aim, against what was in many regards unfair criticism from the rationalistic-liberal side, to show that the Christian faith is not contrary to reason and does not require sacrifice of the intellect.

Barth would certainly agree fully with these latter statements. He has very often been charged with anti-intellectualism and

---

22. *K.D.*, IV, 3a, 1959, p. 95.
23. L. Berkhof, *Introductory Volume to Systematic Theology*, 1932, p. 156.

irrationalism, but this charge does not at all correspond with his views. In connection with the fact that God's revelation comes to man in the form of language ("God's Word" means "God speaks") he emphatically *rejects* all anti-intellectualism of the sort that had been in vogue for so many years.

> We might very well be of the private opinion that it would be better and nicer if God had not spoken and did not speak with such deliberate "intellectualism" and that it would be more appropriate to God if "God's Word" meant all sorts of different things, apart from the meaning "God speaks."[24]

But our opinion is not decisive. We have to accept the fact that God *does* speak. God has chosen this way of communication, for "the form in which reason communicates with reason, person with person, is language; so too when it is God's language."[25] Of course we have to add immediately that in this case "it is divine reason that communicates with human reason, the divine person with the human." But none the less it is language. "The Word of God — we should not evade the concept so much tabooed today — is a rational and not an irrational event."[26] Later on, in dealing with the relation between the Word of God and experience, Barth speaks of the "extra-ordinary polemic which it has been fashion in recent years to wage against the so-called 'intellect' of man, his powers of comprehension and thought, as a center of possible religious experience of the Word of God."[27] Here Barth asks the question whether this anti-intellectualism is not an entirely wrong effort after holiness, as if other anthropological possibilities (for example, man's feeling or his conscience) would constitute a more suitable instrument to appropriate the revelation. Barth sees in modern anti-intellectualism nothing else than a form of *hubris,* the pride of sinful man, who in some way or other wants to be independent of God. After realizing that the way of rationalism leads nowhere, man now tries to reach this goal by anti- or irrationalism. And so Barth can say:

> Even the idea of the *sacrificium intellectus* is but a last desperate attempt to make of the knowledge of God a work of man,

---

24. *C.D.,* I, 1, 150.
25. *Ibid.,* p. 152.
26. *Ibid.*
27. *Ibid.,* p. 231.

to have a human possibility correspond to what is the sole work of God.[28]

From these sketchy remarks it is altogether obvious that Barth would fully agree with Berkhof, when the latter contends that the Christian faith is not anti- or irrational. Yet there is a decisive difference between Barth and the above-mentioned Reformed apologists. The latter, in their apologetic endeavor, actually place themselves on the level of their antagonists. They try to vindicate the Christian faith before the bar of human reason. Apparently Berkhof himself felt the essential impossibility of this attempt, for immediately after the apologetic argument he continues:

> It is a question whether the circle referred to is really as vicious as some would have us believe. Jesus evidently did not think so, when a similar objection was raised against His testimony concerning Himself as the incarnate Word of God, John 8:13ff.[29]

This passage from John is most appropriate. Though its concern is with the person of Jesus Christ, it concerns Him (to use Barth's phraseology) as the Revealed Word and consequently it applies also to the written Word of God, which is the Word about Him. Jesus is charged here by the Pharisees of bearing witness to Himself and that this witness is not true (v. 13). And what is Jesus' defense? Does He appeal to any earthly authority to "prove" His own authority? Does He adduce rational or emotional or experiential "proofs" for His self-witness and self-assertion? No, He only points to His origin from God and His going to God. "I know whence I came, and whither I go" (v. 14). He appeals to His being sent by the Father: "I am not alone, but I and the Father that sent me" (v. 16). In other words:

> His only answer to the Pharisees' incredulity was latent in His original declaration, that He was the light of the world, be-

---

28. *Ibid.*, p. 283. We could also point to Barth's work on Anselm's proof of the existence of God, *Fides Quaerens Intellectum*, 1931. Here Barth defends Anselm against the criticism of natural theology and asserts that Anselm's whole argument is an argument on the basis of faith. The order of Anselm would be: revelation-faith-reason. *"Fides* quaerens intellectum"!

29. Berkhof, *op. cit.*, pp. 156, 157. Cf. p. 125: "If there is a revelation then this itself must shed light on its essential nature and thus supply us with a standard of judgment."

cause light needs no witness; it demonstrates its reality by its own radiance.[30]

We find the same in the sequel of the conversation, when the Jews, helpless in their lack of understanding, ask Jesus: "Who art thou?". Jesus' answer consists only in an immediate appeal to His being sent by the Father: "Even that which I have spoken unto you from the beginning . . . howbeit he that sent me is true; and the things which I heard from him, these speak I unto the world" (vv. 25, 26). Another "proof" than this authoritative testimony cannot be given. Jesus' words are true and "prove" themselves to be true, because He is the Son of God. His words are God's Word and this equation constitutes their authority in an altogether final way. And the same applies to the Bible as the Word of God and thus as the only and final ground of the Christian faith.[31]

Sometimes this unique starting point of the Christian faith regarding the Bible has been called an *axiom*, and has been compared with the axioms that underlie the various sciences.[32] But the resemblance is purely formal and can easily mislead. Materially there is an essential difference. In science axioms are truths which are self-evident and self-evidenced. They cannot be proved, but they need not be proved either. Every thinking being is immediately convinced of their truth. Now it is certainly true that the Bible as the Word of God is also self-evident, but this self-evidence is of an entirely different nature. For natural man does not see it at all. Only when the Holy Spirit has opened his blind eyes does this self-evidence of the Bible become visible to him. We therefore fully agree with Barth when he says:

> The astonishing statement that the Bible is God's Word has been called an axiom. But it is such only in its logical form. In content its certainty is wholly unlike the self-evidenced certainty of mathematical axioms. It expresses rather the self-evidenced *revelation* which God gives simultaneously to his Biblical

---

30. Merrill C. Tenney, *John, The Gospel of Belief*, 1954, pp. 144, 145. Cf. Calvin *ad locum*: "By these words (I know whence I came) he declares that his origin is not from the world, but that he proceeded from God, and therefore that it would be unjust and unreasonable that his doctrine, which is divine, should be subjected to the laws of men."
31. Cf. Alan M. Stibbs in *Revelation and the Bible*, ed. Carl F. H. Henry, 1958, p. 108.
32. Cf. Bavinck, *op. cit.*, pp. 558f.

witnesses and to those who accept their witness. It expresses obedience to the *testimonium Spiritus Sancti internum* (the internal testimony of the Holy Spirit), to the Spirit of God, in which the human spirit of the writer and the reader become one in common adoration.[33]

In these last words we indeed have come to the moving cause of our faith in Holy Scripture: the *testimony of the Holy Spirit in the heart of the believers*. Calvin, in particular, has from the beginning stressed the necessity of this testimony:

> For as God alone can properly bear witness to men, so these words will not obtain full credit in the hearts of men, until they are sealed by the inward testimony of the Spirit. The Spirit, therefore, who spoke by the mouth of the prophets, must penetrate our hearts, in order to convince us that they faithfully delivered the message with which they were divinely entrusted.[34]

No wonder, therefore, that Barth in his discussion of the Bible as the Word of God also refers to this testimony.[35] Yet there is also the remarkable fact that he only mentions it, but does not give a detailed description of it.[36] The only function it has here is to stress "the free and gracious act of God's turning to us. When we say: 'by the Holy Spirit' we say that in the doctrine of Holy Scripture we are content to give the glory to God and not to ourselves."[37]

* * *

Finally, there is still this question: Is there any room for the so-called *"motiva credibilitatis"* in Barth's conception? In this regard there is to be noticed a slight shift in Barth's views in the years between 1925 and 1938. In 1925 in his lecture on "The Scriptural Principle of the Reformed Church" he points out that already in the sixteenth century Calvin (later followed by many other theologians) liked to mention other things which would also point to the divine nature of the Bible. Cal-

---

33. Barth, *The Word of God and the Word of Man*, p. 244. Cf. *Zwischen der Zeiten, op. cit.*, p. 240.
34. Calvin, *Instit.*, I, vii, 4.
35. *C.D.*, I, 2, 537.
36. *Ibid.*, pp. 538ff., where he deals with the authority of the Bible, he again mentions it a few times. No doubt the reason is found in Barth's own conception of the inspiration as consisting of two phases, together forming the one act of divine inspiration: the first in the writers of the past, the second in the readers of the present. Cf. Ch. VI of this book.
37. *C.D.*, I, 2, 537.

vin even devotes a complete chapter of his *Institutes* to them.[38] His view could aptly be summarized in the enumeration of the Westminster Confession, which in this respect is a true disciple of Calvin:

> the testimony of the church, the heavenliness of the matter, the efficacy of the doctrine, the majesty of the style, the consent of all the parts, the scope of the whole (which is to give all glory to God), the full discovery it makes of the only way of man's salvation, the many other incomparable excellencies and the entire perfection thereof, which are all arguments, whereby it doth abundantly evidence itself the word of God (Ch. I, 5).

Barth then points out that Calvin's appeal to these facts in no way undercuts the testimony of the Holy Spirit. Calvin himself calls them "secondary helps to our weakness,"[39] and is fully aware of their relative value. They are only "small apologetics"[40] within the confines of the one and final ground. Later on, however, it became customary to co-ordinate them with the one ground. The difference between *the* ground and the grounds was fully lost sight of and then *the* ground was seen merely as *a* ground. Thus the "small apologetics" became the Trojan horse, dragged within the walls of Christian theology. In 1925 Barth added these words:

> Once we have accustomed ourselves again to the defenseless power of the one ground . . . and thus have found the sober, realistic distance over against all the other grounds, we, too, might again do some apologetics.[41]

It is clear that here Barth, too, upholds the relative value of the so-called *motiva credibilitatis*. But in 1938 this addition is not found any more. Actually we find disapproval only. He calls it "unfortunate"[42] that Calvin developed these secondary grounds, though it is still admitted that in Calvin's own view they had no competitive function at all.

In our opinion the earlier Barth is more correct and more balanced here than the later Barth. Though admittedly these secondary grounds have no power to convince any man in a definite way, yet they have their own limited value within the

---

38. Calvin, *Instit.*, I. viii, *passim*.
39. *Ibid.*, I, viii, 13.
40. *Zwischen der Zeiten, op. cit.*, p. 238.
41. *Ibid.*, p. 239.
42. *C.D.* I, 2, 536. The same in *C.D.*, I, 1, 191. Cf. the judgment of T.H.L. Parker, *Calvin's Doctrine of the Knowledge of God*, 1959, p. 43.

confines created by the testimony of the Holy Spirit. This was the view of Calvin. He openly admits that they

> cannot of themselves produce a firm faith in Scripture until our heavenly Father manifests his presence in it, and thereby secures implicit reverence for it. Then only, therefore, does Scripture suffice to give a saving knowledge of God when its certainty is founded on the inward persuasion of the Holy Spirit. Still, the human testimonies which go to confirm it will not be without effect, if they are used in subordination to that chief and highest proof, as secondary helps to our weakness.[43]

How much Calvin is in earnest with regard to their relativity, appears from the fact that he immediately continues: "But it is foolish to attempt to prove to infidels that the Scripture is the Word of God. This it cannot be known to be, except by faith." The situation is quite clear here. The *motiva credibilitatis* are anchored in the one and final ground. All their significance comes to them from this one ground. But at the same time they themselves point emphatically to the absolute necessity of the one, decisive ground. To say it again in Calvin's words: The real conviction is "the conviction which revelation from heaven alone can produce."[44]

---

43. Calvin, *Instit.*, I, viii, 13.

44. Calvin, *Instit.*, I, vii, 5. It should be noted that in Calvin the *motiva credibilitatis* do not precede the testimony of the Holy Spirit, but follow it. In other words, it is not one sequence of which the *motiva* are the first components, leading to the testimony of the Spirit as the last and final component, so that essentially they are of the same nature, the difference only being one of degree. But the *motiva* obtain their function only after the decisive change has been wrought already by the Holy Spirit. Actually, therefore, the *motiva* have a real meaning only for those who have been convinced already by the Spirit.

On this point Calvin's scheme is to be preferred to that of the Westminster Confession, which in its formulation is in danger of giving the wrong impression that the testimony of the Holy Spirit is the final addition to the preceding sequence of *motiva*.

Cf. also H. Henry Meeter, who, in his *The Basic Ideas of Calvinism* (1956), mentions three methods to know that the Bible is the Word of God.

The first is the study of comparative religion of which he says that one will have "difficulty" (sic!) in coming to the required conviction. The second method is that of Christian apologetics (i.e., the *motiva credibilitatis*). And then we read: "There is still a third way, namely that of the testimony of the Holy Spirit" (p. 55). True, he adds immediately that "this is the basic method," but nevertheless this means that the testimony of the Holy Spirit has again become one way among other ways. Note also that it is mentioned last. It seems to be the highest mark of a progressive scale!

CHAPTER II

SCRIPTURE AS A WITNESS TO DIVINE REVELATION

Barth divides his discussion of the doctrine of Holy Scripture into two sections: Scripture as a Witness to Divine Revelation, and Scripture as the Word of God. This distinction is a crucial one; as we shall see later on, it contains implicitly the whole of Barth's doctrine of Scripture. We turn now to the first thesis: Scripture is a *witness* to divine revelation. According to Barth this basic statement contains two elements, both of which are indispensable for a correct view of the Bible.

In the first place, the term "witness" means an undoubted *limitation*. When we call the Bible a witness to revelation we make a distinction between the Bible as such and revelation:

> A witness is not absolutely identical with that to which it witnesses. This corresponds with the facts upon which the truth of the whole proposition is based. In the Bible we meet with human words written in human speech, and in these words, and therefore by means of them, we hear of the lordship of the Triune God. Therefore when we have to do with the Bible, we have to do primarily with this means, with these words, with the witness, which as such is not itself revelation, but only — and this is the limitation — the witness to it.[1]

But this is not the only meaning of the word "witness." It is not even the primary meaning, which must be positive rather than negative. Keeping in mind the above-mentioned limitation, we continue immediately:

> In this limitation the Bible is not distinguished from revelation. It is simply revelation as it comes to us, mediating and therefore accommodating itself to us — to us who are not ourselves proph-

---

1. *C.D.*, I, 2, 463.

ets and apostles, and therefore not the immediate and direct recipients of the one revelation, witnesses of the resurrection of Jesus Christ. Yet it is for us revelation by means of the words of the prophets and apostles written in the Bible, in which they are still alive for us as the immediate and direct recipients of revelation, and by which they speak to us. A real witness is not identical with that to which it witnesses, but it sets it before us. Again this corresponds with the facts on which the truth of the whole proposition is founded. If we have really listened to the biblical words in all their humanity, if we have accepted them as witness, we have obviously not only heard of the lordship of the triune God, but by this means it has become for us an actual presence and event.[2]

So "witness" in this context has a double function. On the one hand it denotes *distinctness*. The witness to revelation is not simply and straightforwardly identical with the revelation itself. But on the other hand there is also an indissoluble *unity*. The revelation cannot be heard or apprehended apart from the witness. Without the witness of the Bible, we today, who have not seen or heard Jesus Christ in the flesh, would not know anything about this revelation.

* * *

For his use of the term "witness" Barth appeals to the Bible itself, where the word occurs frequently and synonyms or related terms occur even more frequently.

In the *New Testament* there is the institution of the *apostolate*.[3] The New Testament describes it as a special creation of Jesus Christ Himself. In Mark 3:14 we read: "And he appointed (*epoiēsen!*) twelve, that they might be with him, and that he might send them forth to preach." And in Ephesians 4:11 Paul says of the risen, exalted, and glorified Lord, that "he gave (*edōken*) some to be apostles; and some, prophets; and some, evangelists. . . ." Of these apostles Jesus Himself declares: "He that heareth you heareth me" (Luke 10:16) and "He that receiveth you, receiveth me" (Matt. 10:40; cf. also John 17:8, 20; 20:21). And these apostles themselves were aware of this special revelation, as is shown, for example, by Paul's words to the Corinthians: "We are ambassadors therefore on behalf of Christ, as though God were entreating by us:

---

2. *Ibid.*
3. *Ibid.*, pp. 487f.

we beseech you on behalf of Christ, be ye reconciled to God" (II Cor. 5:20).

The same holds true of the *Old Testament prophets*.[4] They, too, were witnesses of Jesus Christ. Barth proves this by pointing to the fact that Jesus proclaims Himself to be the fulfilment of the Old Testament: "This day," says Jesus when He first appears, "is the scripture fulfilled in your ears" (Luke 4:21). And when after His resurrection He appears to the two lonely travellers to Emmaus, we hear Him rebuking them for their unbelief, after which, "beginning from Moses and from all the prophets, he interpreted to them in all the scriptures the things concerning himself" (Luke 24:27; cf. 18:31; John 1:45; 5:39, 46; Rom. 1:2; 3:21; etc.). All this does not mean that there is no *difference* between the Old and New Testament witnesses. There certainly is. The Old Testament prophets are witnesses of the coming Christ, their witness is one of expectation, while the New Testament apostles are witnesses of the Christ who did come, their witness is one of recollection. But in spite of this undeniable difference, their intrinsic *unity* is much greater: they have the same object, they all witness to the one Jesus Christ.[5]

In being witnesses to Jesus Christ the *unique position* of the biblical writers is founded. They are "the men who in face of the unique and contingent revelation had the no less unique and contingent function of being the first witnesses."[6] Only because there were and still are those first witnesses, could and can there be second and third witnesses. Time and again Barth stresses this unique position of the biblical writers. At another place, for example, he distinguishes between three different *times*[7]: First, the time of the direct, original utterance of God Himself in His revelation, the time of Jesus Christ. Second, the time of the witness, of the prophets and the apostles. Finally, the time of the Church, the time of derivative proclamation, related to the words of prophets and apostles and regulated by them. These three times may not be identified. To be sure, Jesus was a man and in this sense not different from the biblical witnesses, but because of His unity with God He stood

4. *Ibid.*, pp. 488f.
5. *Ibid.*, pp. 481f.
6. *Ibid.*, p. 486.
7. *C.D.*, I, 1, 164f.

absolutely over against them as a master over against his slaves. The prophets and apostles, again, were men like ourselves, yet their office as witnesses is entirely unique in the Church. We who live after them can be related to revelation only through their witness, i.e., through Scripture. Here again the unique place of the biblical witnesses is upheld. They stand between Christ and us, and only through them we have access to the revelation in Jesus Christ.

* * *

There remains one question that still demands an answer: Why does Barth emphasize the idea of *limitation* so strongly with regard to the term "witness"? As we saw, Barth mentions this idea first even though he admits that it is logically secondary.

The answer is found in Barth's concept of *revelation,* which he had worked out already in the first part of Volume I. In particular, two aspects of this concept will help us to understand what he means by "limitation" and why he stresses it.

The first is the oft-repeated proposition that revelation is always an *event* ("Ereignis"). According to the context this proposition is directly linked up with the witness-idea. Here, too, Barth begins with the distinction between the Bible and revelation. Again it is said: The Bible is not itself God's past revelation. The Bible attests to the past revelation in Jesus Christ, and this word "attests" involves a definite distinction. To attest always means to point in a definite direction beyond oneself to something else. The Bible is no exception to this rule. The biblical witnesses do indeed point beyond themselves. They are all to be compared with the figure of John the Baptist on Grünewald's famous picture on the altar at Isenheim. There we see John pointing with a prodigious index finger to the One on the cross.[8] That indeed is the function of the biblical witness: to point completely away from himself and completely toward Jesus Christ. There is, therefore, *no direct identity* between the Bible and revelation. We have no right to presuppose or to anticipate such an identification. It is something that must be *brought about,* through an act of God. Revelation, then, is an event:

> It takes place as an event, when and where the word of the Bible becomes God's Word, i.e., when and where the word of

---

8. *Ibid.,* p. 126; cf. I, 2, 125.

the Bible functions as the word of a witness, when and where John's finger points not in vain, but really pointedly, when and where by means of its word we also succeed in seeing and hearing what he saw and heard. Therefore, where the Word of God is an event, revelation and the Bible are one in fact, and word for word one at that.[9]

It is an event. That means it is wholly God's affair. We can also say it in this way: Revelation is the revealing God. Therefore there is but one direct revelation: the revelation in Jesus Christ. In Him God really spoke His word directly. This was fully "Deus dixit" (God spoke),

> But in the Bible we are invariably concerned with human attempts to repeat and reproduce, in human thoughts and expressions, this Word of God in definite human situations, e.g. in respect of the complications of Israel's political position midway between Egypt and Babylon or of the errors and confusions in the Christian Church at Corinth between A.D. 50-60.[10]

So in the one case we have the "Deus dixit," in the other case it is "Paulus dixit." These are really *two different things*. And yet in the *event* of God's Word they are *one*.

The Bible, therefore, must time and again *become* the Word of God. Barth likes to compare it with the water of the pool of Bethesda (John 5).[11] This water had no healing power in itself, but only when it was moved from on high. Nobody had control over this event. It just happened from time to time. And this same "from time to time" holds true of the Bible. Our evidence for saying this does not rest upon human experience. It is not that we have so often heard God's Word in the Bible. Our human experience can never be constitutive for the reality of God's Word. No, this "from time to time" is the result of the *freedom of God's grace*.[12] Its secret is the divine pleasure. *Ubi et quando visum est Deo* (where and when it pleases the Lord). God is and remains the sovereign in His revelation. It is and remains His revelation, and never becomes human possession.

* * *

There is, however, yet another aspect of Barth's concept of

---

9. *Ibid.*, p. 127. The event-idea is even extended to Jesus' human nature. Cf. McConnachie, *The Barthian Theology and the Man of Today*, pp. 316, 317.
10. *Loc. cit.*
11. *Ibid.*, p. 126; cf. I, 2, 125.
12. *Ibid.*, pp. 131f.

revelation which also accounts for the idea of limitation. It is what he himself calls the *worldliness* ("Welthaftigkeit") of the language of God.[13] The meaning of this term is that God's revelation always comes to man in forms derived from and belonging to this world.

> When God speaks to man, this happening is never so marked off from the rest of what happens, that it might not promptly be also interpreted as part of this or that other happening.[14]

This holds true of all God's "words" to man. The Church e.g. is also a sociological entity with definite historical and structural features and therefore may easily be mistaken as being merely such a sociological entity. Preaching in fact is also an address. The sacraments in fact are also symbols, just like other symbols, and their dissimilarity in the similarity can easily be overlooked. The Bible in fact is also the document for the history of the religion of a tribe in Nearer Asia and of its Hellenistic offshoot. It even holds true of Jesus Christ Himself.

> Jesus Christ in fact is also the Rabbi of Nazareth, historically so difficult to get information about, and when it is got, one whose activity is so easily a little commonplace alongside more than one other founder of a religion and even alongside many later representatives of His own "religion."[15]

So we never have God's Word otherwise than in the mystery of its worldliness. Or to say it in a positive way: "We always have it in a form which as such is *not* the Word of God, even does not *betray* that it is the form precisely of the Word of God."[16] Yet, even here we cannot stop. We have to take another step and say: "Its form is not a suitable, but an *unsuitable* means for the self-representation of God. It does not correspond to the matter, but it contradicts it. It does not unveil it, but veils it."[17] The reason for this last assertion is, that God's Word not only comes in the form of creaturely reality, but in the form of fallen creaturely reality. There is therefore a *twofold indirectness*: God's Word comes in the form of creation and in the form of fallen creation.[18]

13. *Ibid.*, pp. 188f.
14. *Ibid.*
15. *Ibid.*
16. *Ibid.*
17. *Ibid.*, p. 189 (italics ours).
18. *Ibid.*, p. 191.

According to Barth we ought not to regret this worldliness of God's language at all. On the contrary, it is a necessity which we should accept gratefully. For we ourselves are in the world, and worldly to the core. If God did not speak to us in a worldly way, He would not speak to us at all. "To get around the worldliness of His Word would be to get around Christ."[19] We ought therefore never to believe "that God was veiled from us by some unfortunate disturbance and then unveiled Himself removing this veiling. . . . The facts are that God Himself veils Himself and in the very process . . . unveils Himself."[20] And these facts mean pure love and mercy. For it would be the end of us and of the whole world, if God's Word were addressed to us in unveiledness. "In its very worldliness it is, therefore, in every respect the Word of grace."[21]

It is obvious from all this *why* Barth stresses the concept of "witness" so strongly. First, he intends to give room to the freedom of God's grace. Second, he wants revelation to be God's act alone. Third, he wishes to remove any occasion for *hubris*, in which man claims to *possess* and *dispose of* God's revelation. In one word: the motive is *Soli Deo Gloria*.

The word "witness" has become more or less fashionable in our century, in connection with the doctrine of Holy Scripture. In particular, the German scholar Martin Kähler coined it in his now-famous work *Der sogenannte historische Jesus und der geschichtliche Christus* (1892). In this work Kähler utterly rejects the whole "Life of Jesus Theology" of the nineteenth century as futile. Its basic error, he said, lay in viewing the Gospels as "historical sources" to be approached with modern historical techniques. In these "sources" we would find the historical Jesus as viewed by the early Christian congregation, and it would be the task of the historian to seek the real historical Jesus *behind* these sources. Against this Kähler asserted that the Gospels are not sources but *testimonies*. Their intention is "tendentious." They want to evoke faith in Jesus Christ. We have no right to go behind the Gospels to find the real Jesus. The real historical Jesus is the biblical Christ,

---

19. *Ibid.*, p. 192.
20. *Ibid.*
21. *Ibid.*, p. 193.

and the only correct attitude is to accept the "witness of faith" given by the Gospels.

It is not our intention to go deeply into Kähler's views. We only mention them to point out that Barth's use of "witness" does not stand alone. In fact, Barth openly expresses his great appreciation for Kähler's disposing of the so-called Life of Jesus Theology. He writes: "It is an abiding merit of Martin Kähler, which cannot be over-praised, that in his work of 1892 — at a time when it cost something to say so — he called the whole 'Life of Jesus Movement' in plain language a 'wrong way.'"[22]

* * *

It cannot be denied that the word "witness" in this connection is a genuinely biblical term. When we study the New Testament we are struck by the frequent recurrence of the word and how it is used precisely to indicate the whole apostolic preaching. The New Testament relates with great emphasis that Jesus Himself called His apostles witnesses. The two key texts here are Luke 24:48 and Acts 1:8. In Luke 24 the emphasis is on the *fact*. Jesus solemnly declares: "Ye are witnesses of these things." The interpretation of "these things" is found in Jesus' preceding words. It is the fulfilment of the Old Testament in His own suffering, death, and resurrection. "These are my words which I spake unto you, while I was yet with you, how that all things must needs be fulfilled, which are written in the law of Moses, and the prophets, and the psalms, concerning me" (vs. 44, cf. 46). But in this passage there is more than a mere statement of the fact only. In the fact the *task* is included, that enormous task already predicted in the Old Testament, namely, "that repentance and remission of sins should be preached in his name unto all the nations, beginning from Jerusalem" (vs. 47). But both fact and task themselves are embedded in the *promise of the Spirit*. "Behold, I send forth the promise of my Father upon you" (vs. 49). In the second text mentioned, Acts 1:8, the main stress is on the *task*. It is primarily a command: "Ye shall be my witnesses both in Jerusalem, and in all Judea and Samaria, and unto the uttermost part of the earth." Here we see Jesus, the risen Lord, to whom by virtue of His resurrection has been

---

22. *C.D.*, I, 2, 164.

given all authority in heaven and on earth (Matt. 28:18), sovereignly appointing His witnesses.[23]

When we ask what the New Testament *means* by "witness" we find two inseparable elements. The first refers to actual seeing and hearing of an event. These men are appointed witnesses because they have seen the great revelational facts which constitute the content of the Gospel of Jesus Christ. For the apostolic preaching is concerned with *facts*. "It is not concerned with some doctrines or other, with myths or speculations, but with facts which occurred at a certain place, at a certain time in the glaring light of history, facts which can be ascertained and relied upon."[24] This gains added force when we bear in mind that the New Testament, like modern usage, relates witnessing to the law court. The witness is the man who is oathbound to speak the truth, the whole truth, and nothing but the truth. He has to promote the course of justice, and on the ground of the indissoluble relation between justice and fact, he can do this only by stating the facts as they are.[25]

There is, however, a second dimension in the New Testament concept of witness. The witness of Jesus Christ does more than state the mere facts of Jesus' life. His task is also to *interpret* them. It is exactly in this disclosure of meaning that the facts achieve their significance as *divine truth*. Says Strathmann: "The facts cannot be testified without simultaneously pointing to their meaning and emphatically requiring their believing recognition. . . . Being a witness of the facts [Tatsachenzeuge] and being a witness of the truth [Wahrheitszeuge] coincide — the unavoidable result of the fact that in the Gospel we are concerned with a historical revelation."[26] Thus the witness of Jesus Christ is the man who does not give a mere proclama-

23. The word "my" can be interpreted in two ways. It can be taken as a genitive objective: witnesses of me, and as a genitive subjective: my witnesses, appointed by me and witnessing on my command. Though probably both meanings have to be retained, yet, on the ground of the place of the word "my" in the Greek text (*esesthe mou martyres*) we first of all have to see it as a genitive objective.
24. R. Strathmann, in Kittel's *Theologische Wörterbuch zum Neuen Testament*, IV, 496.
25. Cf. R. Schippers, *Getuigen van Jezus Christus in het Nieuwe Testament*, 1938, p. 198 and *passim*.
26. *Op. cit.*, pp. 195-196.

tion of the facts, but calls his listeners to take a decision of faith over against Him who was the subject of these facts.

In particular the writings of Luke contain great stress on the twofold idea of witness. No wonder, therefore, that the two key texts mentioned above were found there. But they are by no means isolated statements: Luke uses the word and concept of witness constantly. Already in the introduction to his Gospel he speaks of those "which from the beginning were eyewitnesses" (1:2). This is nothing less than the foundation stone of his Gospel. But the notion of eye- and ear-witness is especially prominent in his second work, the book of the Acts of the Apostles. When Judas Iscariot's place is to be filled by the choosing of an apostle, Peter tells the congregation to put forward only those "that have companied with us all the time that the Lord Jesus went in and went out among us, beginning from the baptism of John, until the day that he was received up from us" (Acts 1:21, 22). Likewise Peter later on says to Cornelius and his company: "We are witnesses of all things which he did both in the country of the Jews, and in Jerusalem" (Acts 10:39).

The apostle John also stresses this witness-idea time and again. He, too, starts his Gospel with it. When he relates the central fact of the Incarnation, "And the Word became flesh," immediately following he mentions the eyewitness: "and we beheld his glory" (John 1:14). It is again John who relates Jesus' words spoken during the last discourses before the crucifixion: "And ye also bear witness, because ye have been with me from the beginning" (John 15:27).[27] Most striking is the opening of his first general epistle, which is nothing but one emphatic affirmation of his being a witness: "That which was from the beginning, that which we have heard, that which we have seen with our eyes, that which we beheld, and our hands handled, concerning the Word of life (and the life was manifested, and we have seen, and bear witness, and declare unto you the life, the eternal life, which was with the Father, and was manifested unto us): that which we have seen and heard declare we unto you also, that ye also may have fellowship with us" (I John 1:1ff.).[28]

27. Cf. also John 19:35; 21:24.
28. Cf. also for the other books of the New Testament: I Pet. 5:1, II Pet. 1:16, Heb. 2:3.

John also stresses most strongly the *interpretative* element in witnessing. It is John who records for us John the Baptist's words: "I have seen and have born witness *that this is the Son of God*" (John 1:34). Again it is John who records for us Jesus' own words: "But the witness which I have is greater than that of John: for the works which the Father hath given me to accomplish, the very works that I do, bear witness of me, *that the Father hath sent me*" (John 5:36). And when in the passion story John records how Jesus' side was pierced by the soldier's spear, he not only mentions the fact, but immediately adds the deepest intention of his witness: "And he that hath seen hath borne witness, and his witness is true: and he knoweth that he saith true, *that ye also may believe*" (John 19:35). The facts of Jesus' life are not "neutral" facts on a par with those of secular history, but they constitute the history of salvation, and therefore every witness, yes the whole Gospel, is one strong appeal to faith: "These are written, *that ye may believe that Jesus is the Christ, the Son of God;* and that believing ye may have life in his name" (John 20:31; cf. also John 21:24).

A special detail, which may not be neglected, is the New Testament concentration of the witness-idea on the *resurrection* of Jesus Christ. On the very day of Pentecost, Peter, in his address to the Jews, declares emphatically: "This Jesus [whom ye by the hand of lawless men did crucify and slay] did God raise up, whereof we all are witnesses" (Acts 2:32; cf. Acts 3:15; 5:30ff.; 10:41ff.; cf. also 1:22 and 4:33). Bearing in mind the unique place of the resurrection in the history of salvation, this concentration is not surprising at all. For according to the New Testament the resurrection is nothing less than the basis of the apostolic preaching. It is the central fact in Jesus' life — the gate, as it were, to His whole life, through which this life can be seen in its essential meaning. In the resurrection the historical ambiguity of Jesus' life is removed and He is "declared to be the Son of God with power" (Rom. 1:4). With the resurrection the whole appearance of Jesus Christ stands and falls. If the witness fails here, he fails everywhere. As Paul said later: "If Christ hath not been raised, then is our preaching vain, your faith also is vain" (I Cor. 15:14).[29]

Because of this focus on the resurrection, Paul can also be

---

29. Cf. Acts 17:18.

called an eye- and ear-witness (Acts 22:14 and 26:16). For did he not meet the risen Lord Himself on the way to Damascus? True, Paul nowhere calls himself a witness, but it is equally true that he claims to be an apostle precisely on the ground of this meeting. He even includes this meeting among the appearances of the risen Lord to His disciples (I Cor. 15:8f). Yet it cannot be denied that when Luke uses the word "witness" to refer to Paul there is a certain shift of accent. Paul cannot be called an eyewitness in the same extensive sense as the first apostles. Paul himself in Acts 13:31 makes a clear distinction in this respect. Here he calls the older apostles eyewitnesses, in the original sense of men who have attended the events of Christ's life, death, and resurrection ("they came up with him from Galilee to Jerusalem"), while he calls himself and Barnabas "evangelists," bringers of the good tidings that God has fulfilled His promises in Jesus Christ. Though admittedly Strathmann makes the contrast too strong when he says: "Paul is not a 'Tatsachenzeuge' [a witness of the facts] in the sense of the first apostles, because he cannot guarantee the history of Christ on the ground of his own experience, but he is a 'Wahrheitszeuge' [witness of the truth] who by his profession canvasses for the faith in Christ",[30] yet it is obvious that for Paul the emphasis is on the *second aspect* of the word witness. This might also be inferred from the formulation of Acts 22:15, where Ananias says to Paul: "Thou shalt be a witness *for him*." The use of the dative instead of the genitive would seem to imply that Paul first of all is a "witness of the truth."

There is yet another special feature which must be mentioned explicitly here. The New Testament witnesses do not validate themselves, but they are expressly *called* and *appointed* by Jesus Himself. Many people had seen and heard Jesus, but only some were called to be witnesses of Him. Rightly H. N. Ridderbos says: "In this respect being a witness and being an apostle coincide."[31] "The witness is the man, who, ap-

---

30. *Op. cit.*, p. 498. Strathmann is rather critical and describes the fact that Luke in Acts 22:14 and 26:16 also calls Paul a witness as "an artificial and not particularly happy attempt" to apply the original witness-idea to Paul (*op. cit.*, p. 497). Luke, however, follows only the line of concentration of the witness-idea on the resurrection, as he found this in all the apostolic addresses, recorded in the first part of his book.

31. H. N. Ridderbos, *Heilsgeschiedenis en Heilige Schrift*, 1955, p. 119.

pointed by Christ and himself belonging to the history of salvation, in the great lawsuit vouches on behalf of God and Christ for the truth and reality of what was said and happened, and who is especially authorized and equipped for this task."[32] Ridderbos also points to the fact that the witness of the apostles and the *witness of the Holy Spirit* are very closely interrelated in the New Testament. He refers here to Acts 5:32, "And we are witnesses of these things; and so is the Holy Spirit, whom God hath given to them that obey him," and to John 15:26, 27, "But when the Comforter is come, whom I will send unto you from the Father, even the Spirit of truth, which proceedeth from the Father, he shall bear witness of me: and ye also bear witness, because ye have been with me from the beginning." Precisely for this reason the apostles are more than witnesses of mere facts only. They are also witnesses of the truth, for it is the Holy Spirit who, according to the promise of Christ, guides them into all the truth (John 16:13), who teaches them all things and brings to remembrance all that Jesus said unto them (John 14:26), who takes of Christ and declares it to them (John 16:14). It is exactly this concurrent witness of the Spirit that gives its penetrating, absolutely binding power to the witness of the apostles.

* * *

This apostolic witness we find in particular in the New Testament itself. The whole New Testament is one great witness of God's mighty works in Jesus Christ. Deliberately we formulate the contents of the witness in this way: God's mighty works *in Jesus Christ*. For in all the various forms in which the witness is given, Jesus Christ is at the center. The Gospels speak especially of His life, death, and resurrection. The book of Acts describes His deeds as the risen and exalted Lord in the origin and first development of His Church, a line which in the Apocalypse is continued up to His second coming. The Epistles are first of all a witness of the unfathomable and immeasurable riches of the salvation brought about by Jesus Christ, but this "witness of the truth" is from beginning to end inseparably connected with the original "witness of the facts" which is and remains its foundation.

But we are not allowed to halt at the New Testament. The

---

32. *Ibid.*

New Testament itself includes the Old Testament in the witness, in the sense that there the person and work of Jesus Christ were predicted and foreshadowed. The Old Testament writers all announced His coming, and in this way their prophetic voices are one great confirmation of the apostolic witness. Thus Peter in his address to Cornelius and his household can link the two witnesses as follows: "And he charged us to preach unto the people, and to testify that this is he who is ordained of God to be the Judge of the living and the dead. To him bear all the prophets witness, that through his name every one that believeth on him shall receive remission of sins" (Acts 10:42, 43; cf. I Peter 1:10, 11). Indeed, it is remarkable to see how from the beginning the entire Old Testament is seen and handled as one powerful testimony to and confirmation of the truth of the apostolic preaching. Continuously there is an appeal to the Old Testament. One psalm after another, one prophecy after another is quoted as proof that the Old Testament is permanently on the side of the apostolic witnesses. Of course this appeal does not mean that the perspective is lost sight of. The Incarnation is the great division between Old and New Testament. There is the difference between expectation and recollection. But this never affects the witness-character, for both groups of witnesses, each in their own way, either in the form of expectation or that of recollection, proclaim the one Jesus Christ as the God-given Redeemer, as the revelation of God the Redeemer Himself.

From all this it is clear that on the ground of Scripture itself no objection can be raised against the term "witness" to refer to Scripture. On the contrary, we must say that the term is highly appropriate, for here the Bible is characterized in a way which reveals its deepest nature. The Bible is indeed the book of the prophetic and apostolic witness of God's unique revelation in Jesus Christ. The Bible is not a mere record of the national history of the Jewish nation and the subsequent history of the Jewish-Christian community. It is not a compendium of philosophical or even theological truths. It is one long, persistent and consistent witness of God's grace in Jesus Christ, and in this quality of witness it calls continuously to faith and conversion, simultaneously announcing eternal judgment to everyone who rejects Him who is the content of its witness.

The word "witness" when applied to the Bible even has great *advantages*. The greatest, perhaps, is that it naturally carries with it the recognition of *Jesus Christ as the center* of all revelation of salvation. Even in Reformed theology this basic idea has not always been sufficiently honored. Too often a doctrine of revelation and Holy Scripture has been developed which does not give due prominence to this central place of Jesus Christ. We recognize, for instance, the validity of some recent criticisms of B. B. Warfield. So John McIntyre writes: "It is inconceivable that any analysis of the Biblical idea of revelation can be adequate which devotes one page to the revelation of God in Jesus Christ, and which does not make that Revelation the clue to the understanding of 'all forms of revelation' (Warfield's phrase), of which the Bible speaks."[33] And J. F. Peter rightly points out that "the use made of such words as *apokaluptō, phaneroō* and *phanerosis* shows that when the thought of New Testament writers ran along lines of God's selfmanifestation they ran at once to the Person of Jesus Christ."[34] Of course Warfield also acknowledges Jesus Christ as the center of all revelation. He even mentions this explicitly in the criticized article. Jesus Christ is "the culminating revelation." "As in His person, in which dwells all the fulness of the Godhead bodily, He rises above all classification and is *sui generis*. . . . The prophets could prophesy only as the Spirit of Christ which was in them testified, revealing to them as to servants one or another of the secrets of the Lord Jehovah. . . . The entirety of the New Testaments is but the explanatory word accompanying and giving its effect to the fact of Christ."[35] Yet it cannot be denied that this central position of Jesus Christ as *the* revelation of God was not the starting point out of which Warfield had in this article built up his doctrine of revelation. In this respect the term "witness" can serve as a permanent reminder for every theologian that in all his thinking about revelation and Holy Scripture the starting

---

33. John McIntyre, in *Reformed Theological Review*, IX, 2, 30. McIntyre refers here to Warfield's article on "The Biblical Idea of Revelation" in *The Inspiration and Authority of the Bible*, 1951, pp. 71-102.
34. J. F. Peter, "Warfield on the Scriptures," in *Reformed Theological Review*, XVI, 3, 78.
35. B. B. Warfield, *op. cit.*, p. 96.

point has to be sought in Him to whom all the Scriptures witness.

* * *

But does the Bible also know of *limitation* in this respect? As we saw, Barth speaks of both unity *and* distinctness. He even mentions the distinctness first. According to him the Bible is not revelation itself but "only" witness to revelation. Every static identification is to be rejected utterly. Bible and revelation must be distinguished, though it is equally true that through the powerful operation of the Holy Spirit the witness can *become* revelation. Is this also true?

We answer, first, that considered in itself there is nothing to forbid distinguishing between the Bible and revelation. But then of course everything depends on what is meant by such a distinction. When we on our side use the word "distinguish" we only mean to say that the Bible is not the *entire* revelation, but only a *selection* of it. Much of what was revealed to the Old Testament believers has not been recorded. The same applies to the New Testament revelation, as is clearly expressed by John at the end of his Gospel: "And there are also many other things which Jesus did, the which if they should be written every one, I suppose that even the world itself would not contain the books that should be written" (John 21:25; cf. also John 20:30).

It is obvious that Barth goes much further. To him the distinction is not merely quantitative, but essentially qualitative. The Bible as such is not to be identified with revelation. In itself it is not part of the event of revelation. In our opinion, however, this use of the word "distinction" finds *no ground in the Bible itself*. It is a preconceived, dogmatical construction to which the Bible itself is a perfect stranger.

To substantiate this assertion we begin with the concept of *eye- and ear-witnesses* as found above. In our study of this term throughout the New Testament we found no limiting aspect in it, but on the contrary detected that it served to confirm and accentuate the special position and task of those who were thus called. The word witness appeared to have two dimensions. First, a *receptive* one (Luke 24:48, "Ye are witnesses of these things"), these men are "witnesses of the facts." Alongside of this, even based on it, there was the second dimension: the *productive* (Acts 1:8, "Ye shall be my witnesses"), these men are also called as "witnesses of the truth" to preach the fact of the Christ-revelation to the world. As such they are "bearers" of this revelation in a very special way. Through their witness this revelation is communicated to the world. In their witness the revelation itself encounters the world, and therein their witness itself is revelation. On the ground of careful analysis of the term "witness" throughout the whole New Testament R. Schippers comes to the following conclusion:

> In Scripture the witness is the rendering of the facts, under the pressure of the consciousness that the course of justice shall be dominated by the rendering. Therefore the witness is eyewitness and earwitness. The witnesses do not bring their faults, their follies, their views, their ideas, but the record of what they heard and saw. The witness fully disappears behind the history he records. Over against the witness all reservation falls away. To violate the legitimate witness is to violate the history. There is a historical necessity for the believers to live with this witness, but there is nothing in it, which has to be seen as "limitation."[36]

To this must be added the weight of the fact that these men are specially *called* and *appointed* to this function, in both its receptive and its productive dimensions. This calling and appointment constitute them as a class set apart. Jesus more than once declares with great emphasis that every reaction to their message is a reaction to Himself. "He that heareth you heareth me; and he that rejecteth you rejecteth me; and he that rejecteth me, rejecteth him that sent me" (Luke 10:16). "He that receiveth you receiveth me and he that receiveth me receiveth him that sent me" (Matt. 10:40). "As the Father hath sent me, even so send I you" (John 20:21). We immediately admit that these words also hold to a certain extent of the present-day witnesses. The preaching of the Church here and now, too, may claim this intimate relation between itself and Jesus Christ, the living Lord. In this respect we fully agree with Barth, when he calls the preached Word also the Word of God. But this can always be said only in a derivative sense. In the case of the preaching of the Church today there is always the binding condition: in as far as it agrees with the original, apostolic witness. However, concerning this latter witness Jesus states in these texts, *without any reservation*, "He that heareth you, heareth me." Here Jesus *identifies Himself* emphatically with these witnesses as to their witness to Him.

---

36. Schippers, *op. cit.*, p. 202.

There is, therefore, but one conclusion possible: These witnesses are *revelational witnesses*. They are not only witnesses to revelation, in a limiting and distinct way, but they themselves *belong to the revelation*. Their speaking and writing *is* revelation. To quote Jesus' own words once again: "He that heareth you heareth me."

All this is emphasized in a particularly strong way by the special revelation between these human witnesses and *the witness of the Holy Spirit*. We encountered this (for example) in Acts 5:32, "And we are witnesses of these things; and so is the Holy Spirit, whom God hath given to those that obey him." We could also point here to Acts 15:28: "For it seemed good to the Holy Ghost, and to us. . . ." At first glance these texts seem to support Barth's idea of distinctness. Are not the two witnesses clearly distinguished here? They certainly are. The divine and the human "factors" are mentioned separately. But is this not to be expected? For the human never, never becomes divine. This holds true even of the human nature of Christ. His humanity is not deified, not even after the resurrection and the ascension. How much the more will it then hold of the human factor in the revelation![37] But this "distinction" is still quite different from Barth's "distinctness"! The mentioning of the two witnesses side by side in the above texts certainly does not carry with it the slightest idea of a limitation. We should not conceive it as two parallel witnesses which have no point of contact, but we have to see it thus, that the witness of the Spirit takes place in and through the human witness. Says F. F. Bruce on Acts 5:32:

37. In our opinion John Murray goes too far when he completely rejects the idea of interpenetration of a human witness by the divine witness. "The term Paul uses represents the concept of 'breathing out' rather than that of 'breathing in' and is far removed from the notion that a human product or witness is so interpenetrated with divine truth that it becomes the word of God." *The Infallible Word*, A Symposium by the Members of the Faculty of Westminster Theological Seminary, ed. by N. B. Stonehouse and Paul Woolley, 1953, p. 30. Admittedly we are not allowed to understand such an interpenetration in an actualistic sense. But this should not lead us to deny all distinction. The human never ceases to be human. The human never becomes divine. Even not in Christ! Cf. L. Berkhof, *Introductory Volume to Systematic Theology*, p. 154, who also speaks of "interpenetration of the divine and the human factors in Scripture."

For they were not only heralds of the good news, but witnesses as well, and not simply witnesses on their individual initiative, but witnesses under the direction of the Divine Witness, the Holy Spirit, imparted by God to all who obeyed the Gospel. In these words we mark again the apostolic community's consciousness of being possessed and indwelt by the Spirit to such a degree, that they were his organs of expression."[38]

The two witnesses constitute such a unity that they, though they can be distinguished, can never be separated. Here, too, the word "identification" would not be too strong. In His witness the Holy Spirit identifies Himself with the human witness, thus creating indissoluble unity. For this very reason Jesus could say to His apostles, that when they would be delivered up by the enemies they should not be anxious what to say. "For it shall be given you in that hour what ye shall speak. For it is not ye that speak, but the Spirit of your Father that speaketh in you" (Matt. 10:19, 20). Here the identification has become so complete that the human witness fully recedes into the background, and only the witness of the Spirit in and through the human is mentioned.

All this is also confirmed by that other word of Jesus, in which He told His disciples that the Spirit would teach them all things and bring into their remembrance all that Jesus had said unto them (John 14:26). We are certainly not allowed to limit the meaning of these words in such a way that they only say that the Holy Spirit will remind the apostles of the mere words and facts only. The Holy Spirit is not to be compared with some modern drugs, the only function of which is to activate the memory! No, the task of the Holy Spirit is far more comprehensive. He will lead the apostles into the inexhaustible riches of the salvation brought about by Christ in His words and acts. To say it in Paul's words: He will teach them "to apprehend with all the saints what is the breadth and length and height and depth, and to know the love of Christ which passeth knowledge, that ye may be filled unto all the fulness

---

38. F. F. Bruce, *The Book of Acts*, New International Commentary on the New Testament, 1956, p. 122. Cf. also the same author in *The New Bible Commentary*, 1955, p. 906: "Note the continued existence of the apostles' personal testimony (cf. I, 8, 22; II, 32; III, 15; IV, 33), with which the witness of the Spirit *in them is* here combined." (Italics ours.)

of God" (Eph. 3:18, 19). Rightly therefore Ridderbos says in reference to the Johannine texts:

> We are concerned here with the witness of the apostles through the Spirit regarding the historical Jesus. In this sense the apostolic witness constitutes the Spirit-made link between the great event of salvation in the fullness of time and the coming Church. Therefore this witness is not only witness to revelation, but it is itself included in this revelation.[39]

* * *

If all this applies to the preached witness of the apostles, it *a fortiori* applies to their witness in its *written* form, as we find this in the New Testament. For this inscripturation took place for no less reason than for "the better preserving and propagating"[40] of the original, basic, apostolic witness. For this reason we may say without hesitation: Here, too, it holds true: He that heareth me, heareth you. Here, too, the Spirit Himself witnesses with the human witnesses. Here, too, we may speak of identification.

That this is not saying too much, is fully confirmed by what Peter says of the "word of prophecy," i.e., the Old Testament, namely, that it did not come by the will of man, "but men spake from God, being moved (*pheromenoi*) by the Holy Spirit" (II Pet. 1:21). The Holy Spirit is behind the prophets when they speak and write, not only in the sense that He provides the impulse, but that they are "borne along, carried onward, as a ship by the wind" (Dean Alford) by the Spirit. Again, the New Testament more than once quotes words of the Old Testament as being spoken by the Spirit Himself. Not David or Isaiah or Jeremiah are the real speakers, but

---

39. H. N. Ridderbos, *op. cit.*, p. 120. Cf. also 122-123: "The difference between this witness and all other earlier or later books, Christian or non-Christian, is not only found in the fact that it comes from those who themselves were witnesses and hearers of the original Word and the original Act of God in the once-for-all Christ-revelation — all this does not give to this witness as such another than human authority — but it is found in the fact that as witness it is included in this Christ-revelation and in that sense also has a once-for-all significance. It is the witness of what is heard and seen and handled concerning the Word of Life, as this witness is authorized by Christ and prepared by the Holy Spirit. From this the New Testament witness derives its revelational character and its significance as foundation of the Church."

40. *Westminster Confession*, Ch. I, 1.

God the Holy Spirit (cf. Acts 1:16; 4:25; 28:25; Heb. 3:7; 10:15).[41]

When in this connection we use the word *"identification,"* we do not mean to suggest that the Holy Spirit is "locked up" in the Bible as in a prison. Such a conception would mean nothing less than a petrification of the witness and activity of the Holy Spirit. We should never forget that the Spirit is *the living God Himself,* who can never be imprisoned, not even in a Sacred Scripture. His sovereignty has no limits. What we mean by "identification" here is that the initiative permanently remains with the Spirit.[42] It is He who in His living, divine dynamics once made the human witness the living Word of God and in His unbounded grace continues to preserve it as such. But exactly for this very reason this human witness *is* the Word of God. And for the very same reason it can be said *without any reservation* of this apostolic witness, now as well as in the days when it was written down: It *is* the revelation of the revealing God.

* * *

Of course all the above-mentioned texts are not unknown to Barth. He explicitly mentions, for instance, Luke 10:16 and Matthew 10:40. He even adds these comments: "We must not weaken this. It does not say: 'also heareth me,' or 'also receiveth me.' The meaning already is, that to hear and receive the disciples is to hear and receive Christ."[43] And on the same page he says with regard to John 20:21 and John 17:8: "In the relationship between Jesus Christ and the apostles there is therefore repeated or reflected in some degree the economy of the incarnation of the Word." But according to Barth these texts reveal only one aspect of the witness: the aspect of *unity.* Besides this there is yet the other aspect, that of *distinctness,* which must be fully honored.

It is remarkable, however, that for this latter aspect *no Scripture proof is adduced.* Barth only appeals to the word "witness," which means: to point beyond oneself to something

---

41. This usage was also followed by Calvin. Cf. *Institutes* I, v, 13 and I, xiii, 23.

42. We therefore prefer the term "identification" to the outwardly similar term "identity." Though it cannot be denied that the former includes the latter, yet it clearly has a different connotation. It points to a dynamic relation.

43. *C. D.,* I, 2, 487.

or somebody else. But is this purely linguistic semantic interpretation of a certain term, used by Scripture itself, sufficient to vindicate such a far-reaching distinction between the Bible and revelation? In our opinion the answer must be a definite No. Barth should have given extensive proof that Scripture itself makes such a fundamental distinction between itself and God's revelation.

* * *

In his earlier works Barth did make an appeal to Calvin. According to him Calvin, too, would have known this distinction between Scripture and revelation. As proof Barth adduces *Institutes* I, vi, 2.[44] Careful reading of the quoted passage however, does not at all confirm Barth's idea of distinctness. On the contrary! Calvin writes:

> Whether God revealed himself to the fathers by oracles and visions, or, by the instrumentality and ministry of men, suggested what they were to hand to posterity, there cannot be a doubt that the certainty of what he taught them was firmly engraven on their hearts, so that they felt assured and knew that the things which they learned came forth from God, who invariably accompanied his word with a sure testimony, infinitely superior to mere opinion. At length, in order that, while doctrine was continually enlarged, its truth might subsist in the world during all ages, it was his pleasure that the same oracles, which he had deposited with the fathers should be consigned, as it were, to public records.

True, in the last words of this quotation we find a distinction between the revelation and its inscripturation, but this distinction is quite different from Barth's distinctness. All theologians will accept the legitimacy of Calvin's distinction, even though it has to be added at once that this distinction only applies to certain parts of Scripture; in the case of many other parts (e.g. the Epistles) revelation and inscripturation coincided. To Calvin, however, this distinction does not imply any limitation. It does not at all detract from the revelational character of these "public records." In the following chapter Calvin writes that it is "the person of God who speaks in it" and that "the Scripture exhibits clear evidence of its being spoken by God."[45] And at the end of the first book, he declares that "our true wisdom is to embrace with meek docility and without

---

44. "Das Schriftprinzip der reformierten Kirche," in *Zwischen der Zeiten*, 1925, p. 219.
45. I, vii, 4. *"Dei loquentis persona."*

reservation whatever the Holy Scriptures have delivered."[46] Here the revelational character of Holy Scripture is fully recognized, and no limitation or distinctness is admitted.

This same also holds true over against W. Niesel.[47] In his recently translated *The Theology of Calvin* Niesel defends the thesis that Calvin would not have known a literal inspiration of Holy Scripture. He adduces a threefold proof.[48] In the first place he points out that in the scriptural exegesis of Calvin there is nothing to support a belief in literal inerrancy. He certainly believed in the inspiration of the Bible, but "only very rarely" spoke of it.[49] Second, Calvin was fond of comparing the word of Scripture with a mirror. Here Niesel quotes Peter Barth, who interprets Calvin as follows: "The mirror clearly reflects an image, but this reflection is not identical with the image itself." Niesel also mentions approvingly Peter Barth's quoting of Calvin's exegesis of II Corinthians 5:7: "We see indeed, but as in a glass darkly — i.e., instead of having the thing itself we have to be content with the message about it."[50] Niesel himself adds that Calvin sometimes calls the Bible an "instrument" of the Spirit. "This means that the Holy Spirit uses the word, but it does not mean that it has so penetrated the word as to be identical with it." Does not Calvin use the term "instrument" also with regard to the elements in the Eucharist?[51] Finally, there is a third series of

---

46. I, xviii, 4. "Without reservation" — *sine exceptione*.

47. W. Niesel, *The Theology of Calvin*, 1956. The original German edition is dated 1938.

48. Niesel, *op. cit.*, pp. 31f.

49. Niesel does not seem to take into account the fact that the inspiration of the Bible was not at stake in those days. Protestants and Roman Catholics alike accepted it.

50. Pringle's translation (ed. Eerdmans) is much more accurate: "We *rest upon* the word" (italics ours).

51. Ronald S. Wallace (*Calvin's Doctrine of the Word and Sacrament*, 1957) argues along similar lines. He, too, draws a parallel between Calvin's doctrine of the Word and his doctrine of the Sacraments. "It seems . . . quite impossible that Calvin, if assailed on this point, would give sanction to any doctrine of inspiration that presupposed a different relation between the divine and human elements than the sacramental relation which is so important a feature in Calvin's theology. In this relation the human action remains throughout real human action, and the divine action remains divine grace throughout. The divine character never becomes inherently and inseparably connected with the human element, though it is true that the human action and indeed the human element can be *spoken* of as if it did so partake of the divine nature" (pp. 113-114).

passages where Calvin says that the word of the Bible is as a dead and ineffectual thing for us, if it is not divinely vivified.

Here we are mainly interested in the second point. It is obvious that Calvin is interpreted in a fully Barthian way. Calvin too would have made the distinction between the Bible and revelation. But Niesel's proofs from Calvin's own writings are not at all conclusive. The appeal to Calvin's exegesis of II Corinthians 5:7, for instance, is very weak. Calvin comments here on Paul's words: "For we walk by faith, not by sight." Paul is concerned here with the appropriation of salvation by the believers here on earth. As long as they are in the body they do not yet have heavenly knowledge, they do not yet see Him face to face (I Cor. 13:12). In this dispensation they can appropriate salvation only by way of faith in the Word. To Calvin this does not degrade the Word but rather elevates it, for it is the way in which believers apprehend salvation. We are not at all surprised, therefore, that Karl Barth, in contrast to Peter Barth and Niesel, quotes precisely these words of Calvin as proof for the unity of the Bible and revelation, rather than for their distinctness.[52]

Further, when Calvin sometimes calls the Bible the "instrument" of the Holy Spirit, his words cannot bear Niesel's interpretation either. When, for example, Calvin in his *Institutes* I, ix, 3 writes: "The word is the instrument by which the illumination of the Spirit is dispensed," we must examine the context of the whole argument. Calvin is here refuting the spiritualists, who appeal directly to the Holy Spirit apart from the Word. Over against them Calvin says that there is no illumination without the Word, and then he follows with the sentence quoted above. Nothing in the context even hints that Calvin meant some sort of limitation by it. On the contrary, in this same paragraph he speaks very convincingly of the indissoluble connection between Word and Spirit. Says he: "The Holy Spirit . . . cleaves to his own truth, as he has expressed it in Scripture," and: "The Lord has so knit together the certainty of His word and His Spirit, that our minds are duly imbued with reference for the word when the Spirit shining upon it enables us there to behold the face of God." When we read the word "instrument" against this background, we find no room for "limitation"; rather, it indicates the intimate, insep-

---

52. *Zwischen der Zeiten, op. cit.*, p. 226. Cf. also *C.D.*, I, 2, 495.

arable relation between the Spirit and the Bible, and between the divine revelation and the Bible (which Calvin in this paragraph calls the "oracles" of the Spirit).

Another of Niesel's examples, *Institutes* IV, xi, 1, is no more successful. Here Calvin speaks of the keys of the kingdom, and exactly in this connection he speaks in a very emphatic way of Holy Scripture. Christ made this statement for two reasons. First of all for the apostles, "that not having Christ the author of their doctrine bodily present on the earth, they might understand that he was in heaven to confirm the truth of the doctrine which he had delivered to them." But secondly also for their hearers, in order that they

> should be most certainly assured that the doctrine of the gospel was not the word of the apostles, but of God himself; not a voice rising from the earth, but descending from heaven. . . . Christ therefore testified that in the preaching of the gospel the apostles only acted ministerially; that it was he who, by their mouths as organs, spoke and promised all; that, therefore, the forgiveness of sins which they announced was the true promise of God; the condemnation which they pronounced, the certain judgment of God. This attestation was given to all ages, and remains firm, rendering all certain and secure, that the word of the gospel, by whomsoever it may be preached, is the very word of God, promulgated at the supreme tribunal, written in the book of life, ratified firm and fixed in heaven.

In the light of these few quotations Niesel's thesis does not seem to be proved, to say the least!

We make the same criticism of John K. S. Reid, who has recently interpreted Calvin in a similar way. Strongly leaning on the works of E. Doumergue, he too asserts that Calvin did not know of a direct identity between the Bible and the Word of God, but only of *"indirect identity."*[53] He even goes so far as to use Barthian terminology to describe Calvin's view: "It is not revelation itself, but only attestation of revelation."[54] Reid is of course familiar with the fact that in Calvin's writings we can find many statements which at least *prima facie* seem to teach a literal, verbal inspiration. He even begins his exposition of Calvin's teaching by quoting them extens-

---

53. John K. S. Reid, *The Authority of Scripture*, p. 36.
54. *Ibid.*, pp. 42, 43.

ively.⁵⁵ But he believes that only the concept of "indirect identity" can account for these statements of Calvin on the one hand, and his detailed criticisms on the other.⁵⁶

This solution, however, looks very much like a construction of embarrassment. Apart from the fact that nothing is left of Calvin's so-called critical disposition (or as Reid calls it, "the apparent deviations") when the adduced places are carefully examined,⁵⁷ there is the much weightier fact that Calvin, if he indeed had accepted such an "indirect identity," never could have spoken in such a pointed, pregnant way as he actually did. Reid tries to solve this difficulty by speaking of a "foreshortening of the perspective"⁵⁸ with Calvin in some places, but then this would be a "foreshortening" which not only gives a wrong impression to the reader, but even *expressis verbis* would clash with his real, deepest intention.

The *basic* error of Reid is that he identifies literal or verbal inspiration with a *mechanical* conception of inspiration.⁵⁹ But this is an identification which has no right to exist. True, it has been defended (e.g. in the early Church and in the seventeenth century), but this does not mean that *every* acceptance of verbal inspiration implies this mechanical conception. Calvin was certainly not an advocate of a mechanical theory.⁶⁰

55. *Ibid.*, pp. 34f.
56. *Ibid.*, p. 36. "If his view really is that there is not an exact identity, but an 'indirect identity,' it is not unnatural that expressions should be used which foreshorten the perspective and which, read in isolation, give the impression of affirming a direct identity. Two kinds of expressions have to be accommodated; and the view that Calvin does not hold verbal inspiration accomodates them more easily than the view that he does. Already the lines of a prima facie case that Calvin is no verbal inspirationist are appearing."
57. Reid mainly appeals to Calvin's comments on the New Testament way of quoting the Old Testament, *op. cit.*, pp. 40, 44.
58. *Op. cit.*, pp. 36, 48, 51.
59. The same is said by Father Hebert in his *Fundamentalism and the Church of God*, 1957. He speaks of "the rigid doctrine that Holy Scripture must be taken to be entirely free from error in every detail. This rigid view coincides with the 'dictation-theory' of Inspiration, that the human writer was a pen with which the Holy Spirit wrote" (p. 56). Cf. also C. H. Dodd, *The Authority of the Bible*, 1938, p. 35; E. Brunner, *Revelation and Reason*, 1946, p. 128; Wand, *The Authority of Scripture*, p. 59.
60. Cf. B. B. Warfield, *Calvin and Calvinism*, 1931, pp. 63f. Wallace, *op. cit.*, p. 107f.

Though he admittedly used expressions which seem to imply this ("dictation," "amanuensis"), yet he also clearly defends the genuinely human aspect of the Bible. He even recognizes an element of "accommodation" to human weakness in the Bible. According to Reid one cannot do the latter and at the same time be a "literalist."[61] But again this is nothing but a supposition. Many Reformed theologians (Calvin himself included) fully accept the verbal inspiration of the Bible and yet acknowledge the human aspect of the Bible. It certainly would clarify theological discussion of Holy Scripture and its inspiration, if literal, verbal inspiration and mechanical inspiration were no longer confused.

Likewise Reid's assertion that the orthodox view would mean that the Holy Spirit is "locked up" within the Bible[62] rests on a complete misunderstanding of the orthodox position. He who fights this, fights windmills. And he who in this way tries to prove that Calvin was not a "literalist" does not prove anything, because neither Calvin nor any other Reformed "literalist" would defend this. We agree with B. A. Gerrish when he writes:

> It cannot (I think) be maintained that Calvin holds "Word" and "Spirit" together in a kind of dynamic relationship — as though authority were vested, not in the Scripture *per se*, but rather in the Spirit "speaking through the Scriptures." This would no doubt be very congenial to our modern ways of thinking. But Calvin seems to be thinking along different lines.[63]

As a matter of fact Reid's own argument is nothing else than the following: Calvin *seems* to say *this*, but in actual fact he *means* to say *that*. This is so often repeated that one wonders

---

61. An ugly term! Reid writes: "Verbal inspiration raises the issue of the nature of God's operations with men. One view is that the Bible is simply a divine datum, something given directly by God to men . . . . Whether the statement is made by Reformed or Roman theology, the Bible is represented as God's Word in a sense which precludes its being at the same time a genuinely human word. When the matter is put in this way, it is fairly clear on which side Calvin must be held to stand. As has already been said, he often points out the humanness of the Bible, but always (or at least in general) without prejudice to the thesis that it is at the same time the Word of God" (*op. cit.*, p. 45).

62. Reid, *op. cit.*, p. 47.

63. B. A. Gerrish, "Biblical Authority and the Continental Reformation," *Scottish Journal of Theology*, X, 355.

whether Calvin was not able to say what he meant.⁶⁴ We cannot possibly accept this. Calvin has expressed himself so clearly on this point that no room is left for such ambiguity.

In the light of Calvin's own words the whole assertion that he did not hold to verbal inspiration cannot be maintained. Rather than demonstrating this point at length here, we will give a few quotations from the last book of the *Institutes* as an example. Here he opposes the doctrine of the Church of Rome, which teaches that councils cannot err and that they may coin new doctrines. Over against this claim Calvin declares "that the servants of God are only to teach what they have learned from himself" (IV, viii, 5), which is immediately followed by the statement that "according to the variety of times, they have had different methods of learning." In the days of the patriarchs the divine Wisdom, i.e. the Son, employed secret revelations and signs. Later on the law was given in written form, followed by the "new oracles" of the prophets, which also had to be committed to writing, and "to be held part of his Word." "To these at the same time were added historical details, which are also the composition of prophets, but dictated by the Holy Spirit" (IV, viii, 6). The whole body of the Old Testament books, therefore, constitutes "the Word of God" to his ancient people, and the teachers of those days were bound to give responses to the people "from the mouth of God." In the fullness of time the Wisdom of God was manifested in the flesh. "Now, therefore, since Christ, the Sun of Righteousness, has arisen, we have the perfect refulgence of divine truth, like the brightness of noon-day, whereas the light was previously dim" (IV, viii, 7). He is *the* revelation, as the Father Himself said: "Hear him" (Matt. 17:5), "ordering us to seek the whole doctrine of salvation from him alone, to depend on him alone, and cleave to him alone." It was the

---

64. Evidently Reid himself is not always too sure. E.g. on p. 38, *op. cit.*, he writes: "But that the problem appears in this form in his pages at all *seems* at least to exculpate him from the charge of verbal literalism" (italics ours). Also on p. 38: "*If it is permissible* to take this metaphorical use [namely the Word is like a mirror] as really normative for Calvin's thought, it yields a clear indication of his view of Holy Scripture." On p. 44 he says of Doumergue, Heppe, Clavier and Pannier, who all defend a similar view, that "they are *probably* right" on a certain point. Sometimes he even contradicts himself. Regarding Calvin's exegesis of Jer. 36:4-6 he says: "It follows that Calvin is not here arguing for verbal dictation, but rather from it" (p. 35). Cf. also p. 103.

task of the New Testament apostles "to show that the things [delivered in the ancient Scriptures] are fulfilled in Christ; this, however, they could not do unless from the Lord; that is, unless the Spirit of Christ went before, and in a manner dictated words to them" (IV, viii, 8). They were "sure and authentic amanuenses of the Holy Spirit; and, therefore, their writings are to be regarded as the oracles of God, whereas others have no other office than to teach what is delivered and sealed in the Holy Scriptures" (IV, viii, 9). From these few quotations one can draw only one conclusion, namely, that for Calvin there is no room for "distinctness." To him the Bible *is* the Word of God, without any restriction or limitation.[65]

* * *

We now return to Barth's concept of "indirect revelation." Here we find the deepest ground for his emphasis on the witness-character of the Bible, and on the limitation implied by this witness-character. The revelation which comes to us through the witness of the prophets and the apostles is always indirect. The "Deus dixit" and the "Paul dixit" do not coincide automatically, nor are they identical as such, but only in the *event* of God's Word do they *become* one. Moreover, the Word of God comes to us in the form of creation, even fallen creation. Therefore we never have the Word of God otherwise than in the mystery of its *worldliness*, that is, in its indirectness.

Considered in itself we have no objection against the combination of the words "revelation" and "indirect"; particularly not where the special function of the prophets and apostles is concerned. It is wholly true that we are accosted by the revelation of God only through these eye- and ear-witnesses. God does not speak directly to us without the mediation of these witnesses.

> The second generation, and all the succeeding generations, receive faith, illumination through the Spirit, *by means of the*

---

65. For more quotations see Reid, *op. cit.*, pp. 34f. In a supplementary note Reid (54f.) also gives an extensive list of those who deny the view of "literal" inspiration to Calvin and of those who defend this. To the former should be added J. A. Cramer, *De Heilige Schrift bij Calvijn*, 1926. To the latter: D. J. De Groot, *Calvijns opvatting over de inspiratie der Heilige Schrift*, 1931, and B. A. Gerrish, *op. cit.* from *Scottish Journal of Theology*.

witness of the first generation, of the Apostles, the eye-witnesses. Jesus Christ is not directly *"here"* for us, as He was for the disciples. We possess Him only in their narrative which tells us about Him. Their narrative and their doctrine are the *means*, which God uses, in order to unite us with Him. This is inherent in the very nature of the historical revelation.[66]

But then it has to be added at once that we *most certainly meet Jesus Christ* through *the medium* of these witnesses. In their witness He Himself is coming to us and revealing Himself unto us. In other words, *their witness is at the same time direct revelation to us*. As we saw in the preceding pages, Scripture itself does not make any restriction here, but: "He that heareth you heareth me; and he that rejecteth you rejecteth me; and he that rejecteth me rejecteth him that sent me" (Luke 10:16). The witness of the prophets and the apostles, that is *in concreto*, the Bible, does not only constitute the area or sphere where the divine revelation *may* take place, but this witness itself is included in the revelation, belongs to it, *is* revelation. For that reason Calvin rightly can say: "In place of the reality we rest upon the word" (ad II Cor. 5:7). Though the "building from God," the "house not made with hands, eternal, in the heavens" (II Cor. 5:1) is still a matter of promise, an eschatological quantity, yet we are not empty-handed. For we have the Word of promise, which is perfectly certain. We can *rest* in it, for it is God's own Word. To be sure it is spoken and handed down by men, but these men did not speak on their own authority; they were His "mouthpieces."

As we observed already, Barth also quotes this word of Calvin. He even does it with strong approval. It is used in support of the thesis that Christianity has been always and only a living religion, when it was not ashamed to be actually and seriously a book religion.[67] With Barth, however, such a statement may never be separated from the notion of indirectness, which must be taken just as seriously. The latter notion, as it were, counterbalances the former, and in our opinion weakens it considerably. Because Barth's view has these two dialectically related poles, he means something different from Calvin even though their words are the same. When Barth says "We rest upon the word," this certainly has to be taken

---

66. E. Brunner, *The Christian Doctrine of God*, Dogmatics I, 1958, p. 33.
67. *C.D.*, I, 2, 495.

quite seriously because for Barth there is only one "word," the Bible; but at the same time it must be remembered that for Barth the word of revelation can come only as an event.

In subsequent chapters we will return to Barth's concepts of "event" and "worldliness." Here we will point to another aspect which is also of decisive importance for Barth's view of the "indirectness" and the "witness" character of the Bible, namely, his *concentration* of all revelation upon the *revelation in Jesus Christ.*

* * *

According to Barth there is only one real revelation, the revelation in Jesus Christ. Only in Him do we have *direct* revelation. "God's revelation is the event of Jesus Christ."[68] In Jesus Christ God has become present to us: *Deus praesens.* We can also say it in this way: In Jesus Christ God has time for us. "The Word became flesh" also means: "The Word became time."[69] On the one hand this time of the incarnate Word is ordinary time, like our time. It is part of what we call "historical" time. Yet, on the other hand, we should not confuse it with any other time. This is the time which God's Son assumed for us. It is the time of the Lord of time and for that very reason *real, fulfilled time.*[70] So we may say: The fulfilled time is the time of the years 1 to 30 A.D.[71]

This time of revelation in Jesus Christ has also a definite pre-time, namely, the time of the witness to the *expectation* of revelation or the time of the *Old Testament.*[72] This pre-time belongs to the time of fulfillment. It is co-ordinated with it.[73] although it is quite a different time. It, too, is revelation-time, though in the sense of the time of expecting revelation. It can be called revelation-time because genuine expectation of revelation does not exist without the latter. Likewise the fulfilled time is followed by a very definite time that is bound up with it.[74] This is the time of the witness to *recollection* of revelation, or the time of the *New Testament.* This time, too,

68. *Ibid.,* **49.**
69. *Ibid.,* **p. 50.**
70. *Ibid.,* **p. 52.**
71. *Ibid.,* **p. 58.**
72. *Ibid.,* **p. 70.**
73. The English translation does not give the exact meaning of the original German word. In German there is an element of subordination in the co-ordination. "Sie ist ihr. . . zugeordnet." (German ed., p. 77.)
74. *Op. cit.,* p. 101.

belongs to the time of fulfillment; we cannot speak of the latter without speaking of the former.

But however much the pre-time of expectation and the subsequent time of recollection belong to the time of fulfillment, they cannot be confused with it. The time of fulfillment is that definite time of the years 1 to 30 A.D., which was the time of Jesus Christ. This was the time of the real revelation. But even here we must apply *yet another concentration*. The revelation-time was the time of the *forty days of the Easter story* (with the story of the transfiguration as prologue and the story of the conversion of Saul as epilogue).[75] Here we have a present without any future, an eternal presence of God in time. This is the "pure presence of God".[76] Here the eschatology has become reality already, though it is at the same time the beginning of a new eschatological expectation. Because in the Easter story we have *God's* eternal time present in this history, it never becomes a fact merely belonging to the past. This is a time which overarches our time and cannot be confined to datable time, with which it is in the first instance related. Or, in other words, "we have His revelation not only behind us; because we have it behind us, we also have it in front of us."[77]

In our opinion this is one of the most *fundamental* aspects of Barth's doctrine of revelation. Jesus Christ and He alone is revelation. Or even better: Revelation takes place only in Jesus Christ. All the rest is not revelation in the real sense of the word, it is only expectation or recollection of this one revelation. And though it is certainly not denied by Barth that this expectation and recollection are parts of the revelation, this admission does not alter the fact that revelation itself remains limited to what happened in Jesus Christ. It is quite natural, of course, that on this standpoint the relation between the Old and New Testament witness on the one hand and revelation itself on the other hand can be expressed only in terms like "indirect identity."

* * *

The great question here is: Is this *christological concentration* of the revelation in conformity with what Scripture itself

---

75. *Ibid.*, p. 114. Cf. *K.D.*, III, 2, 529ff.
76. *Die Reine Gegenwart Gottes.* (German ed., p. 125.)
77. *C.D.*, I, 2, 116.

teaches? Does it have any ground, for instance, in the terminology used by Scripture? Or does it actually mean an unpermitted *narrowing* of the scriptural idea of revelation? Is the often-mentioned accusation of "Christomonism" in place here?

In the first place we reply that there is nothing in the *terminology* of Scripture that warrants such a limiting concentration. Very often the attempt has been made to single out one special word as indicative of *the* revelation, which would be the revelation in Jesus Christ. But all these attempts have been failures. Scripture uses several words side by side and interchangeably, and in *all* these several words it "points to God's active revealing of Himself as an all-powerful reality, which may be expressed as transcending of the mystery, as a *speaking* or *showing* or *making known*."[78] Whether it is used of the revelation in the Old Testament days, or of the revelation in Jesus Christ in the fullness of time, everywhere we find this same meaning. We therefore have no right "to arrive in a simplistic manner to one New Testament word for revelation as the only actual one," but the only conclusion can be: "How broad and wide Scripture speaks of God's revealing activity."[79]

In the second place Berkouwer has pointed out "that in the revelation God *Himself* comes to us."[80] And then he immediately adds: "This sheds light on the conception that *only in the incarnation* God *Himself* comes to us and that we, therefore, only in this respect are dealing with real revelation." He calls this a dogmatic reflection which is nowhere found in Scripture itself. Scripture nowhere makes a distinction between real or actual revelation, which would have taken place in the incarnation, and all the other things which are grouped around this, which participate with it in a certain way but are still not revelation in the *real* sense of the word.

> The consistent conclusion from this [Barth's] conception must be, then, that there is not only no revealing activity of God in nature and history but neither can there be any real revelation of God under the Old Covenant. Usually a "participation" of God's revelation by the Old Covenant is mentioned — as a foreshadow — but in the light of the uniqueness of revelation

---

78. G. C. Berkouwer, *General Revelation*, 1955, p. 99.
79. *Ibid.*, p. 100.
80. *Ibid.*, p. 101.

this can never mean that also under the Old Covenant there was *real, actual* revelation of God.[81]

Such a conception, however, is in flagrant contradiction with the clear language of Holy Scripture itself. We can point here particularly to the beginning of the Epistle to the Hebrews, where the author says: "God, having of old time spoken unto the fathers in the prophets by divers portions and in divers manners, hath at the end of these days spoken unto us in his Son. . ." (Heb. 1:1, 2). These words are the more remarkable because it is this epistle that emphasizes so strongly the once-for-all-ness of the salvation brought about by Jesus. All the rites and ceremonies of the law have found their fulfillment in Jesus Christ, who as the great high priest "now once at the end of the ages hath been manifested to put away sin by the sacrifice of himself" (Heb. 9:26, cf. 28). It is the entirely unique act of Jesus that "by one offering he hath perfected for ever them that are sanctified" (Heb. 10:14). And yet this same epistle also emphatically maintains the fully revelational nature of the Old Testament. Surely there *is* a difference. The revelation in the Son, which takes place "at the end of these days," is *the eschatological revelation,* the *consummation* of all previous revelation. But there is no indication that this also implies a difference between real and non-real revelation. On the contrary, in both instances it is *God* who spoke, and in both cases the Greek original uses the *same verb* to denote this divine speaking *(lalēsas, elalēsan).* Berkouwer therefore rightly says:

> The difference between the former and the latter speaking of God is not that the former was less trustworthy or would less contain the nature of *actual revelation.* All such inferences are completely ruled out. Grosheide correctly states that we find in Heb. 1:1 "that the revelation under the Old Covenant was not inferior (cf. I Peter 1:11), but that the prophets are under the Son."[82]

The New Testament can still speak in such an unproblematical way because it does not know of any incarnational scheme that is imposed upon the divine revelation. Without any exaggeration we may say that the New Testament as a whole is a complete stranger to the idea that the actual revela-

---

81. *Ibid.,* p. 102.
82. *Ibid.,* pp. 105-106.

tion would commence with Jesus Christ. True, it emphatically declares that all preceding revelation pointed to Jesus Christ and that in Him it reached its zenith, its fullness, but this never means a derogation from the reality of the preceding revelation.

> While the revelation of the Old and the New Covenant are thus sharply distinguished, God is the one Author of both. He spoke in old time, and He spoke in the last time. In the former case His speaking was upon earth and in the latter case from heaven, but in both cases the words are alike His words.[83]

It is striking, indeed, that the Bible itself is not afraid of speaking of "direct revelation" in the Old Testament. The New Testament repeatedly quotes the Old Testament as spoken by God Himself.[84] The New Testament writers time and again point to the fact that it was God who spoke, who revealed Himself through the Old Testament prophets.[85] And the Old Testament prophets themselves also spoke to Israel with the consciousness of being messengers of God, bearers of His revelation. Time and again they introduced their messages with the weighty words: "Thus saith the Lord. . . ." To make a distinction here between "direct" and "indirect" revelation is altogether out of place. It is nothing but a preconceived scheme which is pressed upon the texts. Brunner (we are inclined to say: against his will) is forced to admit this:

> In the prophetic revelation the revelation of the Old Testament attains its highest point. . . . [Here] God Himself actually speaks, using human words, in formulated sentences, which like other sentences, are formed of intelligible words. Thus here the Word of God is present in the form of revealed human words, not behind them — which human words merely seek to express, just as a poet tries to express in words what an impression of nature or of a musical work of art "says" to him — but in direct identity, in the complete equation of the human word with the "Word of God."[86]

As a matter of fact there is neither in the Old nor in the New Testament the slightest indication that the prophets and apos-

---

83. B. F. Westcott, *On the Epistle to the Hebrews*, The Greek Text with Notes and Essays, p. 4.
84. For example: Rom. 3:2 ("the oracles of God"), Acts 4:24, 25; 13:34, 35; Heb. 1:6; etc.
85. For example: Acts 3:21; I Pet. 1:11.
86. Brunner, *The Christian Doctrine of God*, pp. 22, 23. Having admitted this, Brunner introduces the contrast between Word and

tles even reckoned with the possibility that they were not speaking the Word of God.[87] In all their words they manifest a clear consciousness of being God's "mouthpieces." Thus, for example, the New Testament apostles address the congregations with the authority of God's ambassadors and representatives. Without any hesitation they impose upon the congregations their own words as the Word of God. Paul does not shrink back from asserting that even if an angel from heaven preached unto the Galatians any gospel other than what he, Paul, had preached unto them, let him be anathema (Gal. 1:8). And to the Corinthians he writes: "We are ambassadors therefore on behalf of Christ, as though God were intreating by us: We beseech you on behalf of Christ, be ye reconciled to God" (II Cor. 5:20). Again there is no distinction whatsoever between a "Deus dixit" and a "Paulus dixit." Not even in the words "as though" (*hōs*). According to Grosheide the meaning is not: "It seems so, but it is not so," but rather: "because," i.e., *we* seem to do it, but in reality it is *God* who does it.[88]

Person in order to escape the threatening consequence of the doctrine of verbal inspiration. In Jesus Christ God's revelation is not a "Word" but a Person: Immanuel, God with us. Now the Kingdom of God has dawned and therefore the old is over and past, even the Old Covenant with all the forms of revelation proper to it (p. 23). The great mistake of Orthodoxy was that it returned again to verbal inspiration, forgetting that with Jesus everything has changed (p. 28). The Word which has been formulated in human speech is now only revelation in an indirect sense: it is revelation as witness to Him (p. 27). Cf. also: "The idea which lies behind the theory of Verbal Inspiration corresponds to some extent with the Old Testament, prophetic level of revelation; but it is not in any way in harmony with the New Testament stage of revelation. And precisely for this reason: that, unlike the revelation of the Old Testament, the New Testament revelation is not to be understood simply and solely as the revelation in the 'Word'" (pp. 31-32).

87. Even a text like I Cor. 7:25 may not be interpreted to this effect. Paul says here: "Now concerning virgins I have no commandment of the Lord; but I give my judgment, as one that hath obtained mercy of the Lord to be faithful." This statement does not mean that here Paul disclaims the guidance and inspiration of the Spirit, but he only declares that regarding this special point ("virgins") he has "no saying of the Lord to quote." Cf. Leon Morris, I Cor., *Tyndale New Testament Commentary*, 1958, p. 115. Cf. also F. W. Grosheide, I Cor., *New International Comm. on the New Testament*, 1953, p. 174.

88. F. W. Grosheide, *De Tweede Brief van den Apostel Paulus aan de kerk te Corinthe*, 1939, p. 214. Cf. also C. Hodge, *Commentary on the Second Epistle to the Corinthians*, "An ambassador is at once a messenger and a representative. He does not speak in his own name.

For this very reason it is according to Peter such a great sin when the "ignorant and unstedfast" wrest the epistles of Paul, as they do also the other Scriptures. In deadly earnest he adds: they do so "unto their own destruction" (II Peter 3:16). Particularly instructive is also what Paul writes in Romans 10:8. In the preceding passage he has spoken of the righteousness of God (v. 3) or the righteousness of faith (v. 6) which has appeared in Christ, "who is the end of the law unto righteousness to every one that believeth" (v. 4). Jesus Christ indeed acquired this righteousness fully. Therefore: "Say not in thy heart, Who shall ascend into heaven? (that is, to bring Christ down): or, Who shall descend into the abyss? (that is, to bring Christ up from the dead)" (vv. 6, 7). We should not act as if Christ still had to come and the righteousness of faith still had to be wrought. But where then do we find Christ? And then the clear answer of the apostle, continuing the quotation of Deuteronomy 30, is: "In the word which we preach." And this word is very near. "The word is nigh thee, in thy mouth and in thy heart: that is, the word of faith, which we preach" (v. 8). "There is a remarkable contrast in this verse. Over against the negative: The Messiah is far away, unreachable, not yet come (of which Paul says that it should not be said), he places the affirmative. Not in this form: Christ is here or there on earth, but thus: The word is nigh thee. That means: *Christ is in the word; it is the Gospel which brings Him nigh.*"[89] Again we must say: There is not a shadow of "distinctness" or "limitation" here. In the word of the apos-

---

He does not act on his own authority. What he communicates is not his own opinions or demands, but simply what he has been told or commissioned to say. His message derives no part of its importance or trustworthiness from him. At the same time he is more than a mere messenger. He represents his sovereign. He speaks with authority, is accredited to act in the name of his master" (p. 146). Cf. "It will be noticed that to be an ambassador for Christ, and that God speaks through us, mean the same thing" (p. 147). In this same sense we have also to read what Calvin writes in *Instit.* I, vii, 1, namely, that the full authority of the Bible is not recognized "unless they are believed to have come from heaven, as directly as if [acsi] God had been heard giving utterance to them." According to Barth this is a "proviso," just like "a Dei loquentis persona" in I, vii, 4. (*C.D.*, I., 1, 128). Such an interpretation violates the clear intention of the very words.

89 J. A. C. Van Leeuwen and D. Jacobs, *De Brief aan de Romeinen*, 1939, p. 200 (italics ours).

tolic preaching Christ Himself with all the treasures of God's righteousness is present. Or in other words: The word of apostolic preaching *is* revelation in the full, deep sense of the word.

* * *

All this does not mean that we want to deny or even to minimize the *unique place of Jesus Christ* in the whole of God's revelation. On the contrary, He is the living center of all revelation of salvation. And that not only in the historical sense of the word — Christ stands historically between the Old and the New Testaments — but also in this sense, that it was He of whom all the prophets and apostles spoke; even more, it was He who Himself spoke in and through these prophets and apostles. Seldom has this been expressed more clearly than by Calvin:

> If it is true, as Christ says, "Neither knoweth any man the Father save the Son, and he to whomsoever the Son will reveal him" (Matt. 11:27), then those who wish to attain to the knowledge of God behoved always to be directed by that eternal wisdom. For how could they have comprehended the mysteries of God in their mind, or declared them to others, unless by the teaching of him, to whom alone the secrets of the Father are known? The only way, therefore, by which in ancient times holy men knew God, was by beholding him in the Son as in a mirror. When I say this, I mean that God never manifested himself to men by any other means than by his Son, that is his own only wisdom, light, and truth. From this fountain, Adam, Noah, Abraham, Isaac, Jacob, and others, drew all the heavenly doctrine which they possessed. From the same fountain all the prophets also drew the heavenly oracles which they published (*Inst.* IV, viii, 5).

And the same is said about the New Testament apostles:

> Nothing else was permitted to the apostles than was formerly permitted to the prophets, namely to expound the ancient Scriptures and show that the things there delivered are fulfilled in Christ: this, however, they could not do unless from the Lord: that is, unless the Spirit of Christ went before, and in a manner dictated words to them (IV, viii, 8).[90]

Jesus Christ is the center, the heart, the foundation of God's revelation of salvation, and as such it was He who spoke through the prophets and apostles. It was His Spirit who was

---

90. Cf. B. A. Gerrish, *op. cit.*, pp. 352ff.

in the prophets and who "testified beforehand the sufferings of Christ, and the glories that should follow them" (I Peter 1:11).[91] But exactly because it was He who spoke through them, they themselves are included in this revelation of salvation. The Old and New Testaments themselves belong to the revelation. They are, as it were, the preludium and the postludium of the sonata of the revelation. As such they have each their own allotted place, which cannot possibly be reversed. They should not be confused with the main central part, but nevertheless they belong to the sonata itself and are indispensable. The prophets and apostles are more than mere witnesses whose only function is to point to what they themselves are not. In their being witnesses they indeed *reveal* God's will of salvation, they reveal *God Himself* in His will of salvation, and therefore it holds true of them, without any reservation: "He that heareth you, heareth me." Therefore also John can conclude his book, containing the revelation of the "things which must shortly come to pass," with those immensely heavy-laden words: "I testify unto every man that heareth the words of the prophecy of this book, If any man shall add unto them, God shall add unto him the plagues which are written in this book: and if any man shall take away from the words of the book of this prophecy, God shall take away his part from the tree of life, and out of the holy city, which are written in this book" (Rev. 22:18, 19).

91. Cf. II Sam. 23:2, Isa. 61:1.

CHAPTER III

THE HUMANITY AND FALLIBILITY OF THE BIBLE

In the preceding chapter we saw that Barth distinguishes between the "Deus dixit" and the "Paulus dixit."

> In revelation we are concerned with Jesus Christ to come, who ultimately in the fullness of time did come. Literally we are, therefore, concerned with the singular Word spoken, and this time really directly, by God Himself. But in the Bible we are invariably concerned with human attempts to repeat and reproduce, in human thoughts and expressions, this Word of God in definite human situations. . . . In the one case "Deus dixit," in the other "Paulus dixit."[1]

This distinction naturally implies that the Bible, at least from one point of view, is a fully *human* book.

In the second part of Volume I Barth works this out as follows:

> We have to say that between the Bible and the other quantities and factors of our human cosmos there is no difference in so far as the Bible is incidentally a historical document for the history of ancient Israel and its religion, in so far as it is also a document for one aspect of the religious history of Hellenism and can therefore be used as a collection of historical sources, although with little prospect of success in view of its peculiar literary form. Again, as a timeless document of the human longing and seeking for the unconditioned, the Bible can, if we like, be read alongside other documents of a similar kind. And we shall find that fundamentally at any rate it is not different from other documents of this kind.[2]

A few pages later he says:

1. *C.D.*, I, 1, 127.
2. *C.D.*, I, 2, 495, 496.

Even here the human element does not cease to be human, and as such and in itself it is certainly not divine. And it is quite certain that God does not cease to be God. In contrast to the humanity of Jesus Christ, there is no unity of person between God and the humanity of the prophets and apostles. Again, in contrast to the humanity of Jesus Christ, the humanity of the prophets and apostles is not taken up into the glory of God.[3]

In this last quotation Barth clearly points out that we have *no right to identify* the "Word becoming Scripture" (ie., the inscripturation) and the "Word becoming flesh" (i.e., the incarnation). There are decisive differences which may not be overlooked. In the incarnation there is a unity of the divine and human nature in the divine person of the Son, that is, the *unio personalis*. In the inscripturation such a unity of person is absent. Yet, on the other hand, there is a very intimate relation between incarnation and inscripturation: they belong together. The word of the apostles *had to* follow the incarnation. If this word had not come, we would know nothing about the incarnation. And so Barth can say in the same breath: "That the Word has become Scripture is *not one and the same thing* as its becoming flesh," and, "But the uniqueness and at the same time general relevance of its becoming flesh *necessarily involved* its becoming Scripture."[4]

We must make yet another step, according to Barth. There is even a *parallel* between the incarnation and inscripturation. Just as Jesus Christ is God and man and not a mixture of the two, so the Bible is also God and man, that is, it is a witness of revelation which itself belongs to revelation, and it is historically a human literary document.[5]

* * *

To acknowledge that the Bible is a fully human document is, however, only the first step. We must go on at once to acknowledge that the Bible as a human document is also a *fallible* document. This is also one of the consequences of the "witness idea."

> The men whom we hear as witnesses speak as fallible, erring men like ourselves. What they say, and what we read as their

---

3. *Ibid.*, pp. 499, 500.
4. *Ibid.*, p. 500.
5. *Ibid.*, p. 501. Cf. p. 499: "It is impossible that there should have been a transmutation of the one into the other, or an admixture of the one with the other."

THE HUMANITY AND FALLIBILITY OF THE BIBLE 59

word, can of itself lay claim to be the Word of God, but never sustain that claim. We can read and try to assess their word as a purely human word. It can be subjected to all kinds of immanent criticism, not only in respect of its philosophical, historical and ethical content, but even of its religious and theological. We can establish lacunae, inconsistencies and overemphases. We may be alienated by a figure like that of Moses. We may quarrel with James or with Paul. We may have to admit that we can make little or nothing of large tracts of the Bible, as is often the case with the records of other men. We can take offence at the Bible.[6]

How realistically this is meant by Barth appears from another quotation:

The prophets and apostles as such, even in their office, even in their function as witnesses, even in the act of writing down their witness, were real, historical men as we are, and therefore sinful in their action, and capable and actually guilty of error in their spoken and written word.[7]

Barth substantiates his assertion by the following points.

In the first place he points to the *biblical world view and view of man*. At this point we clearly see that the biblical writers shared the culture of their own age and environment. "In the Biblical view of the world and of man we are constantly coming up against presuppositions, which are not ours, and statements and judgments we cannot accept."[8] It cannot be denied that this gives many tensions. Barth deliberately expresses himself very carefully here. He does not speak plainly of "errors" but prefers to say: there is with the biblical authors a "capacity for errors" in this regard. For is our present-day view fully correct? Our insight is no more divine or even solomonic than that of the biblical authors. Nevertheless, it is obvious that there are real difficulties at this point. Here certainly is an "offense," and we must believe in spite of it.

Second, Barth mentions the writers' *understanding of history*.

Like all ancient literature the Old and New Testaments know nothing of the distinction of fact and value which is so important to us, between history on the one hand, and saga and legend on the other.[9]

6. *Ibid.*, p. 507.
7. *Ibid.*, p. 529.
8. *Ibid.*, p. 508.
9. *Ibid.*, p. 509.

Again Barth adds that we cannot attach any final seriousness to this distinction, but this does not alter the fact that it causes difficulties and doubts. Again there is only one thing to do: we must face up to them and believe the Word of God, even if it meets us in the form of saga and legend.

Third, Barth says that there are difficulties as to the *contents* as well. "The vulnerability of the Bible, i.e., its capacity for error, also extends to its *religious or theological* content."[10] The biblical authors did not speak a special language of revelation radically different from that of their time. They often resemble their contemporaries so closely that it is impossible to distinguish between them. Many parts of the Old Testament, for example, seem to be nothing else than documents of secular legislation and history and practical wisdom. Moreover, none of the authors has given us a more or less complete and thoroughgoing theological system. And all together they do not give such a system either:

> There are obvious overlappings and contradictions — e.g. between the Law and the Prophets, between John and the Synoptists, between Paul and James. . . . Within certain limits and therefore relatively they are all vulnerable and therefore capable of error even in respect of religion and theology. In fact, of the actual constitution of the Old and New Testaments this is something which we cannot possibly deny, if we are not to be guilty of Docetism.[11]

With this last word, "Docetism," we touch one of the deepest motives behind Barth's view of the Bible. It is according to Barth (and rightly so!) one of the most dangerous heresies which threaten the Christian faith. Therefore he combats it time and again in his christological[12] and pneumatological[13] expositions. Therefore he combats it also in the doctrine of Holy Scripture. If we take away or derogate from the humanity of Scripture, we destroy the divine miracle of revelation. It would be foolish to think that in a docetic fashion we are putting the revelation on a much higher level. The only result would be that we would be left without any revelation whatsoever.

Finally, Barth mentions as a proof of the vulnerability of

10. *Ibid.*, Italics mine.
11. *Ibid.*, pp. 509, 510.
12. *Ibid.*, pp. 17f., 147f.
13. *Ibid.*, p. 266.

The Humanity and Fallibility of the Bible 61

the Bible the fact "that the Bible as the witness of divine revelation is in its humanity a product of the Israelitish, or to put it more clearly, the *Jewish spirit*."[14] This matter, which the Church has only begun to recognize in our day, constitutes, perhaps, the greatest stumblingblock. For the Jewish people is "a hard and stiff-necked people, because it is a people which resists its God, the living God. It is characterized as the people which in its own Messiah finally rejected and crucified the Saviour of the world, and therefore denied the revelation of God. It is in this way that the Bible is a Jewish book, the Jewish book."[15] And this offense, that is, the anti-Semitism in us all, can also be overcome only through faith.

How essential this vulnerability of the Bible is to Barth appears when he takes up the parallel between incarnation and inscripturation. Emphatically he says:

> This offence [viz. the fallibility], like the offence of the cross of Christ, is based on the fact that the Word of God became flesh and therefore to this very day has built and called and gathered and illumined and sanctified His Church amongst flesh. This offence is therefore grounded, like the overcoming of it, in the mercy of God. For that reason it must not be denied and for that reason, too, it must not be evaded. For that reason every time we turn the Word of God into an infallible biblical word of man or the biblical word of man into an infallible Word of God we resist that which we never ought to resist, i.e., the truth of the miracle that here fallible men speak the Word of God in fallible human words — and we therefore resist the sovereignty of grace, in which God Himself became man in Christ, to glorify Himself in His humanity.[16]

These words do not need any clarification. The offense of the Bible is grounded in the offense of the incarnation. God became "flesh," real, true flesh. According to Barth that means with regard to the Bible: a fallible Bible.

* * *

On the ground of all this it is not surprising that Barth wholeheartedly defends the right of *higher criticism*. It is a natural

---

14. *Ibid.*, p. 510.
15. In this connection (Barth wrote this in 1938! Unfortunately it becomes timely again in our day, as we seem to observe a new eruption of anti-Semitism all over the world) Barth makes some very profound and far-reaching remarks about the deepest motives of anti-Semitism (Cf. pp. 510f.
16. *Ibid.*, p. 529.

consequence of his entire view. But we must distinguish carefully here. Barth does not defend every form of higher criticism. Deliberately and emphatically he rejects those ideas which were behind nineteenth-century criticism. Those critics generally viewed the Bible as a purely human book. They did not seek for the message which is conveyed by the text, but tried to find the facts which *lie behind* the text. "Thus a history of Israel and of Old Testament religion is found behind the canonical Old Testament, a history of the apostolic age, i.e., of primitive Christianity, behind the canonical Acts and epistles."[17] In this way the canon was read quite differently from the way it was intended to be read, and the relationship between theme and text was completely dissolved. The critics acted as if the interest in antiquities was the only legitimate interest, and theology lost its own essential nature by allowing itself to be changed into a purely historical science.

Barth sounds a vigorous protest against this whole attitude. But his protest is qualified:

> There cannot . . . be any question of sealing off or abandoning socalled "criticism," as it has been so significant for this investigation. All relevant, historical questions must be put to the biblical texts, considered as witnesses in accordance with their literary form. . . . When the foolish pursuit of an historical truth *supra scripturam* is on all sides abandoned in favour of a circumscribed investigation of the *veritas scripturae ipsius,* then we can and must give the freest possible course to critical questions and answers as demanded by the character of the biblical witness as a human document, and therefore an historical quantity.[18]

That this has been Barth's attitude from the beginning, clearly appears from the first three prefaces of his *Römerbrief* (Epistle to the Romans), in all of which he explicitly deals with this problem of biblical criticism. In the preface to the first edition (Aug. 1918) he declares at the outset:

> The historical-critical method of Biblical investigation has its rightful place: it is concerned with the preparation of the intelligence — and this can never be superfluous. But, were I driven to choose between it and the venerable doctrine of Inspiration, I should without hesitation adopt the latter, which has a broader, deeper, more important justification. The doctrine

17. *Ibid.,* p. 492.
18. *Ibid.,* p. 494.

of Inspiration is concerned with the labour of apprehending, without which no technical equipment, however complete, is of any use whatever. Fortunately I am not compelled to choose between the two.[19]

Barth clearly defines and limits the task of criticism. It has only a preliminary function. The true task of exegesis is to penetrate into the message conveyed by the text.

Many of his readers, however, expressed their doubt whether Barth indeed had a proper appreciation of criticism. For why did he nowhere criticize even one of Paul's thoughts? Some of his opponents went so far as to call him an "enemy of historical criticism." To make things clear Barth in the preface to the second edition (Sept. 1921) emphatically repeated: "I have nothing whatsoever to say against historical criticism. I recognize it; and once more state quite definitely that it is both necessary and justified."[20] But then he adds at once that many critical commentators think that they have interpreted a book of the Bible when they have completed the preliminary work of criticism. In his opinion the work of the interpreter begins exactly then and there! "There is no difference of opinion with regard to the need of applying historical criticism as a prolegomenon to the understanding of the Epistle."[21] But it should be seen clearly that it is a prolegomenon and no more. "By genuine understanding and interpretation I mean that creative energy which Luther exercised with intuitive certainty in his exegesis; which underlies the systematic interpretation of Calvin; and which is at least attempted by such modern writers as Hofmann, J. T. Beck, Godet, and Schlatter."[22]

In this same preface he also enters into a discussion with the German scholar P. Wernle, who had charged him with "Biblicism." Wernle had said: "No single aspect of Paul's teaching seems to cause Barth discomfort. . . . There remain for him no survivals of the age in which Paul lived — not even trivial survivals."[23] What, however, does Wernle mean by "uncomfortable points" or "survivals," which should be permitted to remain relics of the past? Barth gives the following

19. Karl Barth, *Epistle to the Romans* (tr. Edwyn C. Hoskyns), 1933, p. 1.
20. *Ibid.*, p. 6.
21. *Ibid.*, p. 7.
22. *Ibid.*
23. *Ibid.*, p. 11.

enumeration: the Pauline "depreciation" of the earthly life of Jesus — Christ the Son of God — Redemption by the blood of Christ — Adam and Christ — Paul's use of the Old Testament — his so-called "baptismal sacramentalism" — the double predestination — his attitude to secular authority. Barth's only answer is — and rightly so! —: "Now imagine a commentary on the Epistle to the Romans which left these eight points unexplained. . . . Could such a commentary really be called an interpretation?"[24]

The critical voices, however, were by no means silenced. In the preface to the third edition (July, 1922) Barth therefore continues his conversation with the critics, this time especially with R. Bultmann. The latter had complained that Barth was too conservative in never criticizing the opinions of Paul himself. Said Bultmann: "Other spirits make themselves heard as well as the Spirit of Christ."[25] Barth's answer is:

> I do not wish to engage in a controversy with Bultmann as to which of us is the more radical. But I must go farther than he does and say that there are in the Epistle no words at all which are not words of those 'other spirits' which he calls Jewish or popular Christian or Hellenistic or whatever else they may be.[26]

The reason why Barth says this is his conviction that we never have the right to set the Spirit of Christ over against other spirits in such a way that we allegedly can distinguish them in two separate groups of texts. According to Barth the whole epistle is under the "Krisis" of the Spirit of Christ. "The whole is litera, that is, voices of those other spirits." But it is equally true that "the whole must . . . be understood in the relation to the true subject-matter, which is — The Spirit of Christ."[27] But all this still allows the right and necessity of historical criticism. Emphatically Barth repeats: "No human word, no word of Paul, is absolute truth. In this I agree with Bultmann — and surely with all intelligent people."[28]

24. *Ibid.*, p. 12.
25. *Ibid.*, p. 16.
26. *Ibid.*
27. *Ibid.*, p. 17.
28. *Ibid.*, p. 19. Cf. also Barth's correspondence with Adolf von Harnack, the great champion of Liberalism, published in *Theologische Fragen und Antworten*, 1957, pp. 20, 24. Cf. also his criticism of the old Reformation orthodoxy (among others F. Burmannus) which inconsistently and untenably limited itself to textual criticism. "Das Schriftprinzip der reformierten Kirche, in *Zwischen der Zeiten*, 1925, p. 227, n. 1.

THE HUMANITY AND FALLIBILITY OF THE BIBLE   65

* * *

We begin our critique by expressing our cordial *agreement* with Barth's great stress upon the *humanity* of the Bible. As a matter of fact this has generally been accepted and defended by Reformed theologians. For this very reason they generally rejected every mechanical conception of inspiration, as if God would have dictated what the *auctores secundarii* wrote: as if these latter would have been mere amanuenses, mere channels, through which the words of the Holy Spirit flowed, while their own mental life was in a state of repose; as if they did not contribute in any way to the contents or form of their writings, so that even the style of the books was not theirs, but of the Holy Spirit.[29] Admittedly some of the Early Fathers[30] and some of the Lutheran and Reformed theologians of the seventeenth century came dangerously near to a mechanical conception, and in some cases even transgressed the limit.[31] In general, however, Reformed theology adopted a more "organic" view of inspiration, according to which the Holy Spirit acted upon the authors in harmony with the laws of their own being. They were not passive, but active.[32]

One of the clearest examples of this human activity we find in Luke 1:1-4. We see Luke here engaged in a thorough in-

---

29. Cf. Berkhof, *Introductory Volume to Systematic Theology*, p. 151.

30. Cf. H. Sasse, "Sola Scriptura: Observations on Augustine's Doctrine of Inspiration," *Reformed Theol. Review*, Vol. XIV, No. 3, 67ff. They followed Jewish theories, as these had developed in the Aramaic and Greek synagogues, and also the profane Greek conception of inspiration, founded by Plato. Cf. Kleinknecht, *sub voce* PNEUMA, PNEUMATIKOS in Kittel's *Wörterbuch zum Neuen Testament*, VI, 345ff., 348 (n. 69).

31. Even one of the Reformation confessions is guilty, namely, the Formula Consensus Helvetica (1675), the last of the greater Reformed confessions. We must add, however, that this confession was never generally accepted by the several Reformed Churches. Even in the few cantons of Switzerland where it was recognized, it was soon set aside. Cf. Schaff, *The Creeds of Christendom*, I, 486.

32. To what extent Reformed theology is prepared to accept this appears from the following words of Charles Hodge: "There is no reason to believe that the operation of the Spirit in inspiration revealed itself any more in the consciousness of the sacred writers, than his operations in sanctification reveal themselves in the consciousness of the Christian. As the believer seems to himself to act, and in fact does act out of his own nature; so the inspired penmen wrote out of the fulness of their own thoughts and feelings, and employed the language and modes of expression which to them were the most natural and appropriate." *Syst. Theol.* I, 157.

vestigation of the various traditions that had sprung up after the resurrection. We see him collecting and sifting his material. We see him considering and weighing one tradition against the other. When he decided, he had reasons. We should not imagine that the Holy Spirit occasionally interfered in this activity as a sort of *deus ex machina,* a scientific lie-detector which told Luke that this is true and that is false.[33] And yet the Holy Spirit was present and active in all the human activities. We believe also of Luke that he was not only enlightened but "moved by the Holy Spirit" (II Peter 1:21), and that therefore the result of his activities was that he spoke "from God." And the same holds true of all the other writings of the Old and New Testaments. Even where we do not read of prior preparations (e.g. the N. T. Epistles) we need not hold a mechanical conception. Leon Morris has worked this out with regard to Paul's Epistle to the Romans as follows:

> I do not envisage a process of revelation wherein, for example, God used Paul to write the Epistle to the Romans by a mere mechanical dictation. The words are not the product of some Divine activity quite independent of Paul's own experience of God. The words are linked inseparably with Paul's experience of God and they arise out of that experience. If God wanted words like the Epistle to the Romans written, then I envisage Him as preparing a Paul to write it. He prepared him in his natural endowment. He prepared him in those years of which we know nothing. He prepared him in the years when Saul of Tarsus was a rising Jewish leader. He prepared him when he persecuted the Church. He prepared him by confronting him on the Damascus Road, and transforming his whole conception of life and of God and of Jesus. He prepared him in the years that followed, in the quiet years of which we know nothing, and in the active years of missionary service of which we know a little. He prepared him in the conflicts he had with the Judaizers and others. He prepared him in his daily discharge of "the care of all the churches." He prepared him in the depths of his soul in the spiritual lessons that all those years taught him. He prepared him by putting him in such a position vis-a-vis the Roman Church that it was the most natural thing for him, the Spirit-filled Apostle, to write as he

---

33. Another fine example of the full humanity of the biblical writings is found in I Corinthians 16:16, where Paul "corrects" a statement made a few lines before (cf. verse 14). This is genuinely human indeed. All of a sudden the apostle remembers that he baptized yet another family, in addition to the persons mentioned in verse 14.

did. Romans is not "a bolt from the blue." In John Baillie's words: It arises from "the living communion with God which had been granted to" Paul.³⁴

It is therefore not surprising to find that all these writings show the personal stamp of the author (e.g., his experiences, his style, etc.), and also the stamp of the time in which he lived. We can even say that in revelation the divine condescends so deeply into the human that outwardly there seems to be no difference between the special revelation and analogous phenomena in other religions. Between the speaking of God in special revelation and the so-called oracles in other religions, between prophecy and mantics, between miracle and magic we sometimes can barely distinguish. Here we agree fully with what Barth has said about the "worldliness" of the language of God (cf. Chapter II). It is indeed true that always we have the Word of God in a form which as such is not the Word of God, even does not betray that it is the form precisely of the Word of God.³⁵ This "ambiguity" is undoubtedly one of the strongest proofs of the true humanity of special revelation as a whole, and of the Bible in particular.

It is also generally accepted by Reformed theologians that this human character of the Bible involves a *limitation*. The fact that God's revelation is communicated to man in and through human thoughts and words, means a definite limitation. Human thoughts and words can never contain the full riches of the divine revelation. They can never do full justice to all the glories of God; to His grace, His justice, His omnipotence; to His sovereign freedom and love in His works of creation and redemption. Here we fully agree with the words of Augustine, aptly quoted by Barth³⁶:

> For to speak of the matter as it is, who is able? I venture to say, my brethren, perhaps not John himself spoke of the mat-

---

34. Quoted from a private paper, with kind permission of the author. Cf. also Auguste Lecerf, *An Introduction to Reformed Dogmatics*, 1949, p. 31; B. B. Warfield, *The Inspiration and Authority of the Bible*, 1951, p. 155; J. I. Packer, *Fundamentalism and the Word of God*, p. 107.

35. *C.D.*, I, 2, 189. In our opinion Barth goes too far when he says that its form is an unsuitable means, because it is the form of the creaturely reality of fallen man. Here the distinction between humanity and fallibility is wiped out so that the two become identical, which is *not an absolute necessity*. See below.

36. *C.D.*, I, 2, 508.

ter as it is, but even he only as he was able; for it was man that spoke of God, inspired indeed by God, but still man. Because he was inspired, he said something; if he had not been inspired, he would have said nothing; but because a man inspired, he spoke not the whole, but what a man could he spoke (*quod potuit homo dixit*).[37]

Indeed, what a man could, he spoke.

But there is yet more to be said here. Again we must take into account the *witness-character* of the Bible, as discussed in Chapter II. We found there that God's revelation in Jesus Christ comes to us through the witness of the biblical eye- and ear-witnesses. But witness always means humanity, even humanity-in-limitation. Every witness is naturally limited, because the eye- or ear-witness can give only those aspects of the matter which struck him personally. Or to put it in another way: Every witness is limited because he can testify only about those things which he could see from his own vantagepoint. Rightly Ridderbos says: As eye-witnesses' account the New Testament is "fruit of an apperception, which was not infinite, and of a reproduction, which did not exceed the limits of human comprehension and human memory."[38] He also points out that this is undoubtedly one of the reasons why not everything seen and heard by the apostles has become apostolic tradition, and also why there is so much uncertainty as to the sequence of events, the circumstances under which something was said and the exact words which were used.

All these things have always been fully recognized by Reformed theologians. They even did not hesitate to use strong expressions like "inadequacy" and "imperfection." Thus Dr. Abraham Kuyper, for example, said:

> The Divine factor of the Holy Scripture clothes itself in the garment of our form of thought, and holds itself to our human reality.... As the Logos has not appeared *in the form of glory,* but in the form of a servant, joining Himself to the reality of our nature, as this had come to be through the results of sin, so also, for the revelation of His Logos, God the Lord accepts *our* consciousness, our human life *as it is....* The forms or types are marred by want and sin. The "shadows" remain humanly

---

37. Augustine, Homily on John 1:1, quoted from the translation of the *Nicene and Post-Nicene Fathers* published by Eerdmans, Augustine's Works, VII, 7.

38. Herman Ridderbos, *Heilsgeschiedenis en Heilige Schrift*, p. 126.

imperfect, far beneath their ideal content. The "spoken words," however much aglow with the Holy Ghost, remain bound to the limitation of our language, disturbed as it is by anomalies. As a product of writing, the Holy Scripture also bears on its forehead the mark of the form of a servant.[39]

This quotation cannot be misunderstood. Both the humanity of Scripture and the limitation connected with it are fully stressed.

To show that these insights were not "discovered" by the critical theology of the nineteenth century, we turn next to the father of Reformed theology, John Calvin. Consider, in particular, the so-called *"accommodatio Dei,"* which time and again we encounter in Calvin's writings. In revelation God accommodates Himself to the situation of fallen men in order to reach them:

> Let us therefore remember that our Lord has not spoken according to His nature. For if He would speak His (own) language, would He be understood by mortal creatures? Alas, no. But how has He spoken to us in Holy Scripture? He has stammered. . . . So then God has as it were resigned: for as much as we would not comprehend what He would say, if He did not condescend to us. There you have the reason why in Holy Scripture one sees Him like a nurse rather than that one hears of His high and infinite majesty.[40]

All this is true, first, of the revelation during the old dispensation.[41] Time and again we see how God stoops down, as it were, in order to reach us. "He adapts Himself to us . . . He makes Himself familiar. He is as it were transfigured."[42] Commenting on Exodus 24:10, where we read that Moses and Aaron, Nadab and Abihu, and seventy of the elders "saw" the God of Israel, Calvin says: "They saw the God of Israel, not in all His reality and greatness, but in accordance with the dispensation which He thought best, and which He accommo-

---

39. A. Kuyper, *Principles of Sacred Theology*, 1954, pp. 478f.
40. *Corpus Reformatorum*, 26, c. 387. Original French in F.W.A. Korff, *Christologie*, De leer van het komen Gods, Vol. I, 1942, 244. Cf. also the quotations from the Sermon on Deut. 30:11-14, Sermon on Deut. 32:8-11, Sermon on Gal. 3:1, given by K. Schilder, *Tusschen Ja en Neen*, 1929, pp. 292ff.
41. Cf. Ronald Wallace, *Calvin's Doctrine of the Word and Sacrament*, pp. 2f.
42. Sermon on Job 1:6-8, quoted from Wallace, *op. cit.*, p. 3.

dated to the capacity of man."[43] But it is also true of the revelation in Jesus Christ. Though His coming means the end of the images and shadows of the Old Testament, and in comparison with these it can be said that in Him "the heavens are opened to us,"[44] yet this contrast is not so absolute that the idea of accommodation should now be discarded. On the contrary, nowhere is the accommodation (though in a different form) greater than here. In Him God Himself comes to us. But — He comes in the flesh! What that means for the mode of revelation comes to the fore in Calvin's exegesis of John 1:14:

> The word *Flesh* expresses the meaning of the Evangelist more forcibly than if he had said that *he was made man*. He intended to show to what a mean and despicable condition the Son of God, on our account, descended from the height of his heavenly glory. When Scripture speaks of man contemptuously, it calls him *flesh*. Now, though there be so wide a distance between the spiritual glory of the *Speech* of God and the abominable filth of our *flesh*, yet the Son of God stooped so low as to take upon himself that flesh, subject to so many miseries. The word *flesh* is not taken here for corrupt nature (as it is often used by Paul), but for mortal man; though it marks disdainfully his frail and perishing nature.[45]

We could summarize Calvin's views thus: It belongs to the essence of the special revelation, as it comes to fallen man, that it is given in the form of accommodation. And this does not only apply to the words spoken and written by prophets and apostles, but to the revelation of the Word Himself in Jesus Christ as well. Yes, the whole incarnation itself means "accommodatio Dei," as Calvin says, appealing to Irenaeus: "The Father, who is boundless in himself, is bounded in the Son, because he has accommodated himself to our capacity, lest our minds should be swallowed up by the immensity of his glory."[46]

---

43. Calvin, *Harmony of Exodus, Leviticus, Numbers and Deuteronomy*, III, 323. Cf. also Commentary on Jer. 31:12, where he points out that the prophets "describe the Kingdom of Christ in a way suitable to the comprehension of a rude people, and hence they set before them external images."
44. Comm. on Jer. 31:12, XIV, 82.
45. Commentary on John's Gospel, I, 45. In another place he says, "That we cannot believe in God except through Christ, in whom God in a manner makes Himself little, that He might accommodate Himself to our comprehension." (Comm. on I Peter 1:21, Vol. on Catholic Epistles, p. 54.)
46. *Institutes* II, vi, 4.

Can the limitation involved in the humanity of the Bible be stressed more strongly than here? To ask the question is to answer it.

* * *

From all this it also follows that Reformed theology on the whole has no objection against the *parallel* between the Word becoming flesh, i.e., the *incarnation*, and the Word becoming Scripture, i.e., the *inscripturation*. We may even say that it always tended positively toward this parallel. So, for example, Bavinck writes:

> In the doctrine of Holy Scripture the doctrine of organic inspiration is the working out and application of the central fact of the revelation, the Incarnation. The LOGOS became SARX, and the Word became Scripture. These two facts not only run parallel to each other, but are very intimately connected with each other. Christ became flesh, a servant without form or comeliness . . . obedient unto the death of the cross. Likewise the revelation of God entered into the forms of creation, into the life and history of men and nations, into all human forms of dream and vision, etc., even into that which is weak and despised; the Word became writing, and as a piece of writing it subjected itself to the fate of all writing. All this happened, that the exceeding greatness of the power, also of the power of Holy Scripture, may be of God and not from ourselves (I Cor. 4:7).[47]

This affinity of Reformed theology for the parallel incarnation-inscripturation no doubt finds one of its main grounds in the fact that it does full justice to both the divinity and the humanity of the Bible. Reformed theology has always wished to maintain both and sacrifice neither.

So far forth, Reformed theology fully agrees with Barth when

---

[47] H. Bavinck, *Gereformeerde Dogmatiek*, I, 405. Cf. also p. 352, and the quotation from Kuyper given supra. B. B. Warfield, *op. cit.*, p. 162, rejects the word "parallel" in this connection. According to him we can only speak of a "remote analogy." It is clear from the context, however, that Warfield does not reject the word "parallel" in the relative sense, as we have used it. He only wants to stress that there are essential differences between the incarnation and inscripturation. "There is no hypostatic union between the Divine and the human in Scripture; we cannot parallel the 'Inscripturation' of the Holy Spirit and the Incarnation of the Son of God. . . . The analogy in the present instance amounts to no more than that in both cases Divine and human factors are involved, though very differently. In the one they unite to constitute a Divine-human person, in the other they cooperate to perform a Divine-human work."

he says that all Docetism (or Monophysitism)[48] is entirely objectionable in the doctrine of Holy Scripture. It also agrees when Barth emphatically points out that the Bible is a product of the Jewish spirit, and it has no difficulty in gratefully acknowledging its indebtedness to the historico-critical studies of the last hundred years for a much better understanding of this aspect of the Bible. We are also quite willing to admit that orthodox theology in particular, wanting to recognize fully the divine character of Holy Scripture, must be fully aware of the permanent danger of Docetism. In reaction against those who onesidedly bring forward the humanity of Scripture at the expense of its divinity, one can easily fall into the other extreme and neglect the human aspect. This has sometimes happened in christology. There have been Reformed theologians who defended the thesis that Jesus had a *human-nature-in-general*, and not a specific, individual human nature.[49] However good the intention may have been, yet we see here the shadows of Docetism falling over christology. Jesus Christ was not a man-in-general, He was the Jew Jesus of Nazareth, born of another human individual, the virgin Mary, from whom He derived His human nature under the overshadowing of the

---

48. Recently the orthodox view of the Bible has been charged with Monophysitism. It would derogate from the truly human nature of the Bible, in a way similar to the derogation from the truly human nature of Christ by the 5th century Monophysites. So e.g., R. H. Fuller and G. Hebert. Cf. Hebert, *Fundamentalism and the Church of God*, pp. 77f. Both authors make this charge, however, because orthodoxy refuses to include the aspect of fallibility into the humanity of the Bible! At the same time we see here how carefully the parallel Incarnation-Inscripturation must be handled. Without any hesitation Fuller writes: "All the way through we have to discern the treasure in the earthen vessels, the divinity in Christ's humanity . . . the Word of God in the fallible words of men" (quoted from Hebert, *op. cit.*, p. 78). For Hebert's own view, see p. 139. Also in Roman Catholic theology the parallel is accepted. It is even found in papal encyclicals. In "Divino Afflante Spiritu" Pope Pius XII wrote: "Just as the substantial Word of God became like to men in all things, sin excepted, Heb. IV. 15, so the words of God, expressed in human language, became in all things like to human speech, error excepted." Cf. J.S.K. Reid, *The Authority of Scripture*, p. 111.

49. So, e.g., A. Kuyper, *Dictaten Dogmatiek*, n.d., Locus de Christo, Pars Secunda, Paragraph 6, De Natura Humana, pp. 7f. Cf. on the other hand, H. Bavinck, *Gereformeerde Dogmatiek*, III, 290, who says that Christ indeed had an individual nature. Though He shared the same human nature with all other men, yet He had His own specific features, which distinguished Him as an individual person from all others.

Holy Spirit. We cannot do better than listen to the Epistle to the Hebrews, which stresses Jesus' humanity so strongly: "Since then the children are sharers in flesh and blood, he also himself *in like manner* partook of the same" (2:14), and *"in all things"* he was made like unto his brethren" (2:17). Likewise we must accept fully that the Bible is indeed a product of the Jewish spirit. We have no reason to be ashamed of this. If God was not ashamed of sending His Son in the form of a Jew and of having His revelation written down by Jews (with few exceptions), why should we be ashamed?

Undoubtedly nothing can save us better from such docetic tendencies than a good apprehension of the parallel between the incarnation and inscripturation. For this parallel says more clearly than anything else: This Bible is on the one hand fully divine, it is God's Word; but it is at the same time fully human, written as it is by truly human beings with all their peculiarities.[50]

*　　*　　*

[50]. This twofold character of the Bible is flatly denied by the Report of the Committee on Inspiration, presented to the Reformed Ecumenical Synod of 1958 (Potchefstroom, South Africa). We read there: "Incarnation means that our Lord is truly God and truly human. He is all that God is and He is all that man is, integrally divine and integrally human. But we may not say that Scripture is both human and divine or that it has a human element and one that is divine. Scripture is wholly divine though given in its entirety through the instrumentality of men" (*Acts* p. 53). This statement is the second of a series of arguments adduced against every parallel between incarnation and inscripturation. The report is even hesitant to speak of analogy, though it admits that an analogy is not "wholly pointless." But the only significance is that it exemplifies the truth that a conjunction of the divine and the human is possible in other spheres as well. The idea of a parallel is rejected for no less than five reasons; among others the absolute uniqueness and distinctiveness of incarnation, and the *unio personalis*. We, of course, fully accept these facts, but as far as we can see they certainly do not rule out all parallelism. They only warn us that every parallel here can only be of a relative nature — which we fully admit! The situation is different with regard to the second argument, mentioned above. If this is true, then there is indeed no room for any parallelism, even not for analogy. However, we cannot possibly agree with the second half of this statement. Though we respect the intentions behind it, viz.: to safeguard the divinity of Scripture, yet we feel compelled to reject it, because it shows a dangerous docetic view of Scripture. The word "instrumentality" only points to the origin of the Bible. But the humanity of the Bible was not only a passing stage. It is a permanent quality. Scripture is wholly divine, indeed. But no less it is wholly human. Cf. Warfield, *op. cit.*, pp. 153, 160. Exactly in this twofold character of the Bible we encounter the mystery and

So far there is full agreement between Barth and ourselves. But then we see Barth take yet another step. Emphatically he declares: True humanity involves *fallibility*. Every denial of this fallibility is a derogation from true humanity. Every such denial brings us back into the shadows of Docetism.

Here we strongly disagree with Barth. In our opinion Barth is guilty of a leap of thought which has no adequate grounding. Humanity and fallibility may indeed coincide on the purely human level, as we all experience daily, but this gives us no right to draw the same conclusion with regard to the Bible. For — and this is the decisive point — we are not on a *purely* human level here. We have to do with the inspired Word of God, i.e., with the Word that came into being not by human activity only, but in and through this human activity by the operation of the Holy Spirit. There is therefore no ground for such a straightforward identification of humanity and fallibility.

It is certainly not out of place to refer once more to the *parallel* between incarnation and inscripturation, also acknowledged by Barth himself. In fact, we can approach the matter from two sides. In the first place we can take our starting point in the *incarnation*. As we have seen, Jesus did adopt a truly human nature. In Hebrews 4:15 we read: "For we have not a high priest that cannot be touched with the feeling of our infirmities; but one that hath been in all points tempted like as we are." Jesus became so truly human that He adopted our human nature, weakened as it is by the Fall. He indeed became "flesh" (John 1:14), "a poor worm of the earth stripped of all good" (Calvin).[51] There is but one limit: He had *no sin*. The author of the Epistle to the Hebrews immediately continues his above-quoted words as follows: "yet without sin." And later on he repeats it emphatically, when he says that Jesus

---

miracle: This book, which is wholly human, is at the same time wholly Divine.

But if this argument is not valid, then there is no reason whatsoever to deny a real, though relative, parallel between the incarnation and inscripturation. Then we can indeed "rely upon the former to illustrate what is entailed in the latter" (*Acts*, p. 54), provided that the limitations of the parallel are never lost sight of. Cf. for the parallel also G. C. Berkouwer, *Het Probleem der Schriftcritiek*, n.d., 354ff.; Packer, *op. cit.*, 82f.

51. Quoted from R. Wallace, *op. cit.*, p. 12.

was a high priest who was "holy, guileless, undefiled, separated from sinners" (7:26).

The question may be asked, of course: What does this sinlessness of Jesus mean? How far does it go? Does it refer only to His spiritual relation to the Father and His moral relation to His fellow men? Or also to His *knowledge,* so that we must say: There was *never one error* on the part of Jesus? We must distinguish carefully here. It is generally admitted by Reformed theologians that Jesus' knowledge was *limited.* It is also acknowledged that there was a *growth* in knowledge on the side of Jesus. Both of these aspects belong to His true humanity. Says Orr:

> No one who thinks seriously on the subject will maintain that, during His earthly life, Jesus carried in His consciousness a knowledge of all events of history, past, present, and future, of all arts and sciences, including the results of our modern astronomies, geologies, biologies, mathematics, of all languages, etc. To suppose this would be to annul the reality of His human consciousness entirely. The incarnation means that Jesus, in becoming man, entered into all the conditions of a true human life, growth and development included. . . . The limitations of His human consciousness were not assumed, but real.[52]

But limitation is quite different from error, and the former certainly does not always naturally and necessarily imply the latter.

> That Jesus should use the language of His time on things indifferent, where no judgment or pronouncement of His own was involved, is readily understood[53]; that He should be the victim of illusion, or false judgment, on any subject on which He was called to pronounce, is a perilous assertion.[54]

It is to be noted that Orr says: "On any subject on which He was called to pronounce." Orr certainly did this deliberately. In the following pages he not only repeats this same expression a few times, but also gives the following specific definition of Jesus' knowledge: It is "that fulness of knowledge and certainty regarding Himself, the Father and the Father's will, His

---

52. James Orr, *Revelation and Inspiration,* reprinted, 1952, p. 150.
53. As an example Orr mentions Jesus' speaking of Moses or Isaiah in quoting the Old Testament. This language of Jesus should not be pressed too much. "He did nothing more than designate certain books, and need not be understood as giving ex cathedra judgments on the intricate critical questions which the contents of these books raise" (*op. cit.,* p. 153).
54. *Ibid.,* pp. 150, 151.

mission and work in the world, which constituted His peculiar revelation."[55] It is no wonder that Orr stresses this so much, for we can speak of Jesus' knowledge and its specific character only in connection with the revelation which takes place in Him — or perhaps we had better say, the Revelation which He is. The Bible itself never speaks of Jesus apart from this revelation and its purpose. Every other interest in Jesus is simply passed over as sterile speculation. We could perhaps say: This too belongs to the knowledge of Christ which is "after the flesh," a knowledge of which Paul says that he does not want to have at all (II Cor. 5:16).[56] All this is also of the utmost importance for our view of Jesus' infallibility "in abstracto." Jesus' infallibility is directly and inseparably linked with His mission as the Revealer of God and His will (cf. John 1:18). Thus Orr can say, without in any way derogating from Jesus' uniqueness: "Jesus certainly had no more knowledge of the methods and processes of modern criticism than He had of modern astronomy or geology."[57]

But with regard to the revelation which was given in and by Jesus, with regard to the above mentioned "fulness of knowledge and certainty," things are quite different. Orr rightly points out that anyone who says that Jesus was subject to "illusion" or "false judgment" must realize the consequences. Illusion and false judgment are not isolated processes of the mind, but the basis for subsequent actions. Jesus, then, would be subject to sin in the spiritual and moral sphere! But since He was sinless, we must conclude that He was infallibly preserved from all error in all that He revealed as the One sent by the Father.

Returning now to the parallel, we must ask the question: If there is a real parallel between the incarnation and inscripturation, are we then not compelled to accept the same view with regard to the Bible? Must we not conclude that it is fully

---

55. *Ibid.*, p. 151.
56. We follow here the exegesis of Grosheide, who relates "after the flesh" to the verb "to know" and not to Christ. (*De Tweede Brief van den Apostel Paulus aan de Kerk te Korinthe*, 1939, p. 206). But even if one prefers the exegesis of R.V.G. Tasker, who combines "after the flesh" with "Christ" (*Tyndale New Testament Commentaries*, II Cor., 1958, p. 87), the result is the same: It is a knowledge which divorces Christ from His Messiahship, His special mission by the Father, His revelation.
57. Orr, *op. cit.*, p. 153.

human but (being inspired by the Holy Spirit) infallible? Is it not free from all "illusions" and "false judgments"? Is it not free from all error in all that it reveals about God and His will, about His grace and judgment? Reformed theology has always said Yes, and rightly so! Otherwise there would not be a parallel at all! Thus Bavinck continues his earlier quotation (see p. 71) as follows:

> Also in Holy Scripture we have to acknowledge the weak and humble, the form of a servant. But as the human nature in Christ, however weak and humble, yet was free from all sin, so also Holy Scripture is *sine labe concepta* (conceived without stain or blemish).[58]

It cannot be objected that the incarnation has its basis in the *unio personalis,* and the inscripturation does not. Though admittedly this difference may never be lost sight of, and we even must say that because of this difference the incarnation is of an essentially different order, yet the inscripturation involves such a close unity between the divine and the human that they can never be separated however much they are distinguished. When therefore the humanity of the Bible is stressed to the extent of fallibility at every point, even in the theological and religious contents, then there is no place left for real unity — which indeed is the case with Barth.[59] To insist upon biblical fallibility along with its humanity is actually to destroy the whole parallel with the incarnation. The only thing that is left is a purely human book which can be used by God to communicate His divine message, but which as such *is* not this message. Again we must say: This is indeed the view of Barth.[60]

* * *

It is also possible, however, to work out the parallel from the other side, from the side of the *inscripturation*. If Scripture is thus human and fallible, and *if* there is a real parallel

---

58. H. Bavinck, *op. cit.,* I, 406. Cf. Calvin, *Instit.* II, xvi, 2, where he speaks of the accommodation of God in His revelation (i.e., the humanity and limitation of the Bible), which is immediately followed by these opening words of the third paragraph: "Though it is said in accommodation to the weakness of our capacity, it is not said falsely (*non tamen falso*)." Cf. also Warfield's conclusion from the "analogy," *op. cit.,* 162f., and Packer, *op. cit.,* 83.
59. See Chapter V, on his vertical dualism.
60. See Chapter V, on the miracle of the Bible becoming God's Word.

(which is admitted by Barth!), are we then not bound to conclude that Christ was also human and fallible, i.e., sinful? But Barth himself rejects the latter thought with all his might.

> This Man would not be God's revelation to us, God's reconciliation with us, if He were not, as true Man, the true, unchangeable, perfect God Himself. He is the true God because and so far as it has pleased the true God to adopt the true being of man. But this is the expression of a claim upon this being, a sanctification and blessing of this being, which excludes sin. In it God Himself is the subject. How can God sin, deny Himself to Himself, be against Himself as God, want to be a god and so fall away from Himself in the way in which our sin is against Him.[61]

With some slight alterations in Barth's own words we could ask him the following questions: If Holy Scripture is "theopneust" (II Tim. 3:16), if here holy men have spoken "from God, being carried along by the Holy Spirit" (II Peter 1:21), how then can there be room for such a fallibility here? How can God be fallible in His revelation to us? How can God deny the truth, His own truth? How can God be against Himself in the revelation of this truth, and so fall away from Himself?

We can only conclude that, on the ground of the parallel accepted by Barth himself, there is no room for his conclusion: Human witness, therefore fallible witness.

* * *

Somewhere else Barth draws yet another parallel to defend the fallible character of Holy Scripture, viz.: the parallel between the *miracles of the New Testament* and the inscripturation. Says he:

> As truly as Jesus died on the cross, as Lazarus died in John 11, as the lame were lame, as the blind were blind, as the hungry at the feeding of the five thousand were hungry, as the sea on which Jesus walked was a lake many fathoms deep: so, too, the prophets and apostles as such, even in their office, even in their function as witnesses, even in the act of writing down their witness, were real, historical men as we are, and therefore sinful in their action, and capable and actually guilty of error in their spoken and written word . . . That the lame walk, that the blind see, that the dead are raised, that sinful and erring men

---

61. *C.D.*, I, 2, 155.

as such speak the Word of God: that is the miracle of which we speak, when we say that the Bible is the Word of God.[62]

In our view this parallel is nothing but a great confusion. We agree, of course, that the Bible writers in themselves were fully human and also sinful, just as the lame were indeed lame, the blind were blind, etc. We also agree with Barth that a miracle, namely, the inspiration, happened to them. But as the result of the miracle, did nothing happen to these human, sinful authors? Do they still go on erring and actually make mistakes, even in the theological parts? Is that not in conflict with what we read about those lame and blind? When the miracle happens to the lame, they walk, and — *are not lame any more!* When the miracle happens to the blind (really blind!), they see, and — *are not blind any more!* When the miracle happens to Jesus in the grave, He arises, and — *is not dead any more!*

It is good and necessary, indeed, to stress the reality of the humanity and sinfulness of the biblical writers in themselves. It is also good and necessary to stress the *absolute* necessity of the divine miracle here. But the miracle has then to be taken in its fullness. A miracle means the complete conquest of the powers of death and destruction by God in His forgiving love. But are not the biblical errors of which Barth speaks, even in theological content, the symptoms of these powers of death and destruction? And what does conquest mean, if the symptoms of the powers are not taken away?

As far as we can see, all this has nothing to do with the "skandalon" of the Bible, as is suggested by Barth. According to him we take the Bible away when we make it an infallible book.

> This offence [viz. that God speaks to us through the fallible words of fallible men], like the offence of the cross of Christ, is based on the fact that the Word of God became flesh and therefore to this very day has built and called and gathered and illumined and sanctified His Church amongst flesh. This offence is therefore grounded, like the overcoming of it, in the mercy of God.

If we make the Bible infallible,

---

62. *Ibid.*, pp. 528, 529.

we resist the sovereignty of grace, in which God Himself became man in Christ to glorify Himself in His humanity.[63]

Is this true? What is the real "skandalon" of the Bible? We can distinguish two aspects here. The first aspect is that the Bible comes to the world with the specific message of salvation by grace alone, condemning man as guilty and wholly without merit. The second aspect is that this message comes in such a plain, human form that it is given by simple fishers and farmers who speak in their own simple language, yet claiming to be God's mouthpieces. Exactly here we discover again the parallel with Jesus Himself. Was He not a "skandalon" in the same two ways? Did He not offend by His message about Himself, His claim to be the Son of God, and the Savior of the world? And did He not also offend by His form, His claim being made by one having the form of a servant? But nowhere do we read of a third aspect (sinfulness), as Barth frankly admits. On the contrary, His sinfulness was part of the first aspect of the "skandalon," as we see in John 8, where Jesus' words to the Jews, "which of you convicteth me of sin" (v. 46), belong to that passage which concludes with the menacing words, "They took up stones therefore to cast at him" (v. 58)!

We would therefore rather say: *The* "skandalon" of the Bible is that God comes to this world through a human book that claims to be His infallible Word, and that claims the absolute, unconditional subjection of all that are addressed by it. *The* "skandalon" is that in this book God gives Himself so completly to the world, that anyone can take this book and weave it into his own system of thought and use it as the vehicle of his own pet ideas. *The* "skandalon" is that God in His revelation stoops down so far that His infallible Word is put at the disposal of men, and yet this same Word openly claims to be the Word of the living God, to be "living, and active, and sharper than any two-edged sword, and piercing even to the dividing of soul and spirit, of both joints and marrow, and quick to discern the thoughts and intents of the heart" (Heb. 4:12). It is this "skandalon" that offends the heart of the natural man, while at the same time it is the great comfort of the spiritual man, for whom this skandalon has been overcome through the overwhelming power of the Holy Spirit, who speaks in and through this Word.

63. *Ibid.,* p. 529, cf. p. 508.

CHAPTER IV

"PROOFS" OF THE FALLIBILITY OF THE BIBLE

After having dealt with Barth's general argument in favor of the fallibility of the Bible, we now will give special attention to the specific proofs Barth adduces to defend his thesis. They are the following: the biblical world view and view of man, the writers' understanding of history (saga, legend), their religious and theological errors, and finally that the Bible is a product of the Jewish spirit. We can omit discussion of the last point since we have seen in the preceding chapter that this says nothing more than that the Bible is indeed a fully human book, an idea which we gladly acknowledge.

The Biblical View of the World and Man

First of all we are faced with this question: Is it correct to speak of such a view? Barth assumes without more ado that the biblical writers "shared the culture of their age and environment," which also implies that they shared the view of world and man which was common to the ancient world. In Reformed circles, however, it has generally been denied that the Bible contains any world view, even one roughly defined.

In this connection we refer to an interesting discussion in Reformed circles in Holland during the twenties of this century. The discussion was started by Dr. W. J. Schouten (a Doctor of Science), who in the *Journal of the Christian Association of Physical and Medical Science* defended the thesis that we indeed can speak of a biblical view of the world. Of course not in the sense of a scientific view — the Bible is not a textbook of science — but in the sense that the authors shared the view of their day. There was definitely a common ancient world view. Following Schiaparelli Dr. Schouten formulated it as follows:

The earth is flat, on all sides surrounded by an ocean. Under the earth there is the primeval sea. This is connected with the land through wells. Under the primeval sea itself is the Sheol. The lowest centre of it is the Gehennah. Above the earth is a dome, which represents the firmament. Low above the horizon are the treasuries of the wind, higher are the treasuries of rain, snow, and hail. Above the firmament is the heaven of heavens.[1]

According to Schouten we must admit that we also find this ancient view in the Bible. But this does not violate or diminish the authority of the Bible in any respect. It is nothing else than a natural and legitimate consequence of "organic" inspiration. God chose men of those days as bearers of His revelation, and it is our task to translate their message and to transmute it into the pattern of our modern world view.

Against this view, Dr. F. W. Grosheide and Dr. G. Ch. Aalders, both Professors of Theology in the Free University of Amsterdam, strongly maintained that one finds in the Bible only the ordinary view of the universe which all people have when they describe what they see with their eyes.[2] Says Grosheide: "Holy Scripture simply renders what all men formerly observed, and still observe in our day." For example, we still see the earth as a flat disc surrounded by water (Ps. 136:6; Prov. 8:27; Deut. 4:18), we still see the heaven as a dome over the earth (Amos 9:6), etc.[3] In addition, most of the texts appealed to are found in the poetical passages of the Old Testament and therefore may not be used to construe a so-called biblical world view.[4]

---

1. Cf. G. C. Berkouwer, *Het Probleem der Schriftcritiek*, n.d., p. 328, n. 62.
2. For literature, see Berkouwer, *op. cit.*, p. 330, n. 66.
3. For Calvin's view, see Kenneth S. Kantzer, "Calvin and the Holy Scriptures," in *Inspiration and Interpretation*, ed. John F. Walvoord, 1957, pp. 146ff. Holy Scripture does not want to teach any science, but uses popular language so that it will be understood by the simplest as well as the most educated people. At the same time Calvin also leaves room for the idea that the biblical writers used words common in those days, even "borrowed" from "a popular and prevalent error," without, however, committing their own judgment to this erroneous statement.
4. Cf. also J. I. Packer, *"Fundamentalism" and the Word of God*, 1958, pp. 96f. "It may be doubted whether these forms of speech were any more 'scientific' in character and intent than modern references to the sun rising, or lightheadedness, or walking on air, or one's heart sinking into one's boots would be. It is much likelier that they were standard pieces of imagery, which the writers utilized, and sometimes heightened for poetic effect, without a thought of what they would imply for cosmology and

In their rejection of the so-called biblical world view Grosheide and Aalders appealed in particular to Exodus 20:4, the second commandment of the Decalogue. Here the Lord God Himself speaks of "heaven above, the earth beneath, and the water under the earth." Accepting the idea that such expressions have to be taken as indicative of the Bible's sharing of the ancient, antiquated world view, one has to assume that God Himself uses a fundamentally wrong scientific view of the world. According to Grosheide the great danger of the so-called accommodation theory unavoidably looms up here.[5] Nor can one solve this problem by appealing to the doctrine of organic inspiration, which must certainly not be used to explain false conceptions of the structure of the universe. This would give it a meaning it was never intended to have.

So we see how in this discussion the theologians, over against the man of natural science, emphatically maintain that we have no right to ascribe to the Bible the common ancient world view. In later years, however, a change can be observed among Reformed theologians of the following generation in Holland. Several of them frankly admit that the Bible writers in some respects did use contemporary presentations of the structure of the cosmos, which suppose a world view different from ours.[6] The great question now is: Is this a legitimate change of position, warranted by the Bible itself? Or is it not only a deviation from the traditional Reformed position,[7]

---

physiology if taken literally. And language means no more than it is used to mean. In any case, what the writers are concerned to tell us in the passages where they use these forms of speech is not the inner structure of the world and man, but the relation of both to God" (*op. cit.*, p. 97).

5. Cf. also V. Hepp, *Calvinism and the Philosophy of Nature*, p. 169.

6. E.g. H. N. Ridderbos, "Wereldbeeld en Geloof," *Gereformeerd Weekblad*, Vol. VI, No. 49. The same author also in *Heilsgeschiedenis en Heilige Schrift*, 142ff. M. P. Van Dijk, "Het wereldbeeld in de Bijbel," *Ad Fontes*, Vol. II, No. 10. Cf. N. H. Ridderbos, *Is There a Conflict Between Genesis 1 and Natural Science?*, 1957, who expresses himself very cautiously as follows: "With regard to the verses 6ff. one can say that the author expresses himself in terms derived from the world picture of the ancient Orient, or to put it differently, in the terminology current in his day" (p. 44). In a note, however, he adds: "There are objections to speaking of the ancient-oriental world picture. See G. Ch. Aalders, *De Goddelijke Openbaring in de eerste drie hoofdstukken van Genesis*, pp. 173ff."

7. See, e.g., H. Bavinck, *Gereformeerde Dogmatiek*, 1928, I, 417.

but also a violation of the revelational and inspired character of Scripture itself?

* * *

Undoubtedly all theologians, both Reformed and non-Reformed, agree that the Bible does not *teach* or *reveal* a definite world view. Apart from the fact that the Bible nowhere provides us with a detailed description of the structure of the universe, and does not even supply outlines for a scientific description of the cosmos, there is the far more important fact that such a use of the Bible would be in utter conflict with the purpose for which it was given. To use the formulation of the Westminster Confession: "The Bible was given to communicate that knowledge of God and of his will, which is necessary unto salvation" (I, 1), or: "The whole counsel of God concerning all things necessary for his own glory, man's salvation and life" (I, 6). But of course this revelation does come to us in human language and using human conceptions. And there are indeed *indirect, incidental* references to the structure of the universe. On the one hand, these references have their indispensable place within the framework of the message of salvation, and on the other hand they themselves function as a framework for this message.

In our opinion, the question whether in this respect the biblical writers sometimes used the common conceptions of their day, can only be answered in the affirmative. The solution given by Grosheide and Aalders is not satisfactory. Admittedly, sometimes the writers did not do more than describe what they saw and what anyone today would still see. Even in our day a professor of astronomy still speaks of the rising or setting of the sun.[8] But this certainly does not explain everything. First, there is the fact that the biblical authors used many descriptions which nobody would use today, even not in everyday language. Why, then, did they express themselves in such a peculiar way? Second, they used many expressions which are completely identical with the common ancient world view which is found in contemporary extra-biblical writings. How are these striking similarities to be explained? The solution of everyday language falls utterly short here. Moreover, is it not true that even behind poetical representations of

---

8. Cf. also II Chron. 4:2, where the proportions of the diameter and compass of the molten sea are given as 10 and 30 cubits. And no wonder, since *pi* was not known yet.

observations by the senses, there are always certain common perceptions hidden, perceptions which have their basis in the common world view of the day? Have we further to imagine that these writers were so fully separated from the world around them, that they did not know about the common views of their contemporaries? Or did they have no conception at all of the structure of the cosmos?

In answer to all these questions we can only admit that the biblical writers did use conceptions common in their day. And this holds true not only for the Old Testament, but for the New Testament as well. In the latter, too, though not as clearly and as frequently, we find traces of them. H. N. Ridderbos mentions as examples Philippians 2:10, where we find the then-accepted tripartition of the world, and also some passages which speak of demons in figures derived from the popular view of the day (e.g. Matt. 12:43).[9]

This also holds true of the biblical view of man, as far as his biological and psychological structure is concerned. When the kidneys, and also the bowels, are seen as the seat of deepest emotions and sympathies, and the heart as the seat of the mind,[10] we again are confronted with the common ancient-semitic view.[11]

* * *

But does not all this violate the *revelational* character of the Bible? Does it not mean that we must accept "errors" in the Bible? Is not this ancient world view clearly antiquated and unacceptable for us today?

Before discussing the relation between world view and revelation, we must first ask the question: Is it correct to speak of an *antiquated* world view? May we speak of an erroneous view which is superseded by the investigations and results of modern science? This is the crucial point indeed. If we are not mistaken, it was this dilemma that forced Reformed theology *generally* to reject every combination of Bible and world view. Re-

---

9. We read here of "waterless places," i.e., the desert, which according to popular belief was the habitation of demons. Cf. Isa. 13:21; 34:14; Rev. 18:2. H. N. Ridderbos, *Heilsgeschiedenis en Heilige Schrift*, p. 143. Cf. the same author, *Matthew (Korte Verklaring)*, ad locum.

10. With the exception of the book of Daniel, the head is never seen as the seat of the mind.

11. Cf. H. Bavinck, *Bijbelse en Religieuze Psychologie*, 1920, pp. 65f. To a certain extent this holds of the N.T. as well. Cf. Ridderbos, *op. cit.*, p. 142.

cently, however, the legitimacy of this dilemma has been severely questioned by F. Kuyper in a stimulating study on *Faith and World View*.[12] He points out first of all that the world view of the Bible (insofar as we can find traces of such a view) is certainly not meant as a scientific world view and that, if it were only for this reason, it is incorrect and dangerous to use the modern scientific world view as a standard for judging it. In addition, the whole dilemma is connected primarily with the idea of a straightforward evolution of the ancient world view into the modern-scientific, whereby the former is bound to be called erroneous.[13]

Building on the principles of the Philosophy of the Law-Idea, originated by H. Dooyeweerd and D. H. Th. Vollenhoven, both Professors of the Free University of Amsterdam,[14] Kuyper himself defends the proposition that in the Bible we meet with a special kind of world view, namely, the *biotic* world view. With the above-mentioned philosophy Kuyper distinguishes several law-spheres, [15] but he combines these distinctions with the idea that different "worlds" are connected with each of them.[16] These "cosmic worlds" would have appeared successively in the course of history, whereby each new "world" means a progressive differentiation and at the same time an integration of the preceding ones.[17] Thus the "pre-historical" man, i.e., man of the primeval period, who did not have a real sense of

---

12. F. Kuyper, *Geloof en Wereldbeeld*, Een cultuur-historische studie, 1956.
13. *Ibid.*, pp. 27f.
14. Cf. H. Dooyeweerd, *A New Critique of Theoretical Thought*, 4 volumes, 1953f. J. M. Spier, *An Introduction to Christian Philosophy*, 1954.
15. Kuyper, *op. cit.*, pp. 74f. The philosophy of the Law-idea starts with the revealed truth that God has placed His whole creation under law. It speaks thereby of a law-order, because there is a multiplicity of divine laws. Every part of creation belongs to a different law-sphere. Spier mentions the following fourteen law-spheres: arithmetical, spatial, physical, biotic, psychical, analytical, historical, linguistic, social, economic, aesthetic, juridical, ethical, pistical (*op. cit.*, 44). All these spheres constitute a sort of ladder, whereby the later spheres presuppose all the earlier spheres. Every creature has its own place and is characterized by the highest sphere in which it lives. A stone is a physical thing, a plant a biological thing, an animal a psychical thing, while finally man is characterized by them all. Yet he cannot be called a physical thing, because in his heart he concentrates all temporal functions into a supertemporal point (*op. cit.*, p. 41).
16. Kuyper, *op. cit.*, p. 121.
17. *Ibid.*, p. 147; cf. p. 163.

history yet,[18] lived primarily in the biotic world. To this man the material world is "object of the biotic life."[19] Here the spatial element plays a dominating part. The earth is seen as the base upon which life is founded and takes place, while the heavenly dome constitutes, as it were, the protective roof. Time and distance measurements are comparatively unimportant, and hence the heaven, like a sheltering tent, belongs as much to this man's world as the earth.[20] Kuyper goes on to contend that this biotic world view, which as such (i.e., in the context of this sphere of life) is fully correct, time and again reappears in the Bible, sometimes in a world which is already more differentiated. For it is characteristic of all the earlier worlds that they repeatedly reappear in later worlds, as is still the case in our own world view, which is even more differentiated. (Cf. Job 37:18; Ps. 104:2; Isa. 40:22.)[21]

This is not the place to examine thoroughly this view with all its philosophical suppositions, even not in its main outlines. But whatever one's judgment may be, one thing at least is perfectly clear: we are not justified to speak too quickly of "errors" and "antiquation" with regard to the world view of the biblical writers. Such qualifications can be maintained only when one judges the pre-scientific world view by the present-day scientific world view. But once again, this is not the correct standard! The pre-scientific view has to be judged on its own merits and within its own context. And then it is quite obvious that the biblical world view is fully subservient to the *revelation*. Whereas outside Israel the world view is wholly permeated by idolatrous, pseudo-religious ideas, it is in the Bible fully qualified by revelation. It is one of the revelational means made use of by the Lord to bring His message to His people of that time.

We need not be surprised that God followed this course. This is the way in which all revelation is given, as clearly ap-

---

18. The author's use of this term has nothing to do with an evolutionistic construction! Cf. "We will call pre-historical, not that which according to historical investigation is not known from written sources, but that which according to the place of history in the logical distinction of the cosmic worlds is pre-historical, because it logically precedes history" (*op. cit.*, p. 159; cf. also pp. 127ff.).
19. *Ibid.*, p. 193.
20. *Ibid.*, p. 199.
21. *Ibid.*, p. 201.

pears from its central fact: The Word became *flesh*. We certainly do not overstep the limit when we say: All revelation is a sort of "becoming flesh." All God's revelation went into the sphere of thought of those who listened. First of all it used their language: Hebrew, Aramaic, and Greek. But language is no abstraction. A language always belongs to a people with its own special way of life, of thinking, of culture and civilization. It means expressing oneself in certain figures and conceptions.[22] When God used them, He did not give divine sanction of these conceptions as to their scientific character, nor did He necessarily accommodate His message to them. Time and again He fully transformed their meaning so that the *language* was adapted to the *divine* purpose.

Nevertheless, God used human concepts in order to transmit His message in understandable language and figures. A good example of this is found in the second commandment. What message does God wish to convey here to His people? This: that *no creature whatsoever* may be used for an image in order to serve Him. But how to express this "no creature whatsoever" to a people that is not used to abstract thinking, but thinks in concrete images derived from the material world? No doubt the most appropriate way to do this was to express it in the figure of the tripartite world: heaven, earth, and the water under the earth. Exactly in this way every Israelite (and every stranger as well) would immediately understand the exclusive claim of this commandment.

This *condescension* of God to the level of His people by using their available conceptions does not mean an approval of these conceptions. Such a conclusion would proceed on a complete lack of understanding of the divine revelation. For the same reason God does not correct them either. Why should they be corrected? Have not these pre-scientific conceptions their own legitimate right of existence? And by what standards should they be corrected? By the standard of the modern scientific world view? But does that not mean a presumptuous absolutizing of this modern world view? Let us rather respect the divine condescension and listen to the divine message, coming to us by the conceptions and figures of speech which God

---

22. It was the great mistake of the Roman Catholic Church in the 17th century that in the famous Galilei case it did not realize this. Cf. G. De Santillana, *The Crime of Galilei*.

in His divine sovereignty deigned to choose as the carriers of His revelation.

* * *

There remains a final question. Does all this not mean a *dualism of form and contents?* As is well known, such a dualism has always been emphatically rejected by Reformed theology. And rightly so! It has often been used to cover up or defend the most severe criticism of Scripture. The form was then labelled as purely human, and accordingly it not only could, but ought to be dropped as superfluous, even detrimental, to the understanding of the contents. This dualism, however, always amounted to a severe reduction of the biblical message itself. Along with the form, the contents themselves suffered a serious curtailment and became increasingly meagre. A very clear present-day example is found in Bultmann's theology of "demythologization."[23]

But not every distinction of form and contents means dualism. The distinction itself cannot be discarded because of possible and actual misuses. Every message happens to be given in a certain form, and message and form, though inseparably related, are not identical. Sometimes the revelational message is given in a form which does not appeal to readers of today. Then there is but one possibility, namely, that of translating it into present-day conceptions. This is nothing new, but it is the basic question of all hermeneutics.[24] Rightly Packer says:

> We must draw a distinction between the subjects about which Scripture speaks and the terms in which it speaks of them. The biblical authors wrote of God's sovereignty over His world, and of man's experiences within that world, using such modes of speech about the natural order and human experience as were current in their days, and in a language that was common to themselves and their contemporaries. This is saying no more than that they wrote to be understood. . . . Sometimes their grammar lapses; often the mental picture of the created order which their phraseology suggests to the twentieth-century mind differs from that of modern science; but these facts do not bear

---

23. Cf. *Kerugma and Myth,* ed. R. H. Fuller, 1953. Bultmann's own paper, pp. 1-44. Cf. also I. Henderson, "Myth in the New Testament," *Studies in Biblical Theology,* VII, 1952.

24. Cf. H. N. Ridderbos, *Heilsgeschiedenis en Heilige Schrift,* pp. 143f.

on the inerrancy of the divine Word which the writer's conceptual and linguistic resources were being used to convey. This distinction between the content and the form of the written Word of God needs more discussion than we can give it here, but it seems clear enough in broad outline, although admittedly it is not always easily applied in particular cases. The question which the interpreter must constantly ask is: what is being *asserted* in this passage?[25]

And this is the case when one accepts the presence of a definite world view (as we do), as well as when one adopts the view of Grosheide and Aalders. In the latter case, too, one has to translate the practical and "common-day" language into our present-day terminology. What modern would understand the second commandment in its literal form, without such a translation?

In the meantime it will have become clear that there is no ground to speak of "errors" in the Bible here, or even of a "capacity for errors," as Barth carefully puts it.[26] Nor is there any reason to speak of the acceptance of a biblical world view as dragging the Trojan horse within the walls of theology and of the Church.[27] All depends here on one's view of the purpose of the Bible, and on the function which this world view has within the context of this purpose.

---

25. Packer, *op. cit.*, pp. 96-98.

26. Rightly Barth points out that the insight and knowledge of our own age is not divine or even solomonic. Is this perhaps a proviso directed in particular against Bultmann, whose entire theory of demythologization is built upon the basic correctness of the "closed world-order"? As a matter of fact, the world view of modern science has undergone far-reaching changes and the basic idea of a closed causality of nature, which since the 16th century had been predominant, has been severely shaken. Cf. Kuyper, *op. cit.*, pp. 29f., and Rogers D. Rusk, *Atoms, Men and Stars*, 1938, pp. 226ff. John Dillenberger, in an article on "Science and Theology Today" in *The Christian Century* (June 17, 1959) writes: "Gone is the notion that science provides us with a picture of reality or even a partial picture. The old conception of a mechanically ordered world of causation is, of course, dead." At the same time he adds: "Causation has not been abandoned in physics; certain conceptions of *rigid* causation have been abandoned. . . . In principle at least we should be open to the possibility that science in some form may in the future be more deterministic than it is at present." He also warns theology against premature exultation, as if all this had anything to do with the concept of free will or miracles. "The new conception of science does not warrant a return to a biblical world view, including belief in miracles, as if nothing had happened in the interim."

27. Cf. A.D.R. Polman in *Het Dogma der Kerk*, ed. G. C. Berkouwer and G. Toornvliet, 1949, p. 102.

The Biblical Understanding of History

The second "proof" of the fallibility of the Bible, mentioned by Barth, is the understanding of history possessed by the Bible writers. According to Barth their understanding was quite different from our modern conception of history. This comes particularly to the fore in their use of *sagas* and *legends*. "Like all ancient literature, the Old and New Testaments know nothing of the distinction of fact and value which is so important to us, between history, on the one hand, and saga and legend, on the other."[28]

What does Barth mean by "saga? Does he mean that the Bible is full of fairy tales, without any historical basis, without any underlying reality? Does he mean that many of the narrated facts never really happened, but are put into this form in order to convey some general truths to the minds of the readers? This is by no means Barth's intention, as appears clearly from the deliberate distinction he makes between saga (and legend) on the one hand, and myth on the other, whereby the latter is utterly rejected as far as the Bible is concerned.

What is the characteristic feature of a *myth?* Simply formulated it is this: the myth is not concerned with history, with historical reality, but it only purports to describe a general (philosophical or theological) truth or principle. And it does so by clothing such a truth or principle in the garment of a seemingly historical event. In this way it is like the fairy tales of Aesop, De la Fontaine, Grimm and Andersen. They, too, seem to describe historical events, but really they are products of pure human imagination whose only purpose is to give some moral advice. Likewise myth is a product of pure imagination, but this time the intention is not to moralize but to reveal some speculative thought about God or man. As Barth himself says: "Myth in fact means the exposition — brought forward in a narrative form, but claiming to be true in itself, irrespective of time and place — of certain basic relationships of human existence which always exist everywhere."[29] A clear example of myth, as applied to the Bible, is what Alan Richardson writes about Adam:

> The time-element in the myths of Creation and Fall (as in all the biblical myths) must be discounted: it is not that once (in

---

28. *C.D.*, I, 2, 509.
29. *C.D.*, I, 1, 376; cf. *C.D.*, III, 1, 84f.

4004 B.C. — or a hundred thousand years ago) God created man perfect and then he fell from grace. God is eternally Creator; he is eternally making man and holding him in being and seeing that his handiwork is good (Gen. 1:31). And just as creation is an eternal activity, so the "Fall" is an ingredient of every moment of human life; man is at every moment "falling," putting himself in the centre, rebelling against the will of God. Adam is Everyman.[30]

Especially the last three words are very revealing. Adam is not an historical person. He is just a figure, a personification of the "eternal" man, the man of yesterday, today, and tomorrow: Everyman.

Barth utterly rejects all such ideas with regard to the Bible. He knows too well that the Christian faith is an "historical" faith, resting on the facts of the history of salvation, i.e., on God's mighty acts in the history of this world. With reference to many chronological and topographical statements in both the Old and New Testament, to the inclusion of the revelatory events in the framework of other events, to the horizon which ancient Egypt, Assyria, and Babylon form for the experiences of the nation of Israel, to the indispensable place of Cyrenius in the story of Christmas and Pontius Pilate in the Creed, Barth says:

> The Bible claims, in its account of revelation, to relate *history,* i.e. . . . it claims to recount not a relationship between God and man existing generally, always and everywhere, or discoverable in process, but an event that took place there and only there, then and only then, between God and certain perfectly definite men.[31]

But what, then, about *saga?* According to Barth saga is quite different. He gives the following definition:

> A saga is a poetically designed picture of a concrete once-for-all pre-historical "Geschichtswirklichkeit" [historical reality], subject to temporal-spatial limitations.[32]

---

30. A. Richardson, *Theological Wordbook,* p. 14, *sub voce* Adam.
31. *C.D.,* I, 1, 375.
32. Quoted from N. H. Ridderbos, *op. cit.* See *C.D.,* III, 1, 81. In this definition Barth speaks of "pre-historical" because in this volume he is dealing with the creation and the creation story. The latter happens to deal with pre-history. But nevertheless it describes a truly historical fact. For this fact is (a) once for all ("einmalig"), (b) subject to temporal-spatial limitation ("zeitlich-raumlich beschränkt"), and (c) Geschichtswirklichkeit. For a more general definition of saga the "pre-" must be omitted, of course.

"Proofs" of the Fallibility of the Bible   93

This definition contains two main elements. The first is that the saga deals with a really historical fact, with an event that did happen. "The Bible always means an unique event, once occurring in that place and at that time."[33] But — and that is the second main point — this event, this historical reality, often cannot be expressed in ordinary human words. The reason for this is that in the Bible we have a twofold history. There are the human acts, but there are also the mighty works of God.[34] These latter are really historical. They occur in this history. They are "geschichtliche" (historical) reality and belong to the succession of time-filling events. But they are not "historische Geschichte" (historical history), i.e., they are outside the reach of all historical observation and record. They cannot be described in our ordinary words and concepts.[35]

Where this is so, it is no wonder that we find much saga in the Bible. Indeed, we even have to say that it is a *must*. Says Barth:

> There seems no good reason why the Bible as the true witness of the Word of God should always have to speak "historically" and not be allowed also to speak in the form of saga. On the contrary, we have to recognize that as holy and inspired Scripture, as the true witness of God's true Word, the Bible is forced to speak also in the form of saga precisely because its object and origin are what they are, i.e., not just "historical" but also frankly "non-historical."[36]

Mostly we find a mixture of history and saga, fully intertwined. Sometimes, however, we have to do with purely divine works, without any activity of man. So, for example, the work of creation, where at least in the first part man is not yet on the scene. Here we have to do with pure saga ("reine Saga"). Surely, the creation was "geschichtlich": it did happen that God created the world. But here we have no "historische Geschichte," it is entirely "unhistorisch." As a rule, however, we have a mixture of the two.

> In accordance with the nature and theme of the biblical witness, it does actually contain a good deal of saga (and even legend

---

33. *C.D.*, I, 1, 374.
34. Cf. *C.D.*, III, 1, 82. In *C.D.*, I, 1, 375, Barth speaks of events which have two sides, a human and divine. They are the events which have taken place between God and man.
35. Cf. N. H. Ridderbos, *op. cit.*, p. 13. Cf. *C.D.*, III, 1, pp. 80ff.
36. *C.D.*, III, 1, 82.

and anecdote). It also contains "history," but usually with a more or less strong wrapping of saga. This is inevitable, where the immediacy of history to God is prominent, as in the histories which the Bible relates. On the other hand, it also contains a good deal of saga with historical wrappings, and this again is not surprising when by far the greater part of the events related by it takes place in the sphere where "history" and "historical accounts" are at least possible in principle. To put it cautiously, it contains little pure "history" and little pure saga, and little of both that can be unequivocally recognized as the one or the other. The two elements are usually mixed. In the Bible we usually have to reckon with both history and saga.[37]

* * *

Can we accept this Barthian concept of saga? With full appreciation we observed that Barth, against the devaluation of history by modern historicism, wants to maintain the historicity ("Geschichtlichkeit") of the biblical events and therefore rejects all myth. But is the concept of saga more acceptable?

The decisive point here is: Does the Bible itself give us the right to work with this concept and approach the biblical narrative with it? Does the Bible itself clearly intimate that its description of God's mighty works takes place in this literary form? In our opinion this would be the only legitimate ground for speaking of saga here. We have no right to derive it from a certain preconceived concept of revelation. Barth himself would certainly agree here. Does he not repeat time and again that we must derive our concept of revelation from the Bible itself? But that also holds true of the form in which the revelatory events are described by the Bible!

Then we must say that *nowhere* does the Bible give us the impression of speaking in the form of saga or legend.[38] True, the Bible often describes the events in a way quite different from what we would do on the ground of our modern conception of history. But the differences are certainly not of such a nature that they warrant the concept of saga. On the contrary, they require an entirely different explanation, as we will see presently.

37. *C.D.*, III, 1, 81/82; cf. 84.
38. Legend is the application of saga to a historical person. It means "the depiction in saga form of a concrete individual personality." *C.D.*, III, 1, 81.

The whole idea of saga is to be *utterly* rejected for several reasons. First, this term is too much tainted. In the ears of modern man it always has the connotation of being poetry, and that in the sense of not corresponding to a truly historical reality.[39] As a matter of fact Barth himself admits that there is a lot of "bad saga: the bad poetry of a vain divination, of a misunderstanding of the genuinely historical origins and roots."[40] He then immediately adds that the form of saga is as little discredited on this account as the form of history is discredited by the fact that there is plenty of "utterly empty, false, worthless and indeed dangerous history." It is to be questioned, however, whether this is indeed a forceful defense of the term "saga." In our opinion the answer must be No.

For — and this is our second point — *even if* the term "saga" is used in a good sense, it is still unacceptable. Saga is always to a large extent a matter of imagination. Admittedly, Barth does not mean that in the case of the Bible this imagination is the result merely of human intuition. He definitely wants to explain it by the miracle of inspiration. But yet, in spite of these safeguards against human subjectivism, saga nevertheless means that what is narrated is largely a product of human imagination. It means that there are certain facts which are truly historical ("geschichtlich") but which are clad in the garment of divinely inspired human imagination, a garment, therefore, which itself is not historically ("historisch") true. In other words: the fact might have happened in quite a different way! Yet it is described as if it had happened in this particular way. According to Barth all this is rather harmless. In contrast to myth, the saga need not necessarily attack the substance of the biblical witness because the saga at least *means* history, and without prejudice to the historical judgment *can be heard* as the communication of history.[41] The question may be asked whether Barth does not make it sound too harmless! For what is left of the fact itself when its description is a matter of poetry? Is it not like a skeleton without flesh? Who would ever recognize the person to whom the skeleton belonged? Does a fact not cease to be *this particular* fact when its *accidentia* are taken away? Does saga not mean a "transsubstantiation," in which

39. Cf. H. Vogel, *Gott in Christo*, 1951, p. 424.
40. *C.D.*, III, 1, 83.
41. *C.D.*, I, 1, 376.

along with the "accidentia" the "substantia" also changes? Is not such a fact a pure abstraction?

In our opinion the term "saga" means a dragging of the Trojan horse of the old form-contents scheme within the walls of the biblical revelation. And in this case the scheme is applied to the *facts* upon which the Christian faith rests. That is the great difference between this and the case of the world view. Saga concerns the facts which constitute the basis of the Christian faith, for Christianity is a thoroughly historical religion. Take away the facts of the history of salvation, and the Christian faith itself has disappeared. It might be objected that Barth does not purport to take away the facts themselves. We fully grant that and gladly acknowledge it. But once again: What kind of fact is it that allows itself to be stripped of all its outward features, and then still is the same original fact? Does all this not actually mean that the narrative is being transformed into a parable with a historical core?

The solution of Hebert, who speaks of a "theological history,"[42] is not a real solution either. Hebert introduces this term with regard to the Gospel of John, and says:

> If he was intending to write a theological history, primarily to show the real inwardness of the mission and work of the Son of God incarnate, it could be that he was allowing himself certain liberties with regard to the mere literal facts. He does indeed lay the greatest stress on the factual character of the story of Jesus, as real history (cf. John 19:35); but we may well be missing much of what he really intends us to learn from his book if we spend our time of study largely in proving the literal and factual character of every detail. Here and in all the books of the Bible we must attend to what the writer is intending to say. We must take the books as they are, and not impose on them our own notion of what they ought to be.[43]

Everyone, of course, will agree with the last part of this statement. But is it not a condemnation of what Father Hebert himself does? He first declares that John lays the greatest stress on the factual character of the story of Jesus, as real history; he even refers to John 19:35.[44] But from whence do we then derive the right to say that in actual fact John writes

---

42. Hebert, *Fundamentalism and the Church of God*, p. 45.
43. *Ibid.*
44. "And he that hath seen hath borne witness, and his witness is true; and he knoweth that he saith true, that ye also may believe."

a theological history, which permits certain liberties concerning the literal facts? Does not Hebert exactly in this way impose upon the Gospel his notions, his scheme (a theological crime of which he charges the Evangelicals!)?

And is it not the same with the term "saga"? From whence does Barth derive the right to lay the notion of saga upon the Bible? And what is the standard to decide what is saga and what not? Barth probably would answer: the right is given me by the fact that the Bible has to speak of God's mighty works and they cannot be described except in the form of saga. And as far as the second question is concerned: I need no standard to determine saga and non-saga, I have only to listen to what is said to me, for exactly through this mixture of saga and history God wants to reveal Himself to me. However plausible these answers may seem to be, yet in fact they amount to imposing upon Holy Scripture our preconceived notion of what the Bible narratives ought to be. The narratives are no longer allowed to speak for themselves, but from a specific conception of revelation they are forced to adopt the form of saga.

* * *

In our opinion it would have been much better if Barth had used the term "prophecy." This term is entirely appropriate to denote the special way in which the Bible describes history, and it has the great additional advantage of being taken from Scripture itself.

It cannot be denied that the Bible writers did have a conception of historiography different from our modern conception. They certainly did not conceive or perform their task as chroniclers according to the ideas of exposition adopted by modern historians. Take, for example, their conception of *chronology*. They permit themselves here a liberty which no modern historian would dare to use. In all peace of mind they take the facts and give them a place in their own scheme. The order of the facts is made fully subservient to the message. Thus Luke does not feel any embarrassment in reversing the order of the second and third temptations as given by Matthew. Calvin already observed here:

> There is no reason why Luke should not narrate in the second place the temptation which Matthew recounts in the third place. For the Evangelists did not undertake to follow the course of history in such a way that the order of time should be scrupu-

lously observed, but merely to compile a summary statement of
the principal points, in order to bring to our attention . . . that
which was most necessary for us to know concerning the acts and
words of Christ. . . . To know which was the second or the third
temptation is not a matter that need worry us unduly.[45]

Harrison even goes so far as to say:

> Generally speaking there is no such thing as an inspired order
> of narration. . . . One may detect a broad chronological pattern
> unfolding in the Gospels, but it is obvious that within that
> framework the writers exercised considerable liberty in the placing of the individual elements of the story.[46]

Likewise the Bible writers had an entirely different conception
of *accuracy*. In the genealogies they easily skip one or more
names and call a grandson or even a great-grandson a son.
Matthew does not feel any pang of conscience when he applies
an artificial scheme of three times fourteen generations to the
genealogy of Abraham unto Christ.

But all this does by no means derogate from their deep sense
of history, nor does it in any way affect the true historicity of
what they narrate. If one thing is evident here, then it is
certainly this, that the Bible writers intended to give us history
and that they did see history as history. There is all the more
force in this observation, when we realize that exactly *in Israel
the idea of history first was discovered.* The entire Old Testament is characterized by an essentially religious interest in history. Israel's faith as faith in the Covenant of God is founded
on historical facts: first, the establishment of the covenant
with Abraham; later on, with the nation at Sinai; still later,
in the fortunes of the nation as a whole and of the members
individually. In this way the history obtains a value of which
the other ancient nations know nothing. True, the latter also
know of a divine interference in the events of life, but in the
mode of a mythology of nature rather than of real history.
Only Israel knows of protology and eschatology. Only in Israel the entire course of events is fully submitted to the will

---

45. Quoted from Lecerf, *An Introduction to Reformed Dogmatics*, p. 312, n. 3.

46. Harrison in *Revelation and the Bible*, ed. Carl F. H. Henry, 1958, p. 245. From the whole article it is clear that Harrison does not mean to say that the order, as actually given by the evangelists, has nothing to do with inspiration. He uses the word "inspired" here in the strict sense of being prescribed, imposed, or dictated by the Spirit.

of God, who is the God of the covenant and of past and future salvation.[47] And for this very reason it is no wonder that the sacred book of Israel first of all is a record of history and of interpretation of history.

We wish to stress this notion of *interpretation* very strongly. Therefore we spoke of "prophetical" historiography.[48] The facts are not recorded because of an abstract interest in facts as such. The record is not an enumeration, as complete as possible, of the fortunes of a nation or its individual members. But the entire record is characterized by a strong selection based on religious motives. For this reason Omri, according to archaeology one of the most important kings of Israel, is hardly mentioned, while his son Ahab, politically an insignificant ruler, receives much attention as the opponent of Elijah, the great prophet of the Lord. Time and again we see that the facts are selected in accordance with a certain theological scheme. Hence, for example, the differences between the author(s) of Samuel and Kings on the one hand, and the "Chronicles," which cover the same period, on the other.

> There is a very clear principle both in his [viz. the Chronicler's] additions to Samuel and Kings and his omissions. His additions concern mainly the temple and its services and such incidents as exalted the religious side of the state in contrast to the civil. Obviously he is concerned mainly with Israel as a religious community. His omissions show that he is concerned with the development of two divine institutions, the temple and the Davidic line of kings. Hence only the death of Saul is mentioned; his reign, David's sin, Absalom's rebellion, Adonijah's attempted usurpation are all omitted. The history of the northern kingdom, which was in rebellion against both of God's institutions, is mentioned only where it touches the fortunes of Judah. That is why Chronicles is said to represent the priestly standpoint; it is concerned with the working out of what God has ordained and not, as Samuel and Kings, with the prophetic standpoint of how God dealt with His people and so revealed Himself.[49]

---

47. Cf. W. Eichrodt, *Theologie des Alten Testaments*, I, 1939, 9/10. Cf. also my book *De theologische tijd bij Karl Barth*, 1955, 218ff., and the literature mentioned there.

48. Cf. the fact that in Israel the so-called historical books were included among the *Nebiim*, the second part of the Jewish canon. Cf. James Orr, *Revelation and Inspiration*, pp. 190ff.

49. H. L. Ellison, in the *New Bible Commentary*, p. 339. Cf. Harrison, *op. cit.*, p. 239.

And the same holds true of the Gospels.[50]

But all this is altogether different from saga. Prophetical historiography does not mean human imagination, even if inspired, but it means *real history*, but then observed, selected, and interpreted from a definite "theological" point of view. The facts are here fully maintained in their literal meaning. There is no place here for any separation of form and contents. The fact and its interpretation are here fully seen as an inseparable unity.[51]

* * *

It may be good to give a few examples of what the concept "saga" actually means for Barth's *exegesis*.

We will first give a few instances from his exegesis of Genesis 3. Is this chapter the historical description of an event? The answer is a clear No. When in 1935 Barth gave lectures on the Apostles' Creed in Utrecht, he afterwards answered several questions. One was the very concrete question, whether the serpent in Paradise had really spoken. Barth's answer was twofold. On the one hand he rejected the term "myth" in this connection, and on the other hand he said: I cannot take this as "historical" in the sense of the science of history, "for a speaking serpent — well, I cannot imagine that

---

50. Cf. e.g., N. B. Stonehouse, *The Witness of Matthew and Mark to Christ*, 1958, pp. 163ff.

51. This does not mean that we may not ask whether e.g. Genesis 1 is meant as a literal description of God's creative acts or as a more or less "symbolical" description of a divine act, which surpasses all human understanding. We think here of the so-called "framework theory" developed by N. H. Ridderbos, *op. cit*. First of all it has to be kept in mind that Ridderbos limits the question to Genesis 1. This chapter indeed has a very exceptional place because it deals with that which precedes all human history with the purely divine act of creation. Secondly, Ridderbos does not approach this chapter with a general standard of interpretation, derived from a specific conception of revelation (as is the case with Barth!), but he wants to derive his standard of interpretation from the chapter itself. In other words, he deals with the hermeneutical question which is presented by a particular chapter. However, when Orr (*God's Image in Man*, 1906, pp. 219f.) and Packer (*op. cit.*, pp. 99, 104ff.) extend the symbolical interpretation to Gen. 3, we wonder whether they are not dangerously approaching Barth's concept of saga. On the other hand, there may be some truth in what the *New Bible Handbook* (ed. G. T. Manley, I.V.F., 1947, p. 127) says: "Chapter II and III [of Genesis] have much in common with the two closing chapters of Revelation, and in both it is hard to say where the literal ends and the symbolic begins."

any more than anybody else."⁵² He then went on to say that we should first of all give attention to *what* the serpent said. However much the latter is true (and the "friends of the speaking serpent," as Barth calls them, indeed have to take this advice to heart!), yet it is not a sufficient reason to make light of the fact that Genesis 3 does record a speaking serpent.⁵³ We must ask the question: Does Genesis 3 itself in any way suggest that we have to do with a saga here? When we remember what Kuyper said about the biotic world view of the prehistorical man, it might well be that a speaking serpent was exactly the most appropriate means to tempt man,⁵⁴ and that by speaking of saga — or by any other symbolical interpretation — we obscure the clear meaning of Genesis 3.⁵⁵

A far more important question is the following: *Did the Fall after all really happen, according to Barth?* He may reject all myth and call the story as narrated in Genesis 3 a saga, that is, a story with a real event underlying it, but is there place for such a fact in his theology? The remarkable thing is that in this regard there is a considerable difference of opinion among the students of Barth's theology.⁵⁶ Undoubtedly this is due

52. *Grundfragen*, n.d., p. 30. If this is the standard, a great part of Scripture could be rejected as unhistorical. This is pure subjectivism, not to speak of rationalism. In 1953 Barth calls it a saga (*C.D.*, IV, 1, 508).

53. Rightly Brunner called this answer of Barth "a clever evasion of a problem, which, in Holland in particular, ought not to be evaded" (*Man in Revolt*, 1953, 88). In 1926 the Reformed Churches of Holland condemned Dr. J. G. Geelkerken, who assumed the possibility that Gen. 3 had not to be taken literally.

54. Cf. F. Kuyper, *op. cit.*, pp. 221f.

55. This also holds true of what Father Hebert says about the Fall. He calls the story of Adam and Eve a "tale." It is not a "factual historical narrative," yet it describes the "historical truth" (*op. cit.*, p. 40). Here one may wonder what the meaning of the words "historical" and "truth" is. It amounts to this, that *the* fall is changed into *a* fall, which is maintained as an historical (i.e., Barth's "geschichtlich") fact but of which we do not know anything further. Hebert rejects the literal interpretation of Gen. 3 on the ground of so-called historical-critical difficulties (*op. cit.*, p. 38). But when we read the following description ridiculing the conservative standpoint: "A serpent did actually stand on its tail and speak with a human voice," we get a strong impression that these so-called historical-critical difficulties stem from a purely rationalistic approach to the text.

56. Cf. my book *De Theologische Tijd bij Karl Barth*, 1955, p. 138. Cf. also N. H. Ridderbos, *op. cit.*, p. 74, n. 18.

to the fact that in Barth's works we find two statements which seem to be mutually exclusive. On the one hand, he emphatically maintains that God did not create man as a sinner. God is not the author of sin and therefore creatureliness is not automatically identical with sinfulness. On the other hand, Barth as emphatically denies the so-called state of integrity. Genesis 1 and 2 do not speak of such a golden age. They only prefigure God's grace in Christ towards man. But what, then, is the Fall? When did it happen? Did it ever really happen? To put the matter with some care, we have the impression that Barth means this: God created man good, but *as soon as* this created man acts as an independent, responsible being, i.e., *as soon as* this man enters into his own history, he acts against God. In his doctrine of the reconciliation, in the context of which Barth deals with the Fall, he writes:

> There never was a golden age. There is no point in looking back to one. The first man was immediately the first sinner.... It is necessary to combine Gen. 3 with Gen. 2:5-25, and therefore to say that man had hardly been formed of the dust of the earth and become a living soul by the breath of God, that he had hardly been put in the garden of Eden and charged to dress it and to keep it, that his creation had hardly been completed by that of the woman as an indispensable and suitable helpmeet, before he followed up and directly opposed all the good things that God had done for him by becoming disobedient to God.[57]

But if all this is the result of "saga" for exegesis, does it then not condemn itself? What is left here of the biblical facts themselves? They are interpreted in a fully arbitrary way, and actually reinterpreted against their own indubitable meaning.

A particularly clear illustration is found in Barth's exegesis of the words "very good" in Genesis 1:31.[58] These words have nothing to do with an actual state of original innocence and peace.[59] They do not indicate what the creation and the creatures are in themselves. It was the great error of sixteenth- and seventeenth-century orthodoxy that it divorced this "valde bonum" from Christ. At some points it spoke fully and loudly about Christ, but in many others, for example, the

---

57. *C.D.*, IV, 1, 508/9.
58. Cf. *C.D.*, III, 1, 369.
59. Cf. *Ibid.*, p. 212.

doctrine of God and predestination, natural theology, the doctrine of the state, the whole doctrine of creation and providence, and in particular also in its explanation of the "valde bonum" of Genesis 1:31, it was silent about Christ. Just like the Roman Catholic theologians, the Lutheran and Reformed fathers, and to some extent even the Reformers themselves, had adopted a dual system of bookkeeping: nature and grace, creation and covenant, the revelation of creation and the revelation of salvation.[60] And exactly in this way it could interpret Genesis 1:31 as if it spoke of an inherent goodness of the creation itself. In reality, however, the "valde bonum," as part of the creation story, has to be interpreted *christologically*. This "very good" expressed God's Yes, God's mercy in Jesus Christ, which is becoming prefiguratively visible in the creation. With a view to Jesus Christ, who is the beginning of all God's ways and works, God can say this of the existing world.

> The created world is . . . right as it is, because in its essence and structure it is an appropriate sphere and instrument of the divine activity, and because man at the heart of it is the true object of the divine work which has its beginning, centre and end in Jesus Christ. Its rightness, goodness, worth and perfection spring from its correspondence to the word of God's own Son as resolved from all eternity and fulfilled in time.[61]

But again, what is left here of the historical facts as recorded in Genesis 1? Does "saga" here not clearly prove to be *detrimental to the exegesis* of the text and, therefore, to the text itself? We can only agree with G. C. Berkouwer, when he says that Barth's dogmatics represents an "extreme phase of the critical tradition with regard to the paradise-story."[62] And our only conclusion must be that the whole idea of saga as used by Barth cannot be adduced as conclusive proof of the fallibility of the Bible. For it is not a problem presented by Scripture itself, but it is created by Barth, who imposes it upon Scripture.

---

60. *Ibid.*, p. 414.
61. *Ibid.*, p. 370. Actually the whole O.T. has to be read as such a christological commentary and illustration. "The Old Testament is the indispensable lens by which we can read in the mirror of the obedience of the Son of God who and what we were before Him and without Him — men of sin and disobedience and pride, and therefore fallen men, guilty before God and radically and totally corrupt" (*C.D.*, IV, 1, 502).
62. G. C. Berkouwer, *Karl Barth en de Kinderdoop*, 1947, p. 120.

Religious and Theological Errors in the Bible

Third, Barth argues that the Bible is fallible because its capacity for error also carries over to its *religious and theological contents.*

> There are obvious overlappings and contradictions — e.g. between the Law and the prophets, between Paul and James. . . . Within certain limits and therefore relatively they are all vulnerable and therefore capable of error, even in respect of religion and theology. In view of the actual constitution of the Old and New Testaments this is something which we cannot possibly deny, if we are not to take away their humanity, if we are not to be guilty of Docetism.[63]

No doubt this is the most serious of the three points mentioned. For if this is so, where then is our certainty? Would this not mean that "the whole religion of Christ is disturbed" (Calvin)?[64] Does it not mean that we the readers have to make a selection? That we have to accept some statements and to reject others? But what is the standard? Is it Christ? Must we apply within the canon the standard which Luther applied to the canon as a whole: divine is that "was Christum treibt"? But does this actually not mean that "our view" of Christ is the standard? For must we not decide first, on the ground of these same writings, what the true doctrine of Christ is?[65] How

---

63. *C.D.,* I, 2, 509/10.

64. Calvin on Hosea 11:1. Calvin deals here with the contention of some "scoffers" who say that Matthew misapplied these words of Hosea by applying them to Christ. In Calvin's view even such a contention means an attempt "to disturb the whole religion of Christ."

65. This same difficulty underlies H. H. Rowley's attempt to distinguish within the Old Testament. Writes he: "All that we learn in the Old Testament that is in harmony with the revelation given in Christ is truly of God. . . . And all that we learn of God in the Old Testament that is not in harmony with the revelation in Christ is not of God. It represents the misunderstanding of God by sincere men, whose view was distorted by the eyes through which they looked upon Him" (*The Relevance of the Bible,* 1944, p. 33; cf. p. 47.) For the Old Testament this may seem to be a valid solution, but Rowley is immediately faced with the question: Is the New Testament indeed a reliable record of God's revelation in Christ? Rightly Merrill Unger asks: "If inspired Old Testament writers transmitted their human failings and errors to their writings, did not the Synoptists and the apostle John do the same in writing about our Lord? Is not the 'perfect revelation' itself imperfect? How can we be sure the portrait of Christ in the New Testament is not one-sided?" (in the article: "H. H. Rowley and the New Trend in Biblical Studies," in *Inspiration and Interpretation,* ed. John W. Walvoord, 1957, p. 193).

can subjectivism ever be avoided here? Does it not all amount to this, that man places himself above Scripture and becomes the judge of Scripture?

Moreover, is Barth correct in the above-cited quotation? Are there overlappings and contradictions between the law and the prophets, between John and the Synoptists, between Paul and James? The difficulty is that Barth does not give any concrete example here. He just asserts it, but does not adduce any Scripture proof.[66] This is the more remarkable because one of the main, generally accepted results of the exegesis and biblical theology of the last quarter century is the rediscovery of the essential unity of the Bible. This holds especially true of the New Testament. We think, for example, of the conclusion of G. Sevenster's *Christology of the New Testament*:

> There are two things that came to the fore in our investigation. First of all, that everywhere the New Testament placed the preaching of Christ in the centre. Further, that as far as the fundamental points of this preaching are concerned, the New Testament constantly gives the same theme. One, powerful testimony of the coming of Christ and of his atoning death meets the ear. . . . From this it follows that we can speak of Christologies of the New Testament, in the plural, *cum grano salis* only. Certainly, there is a diversity, which somewhat justifies such a usage. Yet the unity in the diversity is much more striking and there is every reason to speak of *the* Christology of

---

66. It is noteworthy that in the eleven volumes of the *Church Dogmatics*, so far published, we hardly find any instance of actual criticism. In III, 1 (*The Doctrine of the Creation*) we read, e.g., that in the two creation stories, compared with each other, we find "painful hiatus and irremovable contradictions" (87), that Gen. 1:3 is related to the mythical tradition (124), that Gen. 2:4a belongs to the "priestly source" and very likely stood originally before Gen. 1:1 (67): and in III, 3, 622f. he rather mildly and somewhat humorously criticizes the New Testament texts which deal with the fall of the angels (Jude 6 and II Pet. 2:4).
But in the whole of his dogmatics these minor criticisms do not have much relevance. Nowhere, as far as we know, does Barth reject any part of Scripture. Barth's "criticism" consists mainly in "re-interpretation" (Umdeutung). It is to be doubted whether he has ever been, or ever shall be surpassed in this "art." Brunner's criticism is much stronger. He openly criticizes Scripture. Cf. his *The Word and the World*, 1931, pp. 94f., 99. We must add, however, that in his later works he seems to be more moderate in his criticisms. But this is merely a matter of degree, for fundamentally his view has not changed. Cf. his *The Christian Doctrine of God*, pp. 14ff., 107ff.

the New Testament. . . . Wherever we listen, in the central things we will always hear the same preaching of Christ.[67]

But not only the essential unity of the New Testament Christology and the New Testament as a whole[68] has been rediscovered, but a similar discovery has been made regarding the Old Testament, though not as unanimously accepted. Th. C. Vriezen, for example, says:

> There is a difference in originality and spiritual atmosphere between the historical writings just as there is also a difference between the various Psalms. This is not to say, however, that the essential internal unity of the Old Testament should or could be denied. There are, it is true, certain differences of vision, and sometimes even contrasts, largely connected with the historical situation in which a piece of writing came into existence. But in spite of these differences and contrasts, there is not only great unanimity among the different authors but especially fundamental spiritual agreement, springing from the certainty of being received into living communion with the same living God.[69]

That does not mean that there are no tensions. Vriezen does not shrink from speaking even of antinomies, but immediately adds: "Even in these antinomies the Old Testament speaks the truth in the form of a divine dialectic."[70]

We are sure that Barth would agree with all this. We have not stressed this unity in order to assert that the basic unity of the Bible was denied by Barth. On the contrary, his whole

---

67. G. Sevenster, *De Christologie van het Nieuwe Testament*, 1946, 355/6. This statement is of more importance since Sevenster called (and still calls) himself a liberal theologian, and therefore cannot be charged with any prejudice regarding the unity of the Bible!

68. Cf. F. F. Bruce, "Trends in N.T. Interpretation," in *Journal of the Transactions of the Victorian Institute*, Vol. LXXXVII, 1955, 37ff. Cf. also C. H. Dodd, *The Apostolic Preaching and its Developments*, 1936; A. M. Hunter, *The Unity of the New Testament*, 1943. H. Diem, *Dogmatik*, 1955, 197f., denies a doctrinal unity. He himself seeks the unity in the proclamation (cf. p. 131). His rejection of the former unity, however, seems to be nothing more than a preconceived, dogmatic idea.

69. Th. C. Vriezen, *An Outline of Old Testament Theology*, 1958, 39/40.

70. *Ibid.*, p. 75. In Vriezen's book this unity unfortunately has some definite limits. Ecclesiastes, Song of Songs, Esther, Ps. 137, e.g., seem to be excluded from this unity. Personally Vriezen would not like to miss them in the collection of O.T. writings, but "one cannot call them a message, a revelation of God, or find in them a trace of that activity of the Holy Spirit, which was revealed in Jesus Christ" (89). Cf. also H. H. Rowley, *The Unity of the Bible*, 1953; R. Abba, "The Unity of the Old Testament," *Reformed Theol. Review*, Melbourne, Vol. 10, No. 3.

theology is built upon the premise of this unity. Yet this rediscovered unity should have made him more careful in his speaking of overlappings and contradictions, without any proof. We ourselves would not go further than speak of *diversities* or *differences in nuances and emphases*. When, for example, Paul over against the Judaizers rejects all work of the unjustified, and James over against the antinominian tendency in some circles urges with equal emphasis the necessity of good works for the justified, then this may lead to a seeming contradiction. Careful analysis, however, will clearly show that in actual fact the statements are not contradictory at all, but rather complementary.[71] A similar situation would present itself when someone heard a Reformed theologian on one day engage in a discussion with an Arminian, and on another day with a hyper-Calvinist. Only a superficial listener would draw the conclusion that there is a real distinction between the emphasis on sovereign, divine election in the former discussion, and the stress on human responsibility in the latter. We should never forget that nearly all the words of the Bible are spoken "by special men in special situations and with a special purpose,"[72] and have to be interpreted within the context of these circumstances. What Dr. A. M. Ramsay, the Archbishop of Canterbury, has said with special regard to the Old Testament, holds *mutatis mutandis* true of the whole Bible: "The faith of Israel did not drop down in a neat pattern from heaven, but was wrought in the ups and downs of a turbulent history."[73]

* * *

Almost involuntarily the question arises here: What is the *deepest background* of Barth's attitude? Though we will discuss this question more fully in the last chapter, it may be wise to make some preliminary remarks at this juncture. As we saw in Chapter III, the rejection of Docetism cannot be the reason. All Reformed theologians have always rejected this. They have always accepted the full humanity of the Bible, though they did not arrive at Barth's conclusion of a fallible Bible. This shows that the rejection of Docetism does not necessarily lead to the acceptance of fallibility.

71. Cf. G. C. Berkouwer, *Faith and Justification*, 1954, pp. 129ff.
72. H. Diem, *op. cit.*, 204/205.
73. A. M. Ramsey, *The Glory of God and the Transfiguration of Christ*, 1949, p. 21.

Are then the "phenomena," namely, the points mentioned in the three so-called proofs of fallibility, the real motive? We have the strong impression that they are not. For they do not have enough emphasis in the whole of Barth's doctrine of Scripture, and in his actual exegesis they never lead him to a clear indication of mistakes or errors.

But what, then, is the deepest motive? The only answer possible is: His view on the *nature of the Bible and of revelation as a whole*. From this view Barth must needs come to a denial of infallibility. For an infallible Bible would mean that man *has* the Word of God. But this is never so, according to Barth. God in His sovereign grace has to *make* it His Word time and again. Revelation is always the revealing God, God in His act of revealing. It is never a static datum, but always an event, a divine act. We could say it in this way: It is never a *datum* (that which has been given), but always a *dandum* (that which must be given again and again, in an always-new divine act). And such a dandum means nothing else than a constantly renewed *miracle of grace*.

> Every time we turn the Word of God into an infallible biblical word of man or the biblical word of man into an infallible Word of God, we resist that which we never ought to resist, i.e. the truth of the miracle that here fallible men speak the Word of God in fallible human words — and we therefore resist the sovereignty of grace, in which God Himself became man in Christ, to glorify Himself in His humanity. . . . If the prophets and apostles are not real and therefore fallible men, even in their office, even when they speak and write of God's revelation, then it is not a miracle, that they speak the Word of God. But if it is not a miracle, how can it be the Word of God that they speak? . . . To the bold postulate, that if their word is to be the Word of God they must be inerrant in every word, we oppose the even bolder assertion, that according to the scriptural witness about man, which applies to them too, they can be at fault in every word, and have been at fault in every word, and yet according to the same scriptural witness, being justified and sanctified by grace alone, they have still spoken the Word of God in their fallible and erring human word. It is the fact that in the Bible we can take part in this real miracle, the miracle of the grace of God to sinners, and not the idle miracle of human words which were not really human words at all, which is the foundation of the dignity and authority of the Bible.[74]

---

74. *C.D.*, I, 2, 529/30.

"PROOFS" OF THE FALLIBILITY OF THE BIBLE

We cannot possibly agree with this.

First of all, what would this argument mean, if applied to Christ? Would it not mean that the incarnation has to be the adoption of a sinful, human nature, if it is a real miracle at all? Does the miracle of the incarnation and consequently of the revelation in the Incarnate not disappear, when we believe with the Church of all ages that the Son of God took upon Himself a true, but sinless human nature?

But even apart from the consequences for christology, the argument itself does not hold water. Actually Barth gives the following syllogism: (a) God's revelation in the Bible must be a miracle of grace. (b) It is such a miracle only when the fallible writers are used so that they remain fallible in their writing. (c) Therefore the biblical writers have been fallible in their writings. No one will have any objection to the first premise. But is the second also correct? Is this not an unproved assertion, an artificial construction? Is it not a miracle as well, if fallible men are so used and influenced by the Holy Spirit that the result of their activities is an infallible Bible? Yes, but then the Bible would *be* the Word of God and that would conflict with Barth's principle of actuality as applied to revelation!

It cannot be denied that all this looks very much like a *dogmatical construction*. First a certain principle is established, namely, the actualistic conception of revelation, and then all the other data and facts are adapted to this principle. It is noteworthy that Barth gives hardly any attention to the *Bible's own testimony* about itself. This is the more remarkable, since his starting point is that there is no higher authority from which the Bible derives its authority. As the Word of God it is the highest authority in itself. We might therefore expect that Barth would give much attention to what the New Testament says about the Old Testament. We think in particular of the attitude of Jesus and the apostles toward the Old Testament.[75] In actual fact, however, Barth does not deal with this at all. For example, John 10:35, where we read Jesus' words that "The Scripture cannot be broken," is mentioned only once, and that in passing.[76] The same holds true of Matthew 5:18, and of the forceful "it is written" against the tempting

---

75. Cf. J. I. Packer, *op. cit.*, pp. 54f., 62f., 86f.
76. *C.D.*, I, 2, 489.

Satan in the wilderness (Matt. 4:4, 6, 7; cf. Luke 4:4, 8, 12). It is impossible to resist the impression that these texts are of no real significance for Barth, because the fundamental decision has been taken somewhere else. And all this is the more to be regretted, because Barth wants to give us a "theology of the Word." But how can such a theology ever pass by the testimony of Scripture about itself? Of course, even after having listened carefully to this testimony, one might still come to the conclusion that the Bible does not speak of its own infallibility. But in that case the conclusion would at least be founded on the Bible itself! The omission of such a discussion in Barth's Dogmatics is the strongest proof that his doctrine is a dogmatic construction, based on decisions which are largely independent of the scriptural testimony itself. The real decision has already been taken before the texts themselves are heard, and after that the texts come forward to be discussed only in the light of those principles adopted beforehand.

* * *

This rejection of Barth's principle of the fallibility of the Bible does not mean, however, that we deny the presence of difficulties here, for Reformed theology as well. Though it is not our task here to give a complete discussion of these problems from a Reformed point of view, it is certainly not out of place to devote a few lines to it.

Reformed theology has always openly admitted that in the doctrine of Holy Scripture we are faced with many difficult problems. More than fifty years ago H. Bavinck wrote in his *Reformed Dogmatics*:

> There remain enough difficulties even for him who subjects himself with childlike faith to Scripture. There is no need to conceal them. There are cruces in Scripture, which cannot be ignored, and which probably never will be solved. But these difficulties, which Scripture itself presents over against its inspiration, are for the greater part not newly discovered in this century; they have always been observed, and nevertheless Jesus and the apostles, Athanasius and Augustine, Thomas and Bonaventura, Luther and Calvin and all Christians of all Churches and throughout all centuries have professed and recognized Scripture as the Word of God. Who wants to wait with his faith in Scripture until all objections are removed and all contradictions are reconciled, never comes to faith. . . . Moreover, objections and difficulties are found in every science. . . . Nature, history, and every science offers as many cruces as Holy

Scripture. . . . There are "enantiophane" (apparent contradictions) in multitude on every page of the book of nature. . . . Who, however, abandons faith in God's Providence for this reason? . . . Of course, here and with regard to Scripture too one can throw oneself into the arms of agnosticism and pessimism. But despair is a *salto mortale* also in the field of science. And with unbelief the mysteries of being do not decrease, while the discord of the heart increases.[77]

It is obvious that Bavinck here writes against Liberalism and not against Barthianism. Barth's view is quite different, even quite the reverse of the liberal view. For Barth infallibility is not a reason to reject, or at least to question, the Bible as the Word of God, but to accept it! Here we see again how in half a century the theological climate completely changed. Which, of course, means that the defense of the faith has to be quite different, too. The citadel of faith remains the same, but the attack comes from quite a different side.

Returning to the admission of difficulties in the Reformed doctrine of Holy Scripture, we must immediately add that for Reformed theology the difficulties have never called the basic doctrine itself into question. The reason for this is that Reformed theology has always insisted upon the use of the so-called *deductive method* in this doctrine and in others. Warfield, in particular, defends this method very ably against the advocates of the so-called inductive method.[78] The deductive method means that in the doctrine of Holy Scripture we take our starting point in the testimony of Scripture about itself. The first question to be answered here is: What does Scripture teach about itself? Only after this question has been answered may we give attention to the so-called phenomena, i.e., the structure of the books, the difficulties which arise from the comparison of several passages, etc. The advocates of the *inductive method,* on the other hand, are of the opinion that we have to start with the phenomena. We find a good example of this method in James Orr's *Revelation and Inspiration.* In this book he begins the discussion of the biblical conception of inspiration with the remark that there are two methods. He himself prefers to follow the second, at least for the purpose of this book. According to him the great advantage of this second method is

---

77. H. Bavinck, *Gereformeerde Dogmatiek,* I, 413.
78. B. B. Warfield, "The Real Problem of Inspiration," in *The Inspiration and the Authority of the Bible,* 1951, pp. 169-226.

that "it assumes nothing, and is not open to the objection of forcing the phenomena of Scripture into harmony with any preconceived theory."[79]

In actual fact, however, this second method is untenable. The first objection is that this method cannot be followed strictly, for if this were done, one would never come to a real *theological* doctrine of Scripture. The examination of the structure of the Bible is a purely historical affair and as such it never leads to a theological doctrine. As a matter of fact Orr does not follow it strictly. He immediately continues the above-quoted words as follows: "Still, some indication of the general view taken of inspiration by the Biblical writers cannot be wholly omitted. It may surprise those who have not looked into the subject with care to discover how strong, full, and pervasive, the testimony of Scripture to its own inspiration is,"[80] and then he gives a short exegesis of II Timothy 3:15-17. But there is yet another objection, much more serious. The inductive method, followed strictly, means that one actually begins from the starting point of unbelief. One refuses to listen first to what the Bible testifies about itself, and approaches it as if it were a merely human book. This is nothing else than unbelief, as Bavinck has already pointed out. "Everyone, who makes his doctrine of Scripture dependent upon the historical examination of its formation and structure, begins already with rejecting its testimony, and therefore does not stand any more in the attitude of faith in Scripture."[81]

There is really *but one correct method,* the *deductive* one, which starts with listening to Scripture's own testimony. Deliberately we write: "starts with." For this method, too, has to consider the "phenomena." These may never be laid aside or disposed of by a strained exegesis. Warfield rightly says that we have "to use these actual characteristics of Scripture as an aid in, and a check upon, our exegesis of Scripture as we seek to discover its doctrine of inspiration."[82] We should never forget that our doctrine of Scripture is a matter of exegesis. No more than in other doctrines does the Bible give a clear-cut, ready-made dogma about itself. We must formulate such a

---

79. Orr, *op. cit.,* p. 159.
80. *Ibid.,* pp. 159/60.
81. H. Bavinck, *op. cit.,* p. 394.
82. Warfield, *op. cit.,* p. 206.

dogma after a careful exegesis of the several statements found in various parts of the Bible. There is therefore always the possibility that our exegesis was not correct on certain points, and the phenomena can indeed serve as a valuable check upon our exegesis.

It may be asked whether Reformed theology has sufficiently used this "check." At any rate it is to be noted that in Warfield's own discussions the phenomena play hardly any role! He is so convinced of the correctness of his exegesis, that in actual fact his statements about the value and function of the phenomena give the impression of a gratuitous admission.

The great question, however, is whether the current Reformed exegesis is correct on all points. We think, for example, of Warfield's own discussion of the "Biblical Idea of Inspiration."[83] In general, as to both method and substance, we highly appreciate this study and basically agree with it. Warfield shows convincingly that the Bible, the entire Bible, from cover to cover, is the inspired Word of God. Yet we feel that some critical remarks can and should be made.

First, Warfield discusses the inspiration of Scripture too much apart from the biblical concept of revelation. Surely he mentions it explicitly at the end of his argument, but it has no decisive significance for the argument. Inspiration is dealt with as an independent datum, instead of from the outset being determined by revelation. Warfield immediately starts with the key texts for inspiration, but does not speak of their decisive background in the idea of revelation.

Second, Warfield limits inspiration too much to the so-called graphical inspiration. He does not make it clear that God's revelation nearly always was accompanied or followed by an act of inspiration, as we clearly see in the "ELALESAN" (holy men of God "spake") of II Peter 1:21.

Third, the concept of authority is used without a more precise qualification, and also apart from the idea of revelation. When he says that Jesus and the apostles made their appeal indifferently to every part of Scripture, to every element in Scripture,[84] the latter is certainly not true. Jesus and His

---

83. *Ibid.*, pp. 131-166. Our choice of Warfield is not without reason. Undoubtedly he is the most accomplished writer on the subject in the English language.
84. *Ibid.*, p. 140.

apostles never appealed, for example, to an element in the sphere of pure science (e.g., astronomy, chronology, etc.), but their appeal was always to the revelatory aspect. To them the Old Testament was the revelation of God and His plan of salvation, and as such they used it.

Fourth, there is a lack of clear distinction between the notions of authority and trustworthiness (i.e., infallibility). Warfield seems not to have realized sufficiently that the latter is a deduction from the former and is fully qualified by the former. This lack of clarity comes clearly to the fore in the fact that Warfield more than once reverses the order by first mentioning infallibility and then authority.[85]

Finally, the concept of infallibility is handled by Warfield in an altogether neutral sense. It becomes a sort of "dictionary" infallibility. We find this in particular in his article on "The Church Doctrine of Inspiration."[86] There we find the following definitions of infallibility: "In all its elements alike — things discoverable by reason as well as mysteries, matters of history and science as well as of faith and practice, words as well as thoughts";[87] "an oracular book, in all its parts and elements, alike, of God, trustworthy in all its affirmations of every kind";[88] "divinely safeguarded in even its verbal expressions, and . . . divinely trustworthy in all its parts, in all its elements, and in all its affirmations of whatever kind."[89] Our great objection is again that this is not a scriptural conception of the word. And the reason is that it is in no respect qualified by the idea of revelation.

In our opinion the whole doctrine of Scripture, its inspiration, its authority and its infallibility, has to be re-thought in direct connection with and derivation from the scriptural idea of revelation. In this regard Barth certainly has shown us the right direction. For only thus will we get a proper view of the claim which the Bible itself presents, namely, to be the

---

85. Cf. *Ibid.*, pp. 150, 158, 161. The same phenomenon can be observed in many other Reformed Dogmatics. E.g., Ch. Hodge, *Syst. Theol.*, I, 153, 161; K. Dijk, *Het Profetische Woord*, 1931, pp. 273, 306. We do not deny that the two are inseparably connected and that from that angle the order can be reversed, but it is incorrect to do this in a fundamental exposition of what Holy Scripture itself teaches about these matters.
86. *Op. cit.*, pp. 105ff.
87. *Ibid.*, p. 113.
88. *Ibid.*, p. 114.
89. *Ibid.*, p. 115.

revelation of God, God's Word. Only in that way, too, will we be able to resist the views of Barth and his followers effectively. This can never be done by ignoring the elements of truth which certainly are present in the Barthian conception. It can be done only by using these elements in such a way that full justice is done to the biblical teaching and at the same time the deficiencies of our traditional view are removed.

We realize that many difficulties may present themselves in this process of rethinking. We think not only of those difficulties which come with every rethinking of a doctrine, but in particular of those which may come up in orthodox circles when certain aspects of the traditional view of the Bible are questioned. We recall Carnell's words: "Contemporary orthodoxy does very little to sustain the classical dialogue on inspiration. . . . The fountain of new ideas has apparently run dry, for what once was a live issue in the church has now ossified into a theological tradition. As a result a heavy pall of fear hangs over the academic community. When a gifted professor tries to interact with the critical difficulties in the text, he is charged with disaffection, if not outright heresy."[90] But it is also good and necessary to listen to what he further says: "Orthodoxy forgets one important verdict of history: namely, that when truth is presented in a poor light, tomorrow's leaders may embrace error for the single reason that it is more persuasively defended."[91]

90. Carnell means the dialogue between the Princeton Theology (e.g. Warfield) and British Evangelical Theology (e.g. Orr). See E. J. Carnell, *The Case for Orthodox Theology*, 1959, pp. 108f.
91. *Ibid.*, p. 110.

CHAPTER V

THE BIBLE AS THE WORD OF GOD

The question with which we will deal in this chapter is: How can the Bible, which according to Barth is a thoroughly human and therefore a thoroughly fallible book, at the same time also be the Word of God? For Barth wants to maintain that with all his might. All his speaking of the humanity and fallibility of the Bible is only the first word. True, it is a necessary word that has to be said, but it is not the final and decisive word. The final and decisive statement is that this Bible, this thoroughly human and fallible book, is indeed the Word of God. "We believe in and with the Church that Holy Scripture as the original and legitimate witness of divine revelation *is* itself the Word of God."[1] But how can Barth say this? In what way does he dogmatically "prove" this claim?

* * *

It is obvious that he cannot found this claim, as the theologians of the Reformation did, on the doctrine of *verbal inspiration*. As a matter of fact — and we are not at all surprised to read this — Barth emphatically rejects this doctrine. According to him this doctrine, as usually taught, is actually a doctrine of *verbal inspiredness,* and the Church may never hold such a view "if she is not to have that false assurance of the Word of God which the Jews and heathen have, by which very fact they betray that the real word of God is strange to them."[2] For verbal inspiredness means nothing else than that we see the Word of God no longer as grace, free grace to be given by God, but as "a bit of higher nature."

1. *C.D.*, I, 2, 502.
2. *Ibid.*, p. 518.

Barth admits that such a view is already found in the Early Church. In the second century, for example, Athenagoras says that the Holy Spirit moved the mouths of the prophets as His organs, snatching away from them their own thoughts and using them as a fluteplayer blows on his flute; and Pseudo-Justin and Hippolytus say that the Logos was the plectrum, by means of which the Holy Spirit played on them as on a zither or harp.[3] From the whole context of their writings it is quite evident why they came to such doctrines. "The obvious aim in all these passages was a stabilizing of the word of man as the Word of God, and an accompanying assurance in respect of the Word of God." But, says Barth, the price which they had to pay for this apparent gain was far too high:

> By, as it were, damping down the word of man as such, by transmuting it into a word of man which is real only in appearance, a Word of God which can be grasped in human speech, the whole mystery was lost, the mystery of the freedom of its presence both in the mouths of the biblical witnesses and also in our ears and hearts.[4]

The same process can be observed again, even in a more pronounced form, in the seventeenth century. Both Lutheran and Reformed Protestantism failed really to take the road newly opened by the Reformers and came to a very definite doctrine of pure verbal inspiredness. The reason was that they lost sight completely of the real nature of God's revelation.

> What was wanted was a tangible certainty, not one that was given and has constantly to be given again, a human certainty and not a divine, a certainty of work and not solely of faith.[5]

But the result for the understanding of the true nature of the Bible was simply devastating.

> This new understanding of biblical inspiration meant simply that the statement that the Bible is the Word of God was now transformed (following the doubtful tendencies we have already met in the Early Church) from a statement about the free grace of God into a statement about the nature of the Bible as exposed to human enquiry brought under human control. The Bible as the Word of God surreptitiously became a part of natural knowledge of God, i.e. of that knowledge of

---

3. *Ibid.*
4. *Ibid.*
5. *Ibid.*, p. 524.

God which man can have without the free grace of God, by his own power, and with direct insight and assurance.[6]

* * *

This clear rejection of verbal inspiration seems to leave but one way open for Barth, namely, that of a *dualistic conception* of inspiration. Though there are different forms of dualism,[7] they all have one basic principle in common: The Bible is not in its totality the Word of God. One must distinguish between the divine and human aspects of the Bible, and try to find out which part belongs to the one aspect and which to the other. Some parts give us divine revelation, others contain merely human opinions. Most of them are a mixture of the two. It is obvious that this means a denial of the authority of the Bible in its totality; the authority is divided (and restricted) by means of selection.

Though it is generally realized that this dualistic conception is not an ideal solution, yet it is still defended by many outstanding theologians of our day.[8] Barth, however, rejects this

---

6. *Ibid.*, pp. 522/23. In *C.D.*, IV, 1, 368 Barth calls this doctrine of verbal inspiration a "product of typical rationalistic thinking." It is "the attempt to replace faith and indirect knowledge by direct knowledge, to assure oneself of revelation in such a way that it was divorced from the living Word of the living God as attested in Scripture, pin-pointing it, making it readily apprehensible as though it were an object of secular experience, and therefore divesting it in fact of its character as revelation."

7. R. Bijlsma in his important doctoral thesis *Schriftuurlijk Schriftgezag* (1959) distinguishes four kinds of dualism: (a) Partial dualism which divides the various books of the Bible into inspired and non-inspired writings. (b) Dualism of degree, which sees some parts of the Bible as more inspired and consequently of a higher authority than others. (c) Formal dualism, which separates form and content, whereby the latter is considered to be the Word of God, while the former is seen as of little or no importance. (d) Material dualism, which regards the religious or religio-ethical message as the real Word of God, to be extracted from the whole.

8. E.g. C. H. Dodd, who on the one hand agrees that "authority belongs to God," but on the other hand also can say: "Not God but Paul is the author of the Epistle to the Romans," a statement which is later followed by this: "The words of the Epistle to the Romans carry just as much weight as we are prepared to allow to Paul as a religious teacher" (*The Authority of the Bible*, pp. 16ff.). Cf. also G. Hebert, who distinguishes between the main outline of the history of God's Purpose of Salvation and its cardinal events, on the one hand, and episodes, such as would never be mentioned in any summary of the history, on the other hand (*Fundamentalism and the Church of God*, p. 43). Cf. also pp. 138f., where he distinguishes between God's own Word and the words of men through which His Word is spoken. "When that distinction is made, it becomes possible to think

"horizontal" dualism emphatically. He did this already in 1922, when in the third preface to his *Römerbrief* he refused to accept Bultmann's criticism. According to Bultmann Barth was too conservative: a real critical attitude "must lead on to the criticism of some of Paul's opinions, because even he fails at times to retain his grip upon what is, in fact, his subject."[9] Barth's answer to Bultmann is:

> From the preface to the first edition onwards, I have never attempted to conceal the fact that my manner of interpretation has certain affinities with the old doctrine of Verbal Inspiration. As expounded by Calvin, the doctrine seems to me at least worthy of careful consideration as capable of leading to spiritual apprehension and I have already made it clear how I have, in fact, made use of it. Is there any way of penetrating the heart of a document — of any document! — except on the assumption that its spirit will speak to our spirit through the actual written words?[10]

All this is repeated with increased emphasis in the *Church Dogmatics*. We have the message of revelation only through the medium of the fallible witness of prophets and apostles. It is impossible to divorce the contents (the revelation) from this form (the witness), as if the former could be heard apart from the latter. No, the two can never be separated, not in one single instance.

> As the witness of divine revelation the Bible also attests the institution and function of prophets and apostles. And in so doing it attests itself as Holy Scripture, as the indispensable form of that content. But because this is the case, in this question of divine revelation the Church, and in and with it theology, has to hold fast to this unity of content and form. The distinc-

---

that there can be errors, of some sort, in the human words, provided that they are not such errors as would make the Bible no longer the Bible. And errors there are. . . ." For H. H. Rowley's view, cf. the summary of Merrill F. Unger: "H. H. Rowley and the New Trend in Biblical Studies," in *Inspiration and Interpretation*, ed. John F. Walvoord, 1957, esp. pp. 192ff. For Brunner, see Paul King Jewett, "Emil Brunner's Doctrine of Scripture," in the same volume, esp. pp. 220f. Even Cardinal Newman, in one of his last articles, accepted the dualistic solution in his theory of the "obiter dicta," i.e., the theory that there are certain incidental statements, e.g. in geographical or historical matters, which do not bear directly upon the revealed truth and do not come under the guarantee of inspiration. Cf. H. Sasse, "Inspiration and Inerrancy," *Reformed Theol. Review*, Vol. XIX, No. 2, p. 34

9. Barth, *The Epistle to the Romans*, p. 16.
10. *Ibid.*, p. 18.

tion of form and content must not involve any separation. Even on the basis of the biblical witness we cannot have revelation except through this witness.[11]

This, of course, means that every student of the Bible is indissolubly *bound to the texts,* as they are found in the Bible. "We are tied to these texts. And we can only ask about revelation, when we surrender to the expectation and recollection attested in these texts."[12] It was the great error of nineteenth century Historicism that it always tried to penetrate behind the texts in order to find the real history. As if we can find that history somewhere else than in the witnesses themselves! And the results have proved the foolishness of this pursuit. How little we have really gained from all this intensive and extensive ploughing of the field of New Testament literature to help us to explain even the simplest individual concepts![13]

Content and form, revelation and witness, God's Word and the Bible are inseparable. Barth does not hesitate to speak here of an "indirect identity." Both the adjective and noun must be fully stressed.

It is *indirect* identity. Under no condition are we allowed to replace this word by its opposite. There is never a direct identity. This is not the case even in the person of Jesus Christ, let alone in the case of the Bible. Says Barth:

> It is quite impossible that there should be a direct identity between the human word of Holy Scripture and the Word of God, and therefore between the creaturely reality in itself and as such and the reality of God the Creator. It is impossible that there should have been a transmutation of the one into the other or an admixture of the one with the other. This is not the case even in the person of Christ where the identity between God and man, in all the originality and indissolubility in which it confronts us, is an assumed identity, one specially willed, created and effected by God, and to that extent indirect, i.e. resting neither in the essence of God nor in that of man, but in a decision and act of God to man. When we necessarily allow for inherent differences, it is exactly the same with the unity of the divine and human word in Holy Scripture.[14]

Here too the identity is assumed. It does not rest in the texts

---

11. *C.D.*, I, 2, 492.
12. *Ibid.*
13. *Ibid.*, 494.
14. *Ibid.*, 499.

themselves, as if there had been a transmutation of the divine revelation into the human witness. The whole identity rests in the decision and act of God.

Yet there is *identity!* God speaks to us through these texts and through these texts only. Here only may we expect His speaking to us. Yes, trusting in His faithfulness, we must *pray* for it. We should never forget that His speaking is not a natural thing. To forget this would mean that in actual fact we replace the indirect identity again by a direct identity. No, we can only come to the texts with a praying heart, realizing that to hear His voice is not in our power, but has to be given to us by Him, in His free grace.

But at the same time we must expect and seek it in *these texts*.

> We are completely absolved from differentiating in the Bible between the divine and the human, the content and the form, the spirit and the letter, and then cautiously choosing the former and scornfully rejecting the latter. Always in the Bible as in all other human words we shall meet with both. And we may differentiate between them as we do in the understanding of a human word. But the event in which the word of man proves itself the Word of God is one which we cannot bring about by this differentiation. The Word of God is so powerful that it is not bound by what we think we can discover and value as the divine element, the content, the spirit of the Bible. Again, it is not so powerful that it will not bind itself to what we think we can value lightly as the human element, the form, the letter of the Bible. We are absolved from differentiating the Word of God in the Bible from other contents, infallible portions and expressions from the erroneous ones, the infallible from the fallible, and from imagining that by means of such discoveries we can create for ourselves encounters with the genuine Word of God in the Bible. If God was not ashamed of the fallibility of all the human words of the Bible, of their historical and scientific inaccuracies, their theological contradictions, the uncertainty of their tradition, and, above all, their Judaism, but adopted and made use of these expressions in all their fallibility, we do not need to be ashamed when He wills to renew it to us in all its fallibility as witness, and it is mere self-will and disobedience to try to find some infallible elements in the Bible.[15]

---

15. *Ibid.*, 531.

In this connection Barth refers again to the old doctrine of verbal inspiration. Although he still feels constrained to reject this doctrine in the form in which it was presented, especially since the Post-Reformation period,[16] yet there was certainly an important element of truth in it, namely, that its advocates full well realized that in the Bible matter and spirit, content and form are inseparable. They saw that the biblical texts are not "sources" from which we have to draw by way of a subjective selection, but they are a witness. A witness that is not a fact somewhere behind the sources, but that is found *in the texts* themselves. Barth calls this the "relative right" of the old doctrine.[17] He even ventures upon a re-interpretation of this doctrine on the ground of his own presuppositions ("indirect identity"). "Verbal inspiration means that the fallible and faulty human word is as such used by God and has to be received and heard in spite of its human fallibility."[18]

All this means necessarily that there is but one way open to us, that of careful *exegesis*. If we can hear God's voice in these texts only, we shall have to concentrate all our attention upon them and study them thoroughly. Of course, here too it holds true that we cannot compel God. It is and remains pure grace, if we do hear Him speaking to us. But this does not alter the fact that we have to stand at this door and knock. "The door of the Bible texts can be opened only from within. It is another thing whether we wait at this door or leave it for other doors, whether we want to enter and knock or sit idly facing it."[19] The Lord comes to those who seek for Him.

16. Cf. H. Diem, *Dogmatik*, 1955, pp. 178f.
17. "Das Schriftprinzip der reformierten Kirche," in *Zwischen der Zeiten*, 1925, p. 226.
18. *C.D.*, I, 2, 533. Similar re-interpretations are quite frequent in modern theology. Cf. John Baillie, *The Idea of Revelation in Recent Thought*, 1956, p. 115: "Nothing could be more artificial than to suppose that these writers were endowed with infallibility in all that they had in mind to say, while the Holy Spirit left them to their own devices as to how they should say it. Hence on the other hand we should have no hesitation in affirming that inspiration extended not only to the thoughts of the writers, but to the very words they employed in the expression of these thoughts." How hollow the term "verbal inspiration" becomes in such a re-interpretation appears immediately, when Baillie continues this quotation with the following words: "though in neither case can we say that the inspiration was plenary." He may, then, on the next page quote I Cor. 2:12f., but such a quotation cannot make amends of the dualism that is involved in the denial of the plenary inspiration. Cf. also G. Hebert, *op. cit.*, pp. 32, 61.
19. *Op. cit.*, p. 533.

From the foregoing it is quite evident that Barth *rejects* every form of *horizontal dualism* which separates one passage from another and then ascribes to the one the "quality" of being the direct Word of God. Barth fully recognizes the dangers involved in such an enterprise, for this inevitably results in an endless subjectivism whereby finally every one has his own Bible. In his lecture on "The Christian Understanding of the Bible" in 1948 he has emphatically repeated this rejection. In it he asks some very pertinent questions. Among others, who is to decide what is God's Word and what not? What standard is to be used? Is it man's reason, as eighteenth century Rationalism asserted? Or is it man's feeling, his "Christian" experience, as Schleiermacher and his followers said in the nineteenth century? But in all these cases God's speaking is not normative any more, but something in man. Man becomes inescapably the measure of revelation.

Against all these dualistic attempts Barth maintains that all biblical passages are fundamentally the same. In themselves they are all witnesses. They can all be used by God to reveal Himself to us. They can all be caught up in His miraculous act of revelation. In actual fact, however, this means that Barth himself creates a new dualism, though of an entirely different kind. His is not a horizontal, but rather a *vertical dualism*, namely, the fundamental separation between man's word and God's Word. The first can become the medium for the latter, but as such and in itself it is not God's Word. Though it is somewhat uncommon to work with graphical figures in a book on dogmatics, we think that the difference could be aptly expressed as follows:

A. Horizontal Dualism.

——— ... ——— ... ——— ... ——— ... etc. (static)

B. Vertical Dualism.

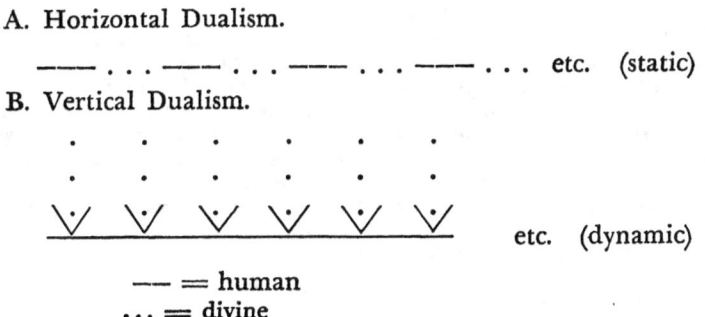

etc. (dynamic)

—— = human
... = divine

It must be granted that Barth has avoided the insurmountable difficulties and inconsistencies of the old dualism.[20] Compared to the latter his conception is indeed a great improvement. Yet it is also burdened with great difficulties. In particular, two questions present themselves.

The *first* is of a *noetic* nature. If the Bible *is* not the Word of God in the sense of direct identity, but has again and again to *become* the Word of God, how then is the Word of God to be recognized? How can we ever be sure that we indeed hear the Word of God and not just a merely human word? Barth has discussed and answered this question at great length in C.D., I, 1, par. 6, where he deals with the "knowability of the Word of God." In the heading which precedes the actual discussion he summarizes his view thus:

> The reality of the Word of God in all its three forms is based only upon itself. So, too, knowledge of it by men can consist only in acknowledgment of it and this acknowledgment can only become real through the Word itself, and can only become comprehensible if we start with itself.[21]

The important point with which Barth starts is, whether the question as to the knowability of the Word of God is a question of *anthropology* or not.[22] Barth means this: Does man in his essential structure have some sort of capacity or faculty which enables him to hear the Word of God? Does the Word of God find a "point of contact" in man, which is given with his nature and functions as "receiving station" for the Word of God? Very often this question has been answered in the affirmative. Rationalism found this faculty in man's reason, Schleiermacher in his experience, and even Brunner speaks of

---

20. John Murray in *The Infallible Word,* 1953, pp. 4, 5. "If human fallibility precludes an infallible Scripture, then by resistless logic it must be maintained that we cannot have any Scripture that is infallible and inerrant. All of Scripture comes to us through human instrumentality. If such instrumentality involves fallibility, then such fallibility must attach to the whole of Scripture." On the other hand, "If infallibility can attach to the 'spiritual truth' enunciated by the Biblical writers, then it is obvious that some extraordinary divine influence must have intervened and become operative so as to prevent human fallibility from leaving its mark upon the truth expressed. If divine influence could thus intrude itself at certain points, why should not this same preserving power exercise itself at every point in the writing of the Scripture?"
21. C.D., I, 1, 213.
22. *Ibid.*, p. 218.

such a "point of contact" in the formal image of God.²³ Barth, however, gives a sharply negative answer.

> God's Word ceases to be grace if grace itself ceases to be grace when we ascribe to man a disposition towards God's Word, a possibility of knowledge independent of it and peculiar in itself, over against this Word.²⁴

It is clear that Barth here again strikes the same chords which sound throughout his entire doctrine of Scripture. Any natural disposition in man means that to hear the Word of God is not a matter of grace any more. But how can God's Word be the Word of *God,* if it is not a matter of free grace? An encounter with the Lord of revelation can only take place from His side! He must come to man! It is not within the competence of man to achieve such an encounter, but it is something entirely new that happens to him. Revelation is God's act. And if man indeed shall hear this revelation, then this is possible only when God Himself creates this hearing through His Word.

> Men can know the Word of God because and so far as God wills that they should know it, because and so far as over against the will of God there is only the weakness of disobedience, and because and so far as there is a revelation of the will of God in His Word, in which this weakness of disobedience is removed.²⁵

All this means that this hearing of the revelation is an "event of faith."²⁶ The introduction of the category of faith does not mean that ultimately Barth also comes to a hidden human capacity. Faith is in no respect a possibility which man on his part contributes to a real knowledge of the Word of God.²⁷ Barth even goes further and says: neither is it "a possibility accruing to man in real knowledge from some source or other as an enrichment of his existence."²⁸ No, faith is nothing more than the openness in man, which God's Word itself creates in its overwhelming power. It is nothing more, indeed. But

---

23. Cf. E. Brunner, "Die andere Aufgabe der Theologie," *Zwischen der Zeiten,"* 1929, and *Gott und Mensch,* 1930, pp. 55f.
24. *C.D.,* I, 1, 221.
25. *Ibid.,* pp. 223-4.
26. *Ibid.,* p. 261.
27. *Ibid.,* p. 271.
28. *Ibid.*

also, it is nothing less. It is a real openness which is created by the Word of God. A real understanding takes place here. And a real knowledge is the result. The well-known statements "finitum non capax infiniti" (the finite cannot hold the infinite) and "peccator non capax verbi divini" (the sinner cannot grasp the Word of God) are no longer the last word. True, they are still valid, but they are only the first word. They are overtaken, bracketed by faith. Man now does really hear and understand.[29]

Barth does not even hesitate to speak now of a "conformity of man with God" and also of a "point of contact" between God and man.[30] A little further on he emphatically says: "Man is the subject of faith. It is not God but man who believes." But immediately he continues:

> The very fact of a man thus being subject in faith is bracketed as the predicate of the subject, God, bracketed exactly as the Creator embraces His creature, the merciful God sinful man, i.e. so that there is no departure from man's being a subject, and this very thing, the Ego of man as such, is still only derivable from the Thou of the Subject, God.[31]

In other words, it is all pure grace. All man's capacity is a capacity which God in the freedom of His grace creates, where and whenever it pleases Him. Man can never dispose of it. He can only receive it as a gift of grace. But again, when this happens, then he does really hear the Word of God. In this connection Barth freely uses even the word "experience." "In faith men have really experience of the Word of God."[32] But, of course, this word fully stands in the context of the revelation as the act of God's free grace. On the last page of this paragraph Barth gives the following final summary of his view: "The Word of God becomes knowable by making itself knowable. . . . The possibility of knowing the Word of God is God's

---

29. *Ibid.*, p. 272.
30. *Ibid.*, p. 273. "Apprehension of the Word of God could not take place, were there not in and along with this event something in common between God who speaks and man who hears, an analogy, a similarity, for all the dis-similarity involved in the difference between God and man, a 'point of contact' — now we may use this concept too — between God and man." The terms used in German are even stronger: "Gottförmigkeit des Menschen" and "Anknüpfungspunkt" (German ed., p. 251).
31. *Op. cit.*, p. 281.
32. *Ibid.*, p. 272; cf. pp. 226ff.

miracle on and in us, just as much as are the Word itself and the utterance of it."³³

* * *

It is not necessary to add much comment. Barth gives a consistent application of his conception of revelation. It is all dominated by his view of God's free grace and gracious freedom. No doubt it means a radical rejection of every theology which ascribes to man a natural capacity for hearing the Word of God. It is also a fundamental refutation of every "theology of experience," whereby the pious man, who thinks that he can dispose of the Word of God, takes the center. As to this we can only agree with Barth. Indeed, to hear the Word of God is a miracle of God's free grace. It is possible only in faith. Rightly Th. L. Haitjema says: "In his view of the 'point of contact' Barth gives us a smart and valuable hint not to have too much attention for the man who receives the revelation."³⁴

Yet there is one important difficulty left. Is there enough room left in Barth's view for the *continuity of faith?* Does the hearing of God's Word not become an endless dotted line with Barth? Where is there room for the genuinely biblical notion of continuity; a continuity which is not anchored in something of man, not even in his faith, but which is anchored in the continuity of the divine promise and of the work of the Holy Spirit?³⁵ Is it not possible in this context even to speak of a "habitus" of faith? We know that this term has fallen into disrepute, mainly under the influence of dialectical theology. From one point of view this is wholesome, since this term often connoted natural or supernatural human capacities which were at man's disposal. But such misuse does not impugn the concept itself. Even Barth himself, in speaking of the seventeenth century doctrine of love as the habitus infused by the Holy Spirit, admits that "the meaning behind this equivocal expression is a right one,"³⁶ namely, that we cannot understand love as consisting in some separate acts only, but "in the being of man as determined in faith by the Word and the Holy Spirit." But if this holds true of love, does it not

---

33. *Ibid.*, p. 282.
34. Th. L. Haitjema, *Dogmatiek als Apologie*, p. 44.
35. Cf. G. C. Van Niftrik, *Sola Fide*, 1940, pp. 252ff.
36. *C.D.*, I, 2, 400.

also apply to faith? Is there not more than an endless dotted line of separate acts of faith? The *term* "habitus" does not interest us so much as the *concept*, which is stated basically in the Canons of Dort, Chapters III-IV, Article 11, namely, that in the miracle of regeneration the Holy Spirit "pervades the inmost recesses of man; He opens the closed and softens the hardened heart, and circumcises that which was uncircumcised; infuses new qualities into the will, which, though heretofore dead, He quickens; from being evil, disobedient, and refractory, He renders it good, obedient and pliable; actuates and strengthens it, that like a good tree it may bring forth the fruits of good actions."

Again, it is possible to criticize some of the expressions (notably "infuses new qualities into the will") as scholastic rather than biblical; we even admit that there is here an ever-latent danger of exchanging the Reformation position for the Roman Catholic doctrine of infused grace. But in spite of all these "criticisms" and dangers, the Canons do stress a point which no theology ever may neglect: the reality and the continuity of the work of the Holy Spirit, and that means also the reality and the continuity of faith. In our opinion, one of the greatest weaknesses in Barth's early works is that he has place for the reality only, and not for the continuity. No doubt this is due to his fierce reaction against the subjectivizing of this continuity in liberal and also in many orthodox circles. But however much it may be understandable, it remains reaction-theology and it results in a serious distortion of the biblical message.

* * *

Barth's vertical dualism evokes yet another question, which is more *ontological*. If the Bible in itself is only a human, fallible witness to revelation, how can Barth nevertheless speak of the Bible as the Word of God? How can the Bible then ever *be* the Word of God? Barth's argument begins when he says:

> We believe in and with the Church that Holy Scripture has . . . priority over all other writings and authorities, even those of the Church. We believe in and with the Church that Holy Scripture as the original and legitimate witness of divine revelation is itself the Word of God.[37]

---

37. *Ibid.*, p. 502.

The great problem, of course, lies in the words "has" and "is." What do they mean here?

Barth first of all says what they do not mean. These two small words do not speak of something which we as men can clearly see or control. They do not say that we have the capacity of ascribing to the Bible this character as the Word of God, or that this character is immediately clear to us. For that would mean that the Word of God is at our disposal, that we can "take" it whenever we like. The real meaning of these two small words is quite different:

> The "has" and "is" speak of a divine disposing, action and decision, to which when we make these statements we have on the one hand to look back as something which has already taken place, and on the other to look forward as something which has yet to do so.[38]

Several words in this statement must be underlined. First of all, it is a "divine disposing, action and decision." It is all God's work and it all remains in His hands. It is free grace. Second, we must look back. We know that in the past God spoke through this Bible. We know that there was a "had" and "was." And therefore, third, we may and must look forward. We may expect to hear God's voice again in this Bible. We may expect a "will have" and "will be." And so, in faith, we can say: the Bible "has" this priority and "is" the Word of God. But now this statement is not about a static state of affairs; we are speaking of the

> divine present, which we do not know, for which we have no word, over which we have no power, of which we cannot say anything except this extravagant "has" and "is," because it is the event of what God Himself decides and wills and does in divine freedom and superiority of power.[39]

These same ideas we find everywhere in Barth's *Church Dogmatics* when he speaks of the Bible. There is always the same emphasis on God's free act. "The Bible is God's Word so far as God lets it be His Word, so far as God speaks through it."[40] The word "is" in the equation of the Bible and the Word of God never denotes an attribute that belongs to the Bible as it lies there, as a book. It can never be used apart

---

38. *Ibid.*
39. *Ibid.*, p. 503.
40. *C.D.*, I, 1, 123.

from faith. Only in the correlation of God's act and man's faith does it become fully real.

> The statement, "the Bible *is* the Word of God," is a confession of faith, a statement made by the faith that hears God Himself speak in the human word of the Bible. . . . The Bible therefore *becomes* God's Word in this event, and it is to its being in this becoming that the tiny word "is" relates, in the statement that the Bible is God's Word.[41]

This stress on the necessity of faith in the correlation of God's act and human faith, does *not* mean that the revelatory character of the Bible is *subjectivized*. It does *not* mean that Barth does not get away from the experimental method introduced by Schleiermacher,[42] and that "his system would inevitably tend to a vast subjectivity in which each man decided for himself just what portion of Scripture had authority for him."[43] Barth does not lay his deepest foundation in a subjective, human faith any more than Reformed theology does. True, in Barth's theology, where the immediate equation between the Bible and God's Word is rejected, this does not become as clear as in Reformed theology. Yet in the whole context of his theology it is quite evident that ultimately faith has the same receptive function. In fact, Barth says this explicitly. After having asserted that the statement "the Bible is God's Word" is a statement of faith, he immediately goes on to say:

> Certainly [it is] a statement which by venturing it in faith we allow to be true quite apart from our faith and above all our faith, allow to be true even and actually against our unbelief, do not allow to be true as a description of our experience with the Bible, but allow to be true as a description of the act of God in the Bible, whatever the experiences may be which we have or do not have in that connection.[44]

The final decision as to the character of the Bible as the Word of God does not depend upon our faith. The Bible has its own character apart from our personal faith. The only element of truth in it is that we personally can discover this character only by faith. But even if we personally, in unbelief, would never discover it, even then it remains true that "the

---

41. *Ibid.*, pp. 123-4; cf. pp. 132f.
42. Cf. L. Berkhof, *Introductory Volume to Systematic Theology*, p. 70.
43. Rolston, *A Conservative Looks to Barth and Brunner*, p. 101, quoted by Berkhof, *loc. cit.*
44. *C.D.*, I, 1, 123.

Bible is God's Word so far as God lets it be His Word, so far as God speaks through it."

* * *

For Scripture proof Barth appeals to the two New Testament passages which are usually quoted in the doctrine of Holy Scripture. The first is II Timothy 3:14-17. This passage clearly speaks of recollection and expectation. It speaks of *recollection* of what Scripture did in the past. Timothy has to abide in the things which he has learned and must remember those from whom he learned them (v. 14). And he has to remember the sacred writings which he has known from a child and of which he knows that they are able to make him "wise unto salvation through faith which is in Jesus Christ" (v. 15). In other words, he has to remember that the Scriptures have played a decisive and definite role in his life and have been the Word of God to him. At the same time Paul also speaks of *expectation* in this passage, for he also speaks of what these Scriptures will do in the future, namely, they will be "profitable for teaching, for reproof, for correction, for instruction which is in righteousness: that the man of God may be complete, furnished completely unto every good work" (vv. 16b, 17). And in the middle, between these two statements of recollection and expectation, we find *pasa graphē theopneustos*, i.e., literally: the whole Scripture is "of the Spirit of God." According to Barth the word *theopneustos* has a passive and an active meaning, and both are to be retained here. Scripture is given and filled and ruled by the Spirit of God and it is actively outbreathing and spreading abroad and making known the Spirit of God. Thus this word, too, points in two directions: to the past and to the future. But in the combination of both, it first of all points out that the relationship between God and Holy Scripture can be understood only as "a disposing act and decision of God Himself, which cannot . . . be expanded, but to which only a — necessarily brief — reference can be made."[45]

The second passage is II Peter 1:19-21. Here too, though not as clearly as in II Timothy 3, we stand between the time of recollection, namely, of the visual witness, and the time of expectation, namely, of the coming dawn. But more clearly than in II Timothy 3, this passage speaks of the *center* from which we

---

45. *C.D.*, I, 2, 504.

look backwards and forwards. For this Scripture is said to be "a light shining in a dark place," to which is added that we should not make it the object of "private interpretation." This no doubt means that we should never think that we can control it. It is God's own decision; time and again Scripture must expound itself; it must control and determine our decision. And this is so (this passage says) because it is not given "by the will of man," but in it men spoke as they were "moved by the Holy Spirit," and thus spoke "from God."[46]

On the ground of this we may indeed say that the Bible *is* God's Word, for God really comes to us through the Bible. But all stress must be laid on the tense of "comes." It happens now, in the present. It is God's free and sovereign act. "The biblical concept of theopneustia points us therefore to the present, to the event which occurs for us: Scripture has this priority, it is the Word of God. But it only points to us. It is not a substitute for it. It does not create it."[47] Or to say it in other words: The presence of God's Word in the Bible is never "an attribute inhering once for all in the book as such." It is not a thing that we simply can say of the books, chapters, and verses as we see them before us.

> Of the book as we have it, we can only say: We recollect that we have heard in this book the Word of God; we recollect, in and with the Church, that the Word of God has been heard in all this book and in all parts of it: therefore we expect that we shall hear the Word of God in this book again, and hear it even in those places where we ourselves have not heard it before. Yet the presence of the Word of God itself, the real and present speaking and hearing of it is not identical with the existence of the book as such. But in this presence something takes place in and with the book, for which the book as such does indeed give the possibility, but the reality of which cannot be anticipated or replaced by the existence of the book. A free divine decision is made.[48]

God Himself takes the Bible *in concreto* in His hands and thus it speaks to us as the authentic witness to divine revelation, and is therefore present as the Word of God.

It may be good to point out here that Barth says this of *the Bible in concreto*. Often he has been charged that according

---

46. *Ibid.*, pp. 504-5.
47. *Ibid.*, p. 506.
48. *Ibid.*, p. 530.

to his view any book could have this function and therefore become the Word of God. This, however, is a serious caricature of what Barth really teaches. As we have seen in Chapter II, Barth repeatedly stresses the fact that the Bible is written by prophets and apostles, i.e., by those who were witnesses to the primary revelation. This being witness gives them a unique position and it also makes their concrete witness, i.e., the Bible, unique. All further witnesses, namely, the preachers of the gospel, are real witnesses only if their message is in accordance with the first and primary witness of the apostles and prophets. To quote Barth again:

> Certain specific men stand in the Bible: that is, the men who in face of the unique and contingent revelation had the no less unique and contingent function of being first witnesses. Because there were and still are those first witnesses, there could and can be second and third witnesses. . . . To try to ignore them is to ignore that unique event. The existence of these specific men is the existence of Jesus Christ for us and for all men.[49]

* * *

Not an inherent quality! These words indeed represent Barth's view fully — at least from the negative point of view. Emphatically Barth says: God's Word is God Himself. And to speak of an inherent quality would mean that we make God an attribute of the Bible! But

> God is not an attribute of something else, even if this something else is the Bible. God is the subject, God is Lord. He is Lord even over the Bible and in the Bible. The statement that the Bible is the Word of God cannot therefore say that the Word of God is tied to the Bible. On the contrary, what it must say is that the Bible is tied to the Word of God.[50]

At this point there is a decisive difference between the incarnation and inscripturation. In Jesus Christ God is present in such a way that we can speak of an immediate identity. "The being of Jesus Christ as the Word of God even in His humanity requires neither promise nor faith. The act in which He became the Word of God in His humanity requires neither repetition nor confirmation."[51] He *is* the Word of God. But in the case of the Bible as the Word of God, we have to do with

49. *Ibid.*, p. 486.
50. *Ibid.*, p. 513.
51. *Ibid.*

a relation of which it cannot be said that it *is* as a "datum." Here we have to do with earthly and temporal human signs, and their being as the Word of God requires promise and faith. There is a constant need of the work of the Holy Spirit in the Church and in its members. The Church cannot grasp at the Bible. It has no control or power over the work of the Holy Spirit. It can only accept the promise, be ready and open to read and understand and expound the Bible, and pray to God that the Bible may be the Word of God here and now. But that this indeed happens is entirely the work of the Holy Spirit.

Only one word is appropriate for this event: it is a *miracle;* a miracle of God Himself, of His free grace.[52] There is no better illustration than the water of the pool at Bethesda.[53] Just as this water was moved by no human action, but from on high, so God Himself makes the Bible His Word. And just as the healing power was not inherent in this water, but was given to it, so the Bible's becoming God's Word is God's act, God's event. And it always happens at God's time. "As to when, where and how the Bible shows itself to us in the event as the Word of God, we do not decide, but the Word of God Himself decides."[54]

* * *

Again we must say that Barth is very consistent in his thinking. The lines are drawn with a firm hand and the basic principles are at no point abandoned. On the contrary, they are applied to the fullest consequences.

There is, in fact, much that appeals here to a Reformed reader. Particularly appealing is Barth's *emphasis on the divine activity* in the miracle of revelation. It is not man who "has" the revelation and can do with it whatever he likes. No, God's Word is God Himself speaking to man. This notion can indeed never be stressed too much.

At the same time, however, many questions present themselves to the Reformed student of Barth's doctrine as a whole. We will not discuss them all at this stage. In the following chapter, which deals with Barth's conception of inspiration, we will refer to them again. At this moment we restrict our-

---

52. *Ibid.,* p. 528.
53. *Ibid.,* p. 530; cf. also *C.D.,* I, 1, 125.
54. *Ibid.*

selves to one aspect only, namely Barth's exegesis of the two well-known passages from II Timothy 3 and II Peter 1. We cannot see it otherwise than that Barth reads into these texts an interpretation which is fundamentally foreign to them. Admittedly, they both do speak of recollection and expectation; in particular II Timothy 3. But there is no indication whatsoever that we have to read the center from these two actions of recollection and expectation. The texts in no way state that the center, as it were, hangs dialectically between them so that it becomes reality only when recollection and expectation flow together in the act of revelation.

Barth can maintain this only by filling the clear and straightforward statements in both texts with his own conception of revelation. Careful and unbiased reading of the texts themselves does not at all confirm Barth's exegesis. Both texts simply speak of a factual situation: "Every Scripture is inspired of God," and "We have the word of prophecy." True, in the first statement the copulative "is" is absent, but this is not a confirmation of Barth's view, for it is a rather usual Greek construction. Paul does indeed speak of an attribute that is inherent in Scripture. It is a "datum." Of course, that does not mean that this datum is effective without the *operation of the Holy Spirit,* or that it may be detached from the *correlation* of Scripture with faith. From that point of view the "datum" is indeed a "dandum." But it remains a dandum which is based on the datum of the *theopneustia,* on the "inspired-ness" of this Scripture. And the same holds true of I Peter 1. This passage does not make any distinction between the prophetic witness and the Word of God. The author simply states: "We *have* the prophetic word," and significantly he adds: "more sure." Yes, he admonishes his readers to give heed to it "as unto a lamp shining in a dark place." The ground for this admonition is the fact that these men spoke "from God." They did not give their own human thoughts, nor did they produce a defective, fallible, human witness, but they spoke "from God." Their witness was nothing less than God's revelation. For — and this is the deepest secret — they were "moved by the Holy Spirit," i.e., borne along as a ship by the wind.[55]

Even so it remains a *miracle* just the same! And the opera-

---

55. Cf. Dean Alford's *Greek New Testament,* IV, 401.

tion of the Holy Spirit remains indispensable for understanding this revelation. Emphatically Peter says that "no prophecy of Scripture is of private interpretation." A man cannot do with God's Word what he likes. It is and remains God's Word, and His is the full control of it. At this point Barth has indeed fully grasped the message of Scripture. At the same time we must say that his main thesis, namely, that there is not a direct, but only an indirect identity between the Bible and the Word of God, has not been proved from these texts. If they say anything about this problem, then it is rather a refutation of this thesis. For they say in plain language, which cannot be mistaken, that this book, this "scripture," this "prophetic word" *is* God's Word.

CHAPTER VI

INSPIRATION OR THEOPNEUSTIA

Barth's conception of *inspiration or theopneustia* is closely related to what we found in the preceding chapter. We saw there that being the Word of God is not an inherent quality of the Bible as a book, but it is always God's work, God's act, God's decision. It is not only a matter of the past — that would mean stabilization — but it is just as much a matter of the present. It is the dynamic of God's actual revealing, revealing Himself here and now. In his conception of inspiration Barth consistently follows the same line. He does not reject inspiration. By no means! But he does re-interpret the old doctrine from his own presuppositions. This is very clear from what he says at the outset:

> The doctrine of inspiration will always have to describe the relation between the Holy Spirit and the Bible in such a way that the whole reality of the unity between the two is safeguarded no less than the fact that this unity is a free act of the grace of God, and therefore for us its content is always a promise.[1]

He calls this the "criterion" which is decisive for our understanding of what Scripture says about inspiration. This means, however, that a dogmatic criterion is imposed upon the texts and that the texts themselves are not allowed to speak first. Or in other words, the concept of inspiration is not derived from Scripture itself, but Scripture is read in the light of a preconceived criterion. According to Barth this is necessary,

1. *C.D.*, I, 2, 514.

because Scripture does not give an extensive or complete doctrine of inspiration.[2]

* * *

Moreover, Barth rejects the idea that inspiration is only a matter of the past. At the conclusion of his discussion of II Timothy 3 and II Peter 1 he said already: "The Biblical concept of *theopneustia* points us to the present, to the event which occurs for us."[3]

He distinguishes two phases or moments in the event of inspiration. *First,* there is the event of inspiration, *when the books were written.* The production of these books was not a purely human affair. The real author of the Bible is the Holy Spirit.[4] The human authors were only "auctores secundarii." Both words must be stressed. They were *genuine authors.* Each of them thought, spoke, and wrote within his own psychological, biological, and historical possibilities; this action was really his own action. Barth here fully agrees with Calvin in his exegesis of II Peter 1:21: "Peter says that they were moved — not that they were bereaved of mind (as the Gentiles imagined their prophets to have been), but because they dared not to announce anything of their own, and obediently followed the Spirit as their guide, who ruled in their mouth as in his own sanctuary." But the latter part of this quotation brings us already to the second emphasis, on the adjective "secundarii." For although it is fully true that their action, like all human action, was their own, yet it acquired a very special function. It was placed under the "auctoritas primaria," the lordship of God. It was surrounded and controlled and impelled by the Holy Spirit, and became an attitude of obedience by virtue of its direct relationship to divine revelation. That was their *theopneustia.*

So far Barth teaches what Reformed theology has always stated as its doctrine of inspiration. But he goes further. This is not the complete inspiration. There is yet a *second moment* in the event of inspiration, namely, *when the books are read and heard.* The readers and listeners need the same Holy Spirit.

2. Cf. H. Diem, *Dogmatik,* p. 177.
3. *C.D.,* I, 2, 506.
4. *Ibid.,* p. 505.

The *theopneustia* of the Bible, the attitude of obedience in which it is written, the compelling fact that in it true men speak to us in the name of the true God: this — and here is the miracle of it — is not simply before us because the Bible is before us and we read the Bible. The *theopneustia* is the act of revelation in which the prophets and apostles in their humanity became what they were, and in which alone in their humanity they can become to us what they are.[5]

* * *

According to Barth this is also the view of Paul. For proof he appeals to two passages from Paul's epistles to the Corinthians. The first is II Corinthians 3:4-18. In this difficult passage Paul speaks about the way the Jews read the Old Testament: a veil lies upon their heart (v. 15). Paul speaks here of the Old Testament in a very remarkable manner. He calls it a "letter" (*gramma*), and then makes a strong contrast between the old and new dispensations. The former is the covenant of the letter which killeth, the latter of the spirit which giveth life (v. 6). Barth rightly[6] says that *per se* there is no disqualification of Scripture in this designation. "This is said in favor of the Spirit, but not against Scripture, or only against a Scripture received and read without the Spirit."[7] Paul himself says that this *gramma* had glory (v. 7). But at the same time he adds that the New Testament dispensation has much more glory, for Jesus Christ has come (vv. 19ff.), a fact which can be recognized only through the Holy Spirit (vv. 6-18). What interests us most of all is Barth's conclusion:

> If, as we can certainly assume, he for his part affirmed a special inspiration of Scripture by God, it was obviously only in connection with his view of the present attestation of the same God by the work of the Holy Spirit. For in II Cor. 3 everything depends on the fact that without this work of the Spirit Scripture is veiled, however great its glory may be and whatever its origin.[8]

The Jews, for example, knew about the "original" inspiration of the biblical writers. In Paul's day there were well-established theories of Talmudic and Alexandrian Jewry concerning the divine-human origin of the Torah. And yet they

---

5. *Ibid.*, pp. 507/8.
6. Cf. F. W. Grosheide, *II Korinthe (Korte Verklaring)*, 1939, pp. 47f.
7. *C.D.*, I, 2, 514.
8. *Ibid.*, p. 515.

did not hear the revelation when they read the Old Testament canon, but they met their condemnation because the present attestation by the Holy Spirit was not there. Precisely this is the great difference between Synagogue and Church. The latter does read and receive revelation — not by virtue of any capacity in itself, but only by virtue of the Lord, who is the Spirit (v. 17). It is the pure grace of the Holy Spirit, an event for the occurrence of which only God can be praised.

The second Pauline passage, which according to Barth is illustrative of his conception of inspiration, is I Corinthians 2:6-16. In this passage Paul speaks of "three keys" which are necessary to know the Lord. (a) Paul says that he received the "wisdom in a mystery" (v. 7), i.e., the revelation of God, which took place in Jesus Christ. This "wisdom" is unknown to the rulers of this world, for otherwise they would never have crucified the Lord. "But unto us God revealed [it] through the Spirit" (v. 10). So the first key is that the revelation came to Paul himself. (b) The second key is that Paul is convinced that he, in turn, can and must express this revelation. Of course this "expressing" has nothing to do with any capacity of Paul himself. It is the work of the same Spirit. "Not in words which man's wisdom teacheth, but which the Spirit teacheth, comparing spiritual things with spiritual" (v. 13). So far Paul has only spoken of what the Spirit does to himself as a witness of revelation. But there is more. (c) There is also an action of the Spirit on the side of the receiver. Only on the basis of the same work of the same Spirit a man can know and receive this witness and hear the revelation through it. "The natural man receiveth not the things of the Spirit of God . . ., but he that is spiritual judgeth all things" (vv. 14, 15).

Barth's conclusion is again:

> The circle which led from the divine benefits to the Apostle instructed by the Spirit and authorized to speak by the Spirit now closes at the hearer of the Apostle, who again by the Spirit is enabled to receive as is necessary. The hearer, too, in his existence as such is part of the miracle which takes place at this point.[9]

Otherwise he would be in the same position as the Synagogue, when it has and reads the *gramma*. Unless the hearer is in-

---

9. *Ibid.*, p. 516.

cluded in the miracle, the mystery of God will remain a mystery for him and the word of the apostle will be foolishness. Only when the same Spirit who created the witness also bears witness of its truth to him, only then he will receive revelation. "This self-disclosure in its totality is THEOPNEUSTIA, the inspiration of the Word of the prophets and apostles."[10]

* * *

Reviewing Barth's position we gladly observe again that there are many points with which we can wholeheartedly agree. We particularly appreciate his emphasis on the *permanent need of the operation of the Holy Spirit* for reading and recognizing, believing and obeying the Bible as the Word of God. This emphasis is not only necessary over against liberalism, with its humanistic doctrine of man's natural capacity for contact with the Supreme Being, but it is also a necessary reminder for orthodoxy. One of the dangers that permanently threaten orthodoxy is that of forgetting that the Bible never becomes our "possession." The Bible belongs to God. It is His Word. He is and remains the Lord and Master of His own Word and He gives it to whom He will.

There have been real exaggerations and deviations in this regard among orthodox theologians. Barth himself points to the Lutheran doctrine of the "efficacy of the Word of God even before and apart from its use."[11] Over against Hermann Rahtmann, minister at Dantzig, who in 1621 published a book in which he asserted that the Word of God alone has no power

---

10. *Ibid.* Similar views are nowadays held by many theologians, e.g. by J.S.K. Reid, *The Authority of Scripture,* R. Bijlsma, *Schriftuurlijk Schriftgezag.* The latter appeals to Bengel, who in his *Gnomon Novi Testamenti* on II Tim. 3:16 writes: *"Divinitus inspirata est, non solum dum scripta est, Deo spirante per scriptores, sed etiam, dum legitur, Deo spirante per scripturam, et scriptura Ipsum spirante."* It is to be questioned, however, whether a Barthian interpretation of these words is in harmony with Bengel's own intention. In our opinion he only stresses that Holy Scripture is still "theopneustos," that the Holy Spirit still sustains and animates Scripture so that it is the living Word of God today. This is a rather common thought in orthodox theology. Cf. Bavinck, *Geref. Dogmatiek,* I, 410/11. Cf. 357, where Bavinck also quotes these words of **Bengel.**

11. *C.D.,* I, 1, 124. *Efficacia Verbi Divini etiam ante et extra usum.* According to Reid, *op. cit.,* p. 201, this view was held by the entire Protestant orthodoxy, even by the Calvinists, Schwenckfeldians and Quakers, and Barth would at this point break with them all. Barth himself, however, rightly states that this was a Lutheran view, "built up in opposition to the Calvinists, Schwenckfeldians, Quakers, etc." *(loc. cit.).*

to convert unless the grace of the Holy Spirit is added, Lutheran theology with one voice defended the above-mentioned efficacy. If they had only meant to prove that the Bible and preaching are the Word of God, in their full compass, as independent of subjective experience and superior to it, then we would have to admit their claim, says Barth. But in actual fact they went much further. Quenstedt, for example, denied that the Bible was an instrument which again and again needs a new motion and elevation in order to produce its effect. According to him the Bible and preaching were media in which the highest power and efficacy were permanently inherent. Hollaz spoke of a "hyperphysical" power, which has an efficacy analagous to the germinative power of a seed. If this is the case there is, of course, no need for a special work of the Holy Spirit.

Reformed theology has always utterly rejected such a view. It is God the Holy Spirit who works through and with the Bible; there is no "hyperphysical power" which is present in the Bible as a kind of deposit. That does not mean that therefore the Bible sometimes is without any power at all. In his discussion of this matter, Bavinck rightly recalls that the Word that goeth forth from God's mouth is always a power that shall accomplish that which pleases God and shall prosper in the thing whereto He sent it.[12] But this, according to Bavinck, is only because it is *God's* Word!

> He is always present with it; He always bears it by His almighty and omnipotent power; He Himself is always the One, who, in whatever form or by whatever means, brings it to men and calls them by it. . . . God's Word is never apart from God, from Christ, from the Holy Spirit; it does not exist by itself; it cannot, in a deistic way, be separated from its creator and author.[13]

* * *

God's Word is *always effective*. It shall never return void. But — it is *not always the same effect!* It may be for a fall

---

12. H. Bavinck, *op. cit.*, IV, 438.
13. *Ibid.*, p. 439; cf. I, 324. We do not think that any present-day Lutheran theologian would defend the views of Quenstedt or Hollaz. At any rate, he would not be compelled to do so by his own confessions, for none of them speaks of such an *efficacia ante et extra usum*. The *Formula Concordiae* stresses only the operation of the Holy Spirit "per verbum." Rightly R. A. Lipsius in his *Lehrbuch der Evangelisch-Protestantischen Dogmatik*, 1879, p. 710, points out that the expression *verbo adest praesens*

or for a rising again. To the one it may be a savour from death unto death, to the other a savour from life unto life. For the latter, Reformed dogmatics has always taught that there is a special operation of the Holy Spirit in the subject. Bavinck says it thus: It is the author of the Word, Jesus Christ, who administers it through the Holy Spirit.[14]

How much Reformed theologians regarded this operation of the Holy Spirit necessary, appears from the strong expressions they sometimes used when they spoke of the Word without the Spirit. Calvin, for example, says that in our present condition Scripture remains "like a dead and ineffectual thing for us."[15] And Abraham Kuyper did not hesitate to say that the Bible in itself is a "lifeless" book without the working of the Holy Spirit.[16] Expressions like these must not be overstressed. Calvin and Kuyper certainly did not mean to deny the ever-present relationship between the Bible and God the Holy Spirit, as indicated above by Bavinck. They only wished to emphasize that no man comes to faith in the Bible, that no man really hears the message of God's Word as a saving message, without the special operation of the Holy Spirit.

As a matter of fact this accent is peculiar to the *whole* Refor-

---

spiritus sanctus is rather against an immanence of the Holy Spirit in the Word. The doctrine of the so-called causative authority of Holy Scripture, i.e., that Scripture (or the Word of God in whatever other form) has the power to convert us, is still vigorously upheld. Cf. Robert D. Preus, "The Word of God in The Theology of Karl Barth," *Concordia Theological Monthly*, XXXI, 2, 112. But this is a far cry from the exaggeration of 17th century Lutheran orthodoxy. For Preus continues: "Scripture is the power of God, it brings Christ, the Spirit of God is always present and operative, *when Scripture is read or preached or used.*" The "per verbum" is retained, the "ante et extra usum" has been fully dropped!

14. Bavinck, *op. cit.*, p. 440.
15. Calvin, *Corpus Reformatorum*, 54, p. 285. Quoted from W. Niesel, *The Theology of Calvin*, p. 24; cf. pp. 36ff. Cf. W. F. Dankbaar, *Calvijn, Zijn Weg en Werk*, 1957, p. 181.
16. A. Kuyper, *Encyclopedie der Heilige Godgeleerdheid*, III, 497. Cf. also the personal statement of Hudson Taylor: "One afternoon, in the course of my usual reading, I came to John IV. It had always been ancient history to me, and as such loved and appreciated, but that afternoon, for the first time, it became a present message to my soul. No one could have been more thirsty, and I there and then accepted the gracious invitation and asked and received the Living Water, believing from His own Word that my thirsty days were all past, not for any present feeling, but because of His promise." Marshall Broomhall, *Hudson Taylor, The Man who Believed God*, 1957, p. 162.

mation, in Luther no less than Calvin. Unceasingly Luther stressed the necessity of the work of the Spirit. In his Shorter Catechism he taught the children of the Church — and it is expressive of his own deepest conviction — "I believe that I cannot of my own understanding and strength believe in or come to Jesus Christ my Lord, but that the Holy Ghost has called me by the Gospel, and illuminated me with His gifts, and sanctified me in the true faith." At another place he writes: "What He did for our sake, He has given to us, but it does not become ours [*non obvenit nobis*] unless the Spirit comes into the heart. The Holy Spirit brings Christ, who reconciles us with the Father."[17] True, Luther speaks here of Christ and not directly of the Bible. But what holds true of Christ holds also true of the Bible, for only through the latter Christ comes to us. It would not be difficult to adduce many statements of Luther where he explicitly speaks of this relation between Word and Spirit. "Time and again Luther asserts that we can have no assurance that the promise of the Gospel is the Word of the living God to us, unless the Holy Spirit says in our heart, 'that is God's Word.' "[18]

We find the same emphasis in Calvin's writings. Calvin always kept Word and Spirit together in an inseparable unity. On the one hand, he rejects the Roman Catholic assertion that the assurance of the divine character of the Bible depends on the testimony of the Church, and calls this "a great insult to the Holy Spirit."[19] On the other hand, he also rejects the Spiritualists' appeal to the Spirit apart from the Word, substituting private revelation for Scripture, and says: "As they [viz.: God's children] feel that without the Spirit of God they are utterly devoid of the light of truth, so they are not ignorant that the word is the instrument by which the illumination of the

---

17. W. A. 48, pp. 27f. Quoted from Philip S. Watson, *Let God be God, An Interpretation of the Theology of Martin Luther*, 1958, p. 185, n. 136.

18. Watson, *op. cit.*, p. 167. Cf. J.S.K. Reid, *op. cit.*, p. 64: "Instead of an authority of a purely objective kind or of a purely subjective kind, Luther maintains that the authority of the Bible lies in an objective-subjective relationship. Spirit and Word go always together — not the Word imposing itself upon the subject externally, but the Word commending itself to the subject and quickening in him that response of faith in which its authority is both recognized and accepted. The Christian is thus not compelled to belief in the Word, *sed verbo trahendus, ut volenter credens sponte veniat.*"

19. *Instit.* I, viii, 1.

Spirit is dispensed."[20] In the same connection he writes that "the Lord has so knit together the certainty of his word and his Spirit that our minds are duly imbued with reverence for the word when the Spirit shining upon it enables us there to behold the face of God; and, on the other hand, we embrace the Spirit with no danger of delusion when we recognize him in his image, that is, in his word."[21] And fully in line with this he writes in a debate with Sadolet: "It is no less unreasonable to claim to give utterance to the Spirit without the authority of the Word than it would be to shelter behind the Word without possessing the Spirit."[22]

This emphasis on the work of the Spirit in connection with the Word is not peripheral but central in the theology of the Reformers. It belongs to the very heart of their theology.[23] In his first period Barth often used the expression: God can only be known [or recognized] by God.[24] This is indeed the language of the Reformation! It was this persuasion which led the Reformers to their view of the relation between Word and Spirit, as summarily indicated above. It is not in man's power to grasp God's Word, God's revelation. God has to give it to him. Bavinck, who uses the very same expression as Barth,[25] goes immediately on to quote the following texts: "Neither doth any know the Father, save the Son, and he to whomsoever the Son willeth to reveal him" (Matt. 12:27, cf. Luke 10:22), and "No man can say, Jesus is Lord, but in the Holy Spirit" (I Cor. 12:3; cf. I John 4:2, 3).

* * *

The theology of the Reformation, however, has never seen this special operation of the Holy Spirit in the subject as part of inspiration, but always conceived it as a separate work of the Spirit and called it *illumination*. This distinction did not mean a separation. The illumination was always seen in such

20. *Ibid.*, ix, 3.
21. *Ibid.*
22. Quoted from W. Niesel, *op. cit.*, p. 38.
23. In this respect the difference between the Lutheran emphasis on "per verbum" and the Calvinistic preference for "cum verbo" does not mean any fundamental disagreement. At least from the Reformed standpoint, the two have never been regarded as exclusive, but rather as mutually inclusive. Cf. Bavinck, *op. cit.*, IV, 437ff.
24. Cf. "Das Schriftprinzip der reformierten Kirche," in *Zwischen der Zeiten*, pp. 220, 231.
25. Bavinck, *op. cit.*, I, 471.

a close conjunction with the operation of the Spirit in the Word that Bavinck, for example, called it a "subjective revelation" which corresponds with and is linked with the objective revelation in the Word.[26] But he immediately adds that in the first instance the word "revelation" is used in a broader sense. "The illumination of the Holy Spirit is not a revelation of mysteries, but the application of the treasures of wisdom and knowledge which are contained in Christ and are shown in His Word."[27]

In the same broader sense it would also be possible to call the illumination *inspiration*. But in this case, too, we would have to add at once that it is not the same as the inspiration of Scripture. While the latter refers to the origin of Scripture, to the *communication* of the revelation, the former or "subjective" inspiration refers to the *reception* of Holy Scripture, the hearing and understanding of the revelation. This same distinction is also behind Calvin's words on the "completion of the inspiration" by illumination. "God employed the same Spirit, by whose agency He had administered the Word, to complete His word by the efficacious confirmation of the Word."[28] The word "complete" does not suggest an extension of the inspiration from the object (Scripture) into the subject (the believer), but over against the Scripturalists Calvin stresses the absolute inseparability of the action of the Spirit in the Word and the heart of the believer. The same Spirit who brought about the written Word applies it to the heart of the believers. From that point of view it can indeed be called one work. And yet at the same time it does not mean that the inspiration in itself is incomplete. Time and again Calvin stresses that the Bible *is* the Word of God, entirely apart from our personal attitude and reaction.

Because of this fundamental dissimilarity of the two operations of the Holy Spirit it is better not to use the same term, for this would only result in confusion. As a matter of fact the term "illumination" is used by Scripture itself, and that in reference to the operation of the Spirit in the subject. So Paul writes to the Corinthians: "It is God, that said, Light shall

---

26. Bavinck, *op. cit.*, p. 321, Cf. also Calvin, *Instit.* I, vii, 5, who speaks of "revelation from heaven."
27. Bavinck, *op. cit.*, p. 367.
28. *Instit.* I, ix, 3.

shine out of darkness, who shined in our hearts, to give the light of the knowledge of the glory of God in the face of Jesus Christ" (II Cor. 4:6). The marginal note of the English and American Revised Versions gives, as the literal translation of "light," "illumination."[29] Paul draws a parallel here between the divine act of the first creation day and what happens in the believer. On the first creation day God dispersed the darkness that originally covered the face of the deep by His divine commandment: Let there be light. In the illumination of the believer the same God dispels the darkness of the human heart. At the same time Paul clearly intimates that the parallel is inadequate. Chrysostom already pointed out: "Then indeed He said: Let it be, and it was; but now He said nothing, but Himself became light for us. For the apostle does not say, "has also now commanded," but "has Himself shined."[30] Indeed, in illumination God the Holy Spirit Himself shines in our hearts and thus makes us see the revelation of God in Jesus Christ, as recorded for us in Holy Scripture.[31]

* * *

This illumination of the believer is very complex. It contains several elements which can be distinguished, but at the same time they are so interrelated that they never can be separated. One of these elements, for example, is the so-called *Testimony of the Holy Spirit*, which was so very much stressed by

---

29. Greek *photismos*. Cf. also John 1:9: "There was the true light, even the light which lighteth (*photizei*) every man, coming into the world," and Heb. 6:4: "Those who were once enlightened" (*hapax photisthentes*).

30. Quoted from R.V.G. Tasker, *II Corinthians, Tyndale New Testament Commentary*, p. 72.

31. Bavinck links illumination immediately with regeneration (John 3:5). While the former is concerned with man's consciousness, the latter refers to man's being (*op. cit.*, I, 321). Although it is certainly correct to distinguish these two actions dogmatically, in Scripture they are not yet sharply distinguished. The illumination of which Paul speaks is an illumination which has a bearing on the entire being of the believer ("shined in our hearts"! Note the aorist!), while the regeneration of which Jesus speaks in John 3:5 (also aorist!) certainly also includes man's consciousness. In both cases we see the miracle in which the Holy Spirit brings a man, blind and dead in sin, to faith in Jesus Christ and through Him to faith in God. Cf. also Calvin in his sermon on Deut. 28:4: "For as often as we ask God to enlighten us through his Spirit, we make the solemn declaration that we come as poor, blind, deaf and ignorant men, until God has recreated us and drawn us near to him," *Corpus Reform.*, LVI, 490, quoted from D. J. De Groot, *De Wedergeboorte*, 1952, pp. 145/46.

Calvin in his doctrine of Scripture. Its special function is to convince the believers of the divine origin and authority of Holy Scripture. By it the faithful come to believe that the Scriptures "have come from heaven, as directly as if God had been heard giving utterance to them."[32] Enlightened by the Spirit, we no longer believe on the ground of any earthly judgment, either our own or that of the Church, but "in a way superior to human judgment, we feel perfectly assured — as much so as if we beheld the divine image visibly impressed on it — that it came to us, by the instrumentality of men, from the very mouth of God."[33]

Unfortunately this testimony of the Holy Spirit has too often been seen as an isolated act of the Spirit. According to Bavinck this is even the case with Calvin himself, who related it onecidedly to the authority of Scripture. This isolation gave it the nature of an extraordinary revelation and was one of the reasons why a rationalist such as Michaelis in the eighteenth century came to the confession that he had never heard such a testimony.[34] Apart from the question whether this criticism of Calvin is correct,[35] it is certainly true that every isolation seriously distorts the unity of the illumination by the Holy Spirit. Bavinck himself rightly sees the testimony of the Holy Spirit in the context of the entire work of the Holy Spirit in the believer. According to him the testimony of the Holy Spirit is first of all an assurance that we are children of God. "That is the central truth, the nucleus and center of

32. *Instit.* I, vii, 1.
33. *Instit.* I, vii, 5.
34. Bavinck, *op. cit.*, I, 563; cf. 554.
35. It may hold true of the *Institutes*, where the testimony of the Holy Spirit indeed is discussed as a more or less isolated action of the Holy Spirit, but in his commentaries Calvin time and again relates this testimony to Christ Himself as the incarnate revelation of God. E.g., Comm. on I John 5:8, where he describes the witness of the Spirit as follows: "It is he who seals on our hearts the testimony of the water and blood, it is he who by his power makes the fruit of Christ's death come to us; yea, he makes the blood shed for our redemption to penetrate into our hearts, or, to say all in one word, he makes Christ with all his blessings to become ours." In his Comm. on II Peter 1:16 he ascribes our certainty of Christ's resurrection to it: "For though Christ had not risen before our eyes, yet we know by whom his resurrection has been handed down to us. And added to this is the inward testimony of conscience, the sealing of the Spirit, which far exceeds all the evidence of the senses." Cf. further K. S. Kantzer, art cit. in *Inspiration and Interpretation* (ed. Walvoord), pp. 133f.

this testimony." And in connection with this, it also seals the objective truths of salvation, among others the divine origin and authority of Holy Scripture.[36]

We wonder whether Bavinck does not unintentionally put too much stress on our own personal assurance. Is that indeed the central truth? Is it not rather our recognition of Him of whom the Bible speaks, namely, Christ as the God-given Saviour, which is the nucleus of this testimony?[37] And does the assurance not flow from this central truth in two directions — in the direction of our own personal subjective sonship and in the direction of the assurance of the divine character of the scriptural revelation and its contents? The latter, of course, should by no means be limited to the so-called religious and ethical truths. It also comprises facts, though not historical, chronological, geographical, etc. data in themselves. As Bavinck says, the Bible is not interested in "nuda facta," bare facts. They are all related to the center of the revelation, Jesus Christ. But for this very reason they, too, are objects of the testimony of the Spirit, and their "divinity" is testified as well.

* * *

This illumination of the Holy Spirit, in the broader sense noted above,[38] is clearly taught by Scripture itself. We think, for example, of the passages quoted by Barth in defense of his own view of inspiration, namely, II Corinthians 3:16-18 and I Corinthians 2:14, 15.

In the first passage Paul intimates a very close relation between Christ the Lord, and the Spirit. He even says: "Now the Lord is the Spirit" (v. 17). This does not mean that Paul confounds the persons of the Trinity by identifying Christ with the Spirit, but by this paradoxical statement he wants to emphasize as strongly as possible that only through the Holy Spirit can the revelation in Jesus Christ be seen and apprehended. The Jews of Paul's day did not see it. "Their minds were blinded" (v. 14). There was a veil over their hearts

---

36. Bavinck, *op. cit.*, I, 564.

37. Cf. Bavinck himself: "The real object to which the Holy Spirit testifies in the hearts of the believers, is nothing else than the *divinitas* of the truth in Christ granted to us" (*op. cit.*, I, 565).

38. How much the testimony of the Holy Spirit regarding Holy Scripture is only part of the whole operation of illumination, also appears from the fact that the entire illumination could be designated as "testimony."

when they heard the Old Testament Scriptures read in their synagogues (v. 15). They did not find Christ in them and that means that they did not understand at all, for Christ is the fulfillment of the Old Testament Scriptures.[39] Only in turning to the Lord is the veil taken away (v. 16), and this is the glorious work of the Spirit. "Where the Lord is, there is His Spirit, and where the Spirit is, there is the Lord. In the presence of the Spirit we see the glorification of the Lord, and in the presence and glorification of the Lord, we see the Spirit and His work."[40] The two are inseparable. Only through the Spirit we see the Lord and accept Him and His righteousness.[41]

The second passage, I Corinthians 2:14, 15, is even more explicit. In both preceding verses Paul has stated that his apostolic preaching, both as to its content (vv. 10-12) and its form (v. 13), is given by the Spirit. And yet there is the undeniable fact that not everyone accepts his preaching. To explain this Paul introduces the distinction between the natural (*psychikos*) and the spiritual (*pneumatikos*) man. The former does not receive the things of the Spirit. They are foolishness to him (v. 14). Yes, even worse, he cannot know them, for these things are judged, examined, discerned in a spiritual way. "The man who has not received the Holy Spirit of God, has not the ability to make an estimate of things spiritual."[42] To say it in the vigorous, pithy words of Luther: In his natural state

> man is like a pillar of salt, like Lot's wife, yea, like a log and a stone, like a lifeless statue which uses neither eyes nor mouth, neither sense nor heart. For man neither sees, nor perceives the terrible and fierce wrath of God on account of sin and death but ever continues in his security, even knowingly and willingly, and thereby falls into a thousand dangers and finally into eternal death and damnation . . . until he is enlightened, converted

---

39. Cf. v. 14, "which veil is done away in Christ." "Few passages in the New Testament emphasize more strongly than this that the Old Testament Scriptures are only fully intelligible when Christ is seen to be their fulfilment," R.V.G. Tasker, *II Corinthians*, p. 66.

40. R.C.H. Lenski, *The Interpretation of St. Paul's First and Second Epistle to the Corinthians*, 1957, p. 946. Cf. H. Sasse, "Inspiration and Inerrancy," *Reformed Theol. Review*, XIX, 2, 42ff.

41. Cf. v. 9, "The ministration of righteousness."

42. Leon Morris, *I Corinthians*, Tyndale Commentary, 1958, p. 60.

and regenerated by the Holy Ghost, for which indeed no stone or block, but man alone, was created.[43]

Only the spiritual man can see the things of God. This spiritual man is not a person who differs only psychologically from the natural man. His "spirituality" is not a matter of natural endowment but the gift of the Holy Spirit; it is the Spirit Himself dwelling in his heart. Therefore this man can examine, judge, discern the things of God. Paul even expresses himself more strongly by saying *all* things. The spiritual man is able to estimate all things, both sacred and secular, at their right value and in their right proportions.

This illumination is, of course, not an event that takes place only once and is then accomplished for good. Both passages clearly show that it is a continuing action of the Spirit. From the beginning to the end the acceptance of the Bible as the Word of God is the work of the Spirit. It is a datum that is and remains a dandum.[44] It may well be that this is not always sufficiently stressed by Reformed dogmatics. When, for example, L. Berkhof writes: "The Testimony of the Holy Spirit is *simply* the work of the Holy Spirit in the heart of the sinner, by which he removes the blindness of sin, so that the erstwhile blind man, who had not eyes for the sublime character of the Word of God, now clearly sees and appreciates the marks of the divine origin of Scripture,"[45] then such a statement easily creates the impression that the work of the Holy Spirit in the illumination only exists in the removal of the "cataract" of sin, and that once the "organ" is repaired, it is further left to man to use it. But the illumination is more than one momentary action of the Spirit. Calvin, in his discussion of the testimony of the Holy Spirit, time and again stresses that it is a much more complicated and permanent operation. This becomes quite clear from his repeated use of the word "to seal." The words of Scripture must be "sealed" in our hearts by the inward testimony of the Spirit.[46] We can never,

---

43. Luther on Psalm 90, quoted from Lenski, *op. cit.*, p. 116.
44. Cf. *supra;* ch. V.
45. Berkhof, *Intro. Vol. to Syst. Theol.*, p. 185 (italics ours!).
46. *Instit.* I, vii, 4, 5. In the Eerdmans edition (1957) on pp. 72, 73 we find this expression three times. The same notion is also behind Luther's distinction between "God's Word as such" and "God's Word for me." "It is all God's Word, indeed, but what use is to me all that talk about God's Word — I have to know to whom it is said." In faith we are al-

not at any time, receive the Word without the Spirit. It is and remains His work.

If this is Barth's deepest motive in his conception of inspiration, we are in full agreement with him. Reformed theology may never forget this. The hearing and understanding never become our "possession." They remain a gift of the Spirit. True, we may believe that it is a permanent gift. For we believe in the continuity of the work of the Spirit. But this continuity never means that the "datum" is not a "dandum" any more. On the contrary, it accentuates it![47]

* * *

All this, however, does not mean that illumination is part of the *inspiration*. The Bible itself clearly indicates that inspiration does not refer to the understanding and receiving of Scripture, but to its origin and being. Actually, we should put the point even more broadly. Inspiration may not be restricted only to the inspiration of Scripture, which is only one part of that work. This fact is usually indicated by calling the inspiration of Scripture "graphical" inspiration. This adjective clearly points to a limitation.

Unfortunately there is much confusion concerning the concept of inspiration. One of the many examples of this confusion is that often *inspiration* and *revelation* are not sufficiently distinguished. Especially the last two of the three modes of revelation mentioned by Warfield, namely, "internal suggestion" (typical of the prophets) and "concursive operation" (typical of the Psalms and Epistles),[48] are easily confounded with inspiration. It is not hard to understand this, for particularly in the case of concursive operation, revelation

---

ways concerned with the "for us." One cannot calculate when the flame breaks out and one cannot help it. "Then the Spirit writes the Word, that is proclaimed to us, inwardly in our heart." Cf. W. J. Kooiman, *Luther en de Bijbel*, n.d., pp. 196f.

47. Cf. Bavinck, *op. cit.*, IV, 74 on the "vocatio interna." "This vocation does not happen once and does not stop, when it has called forth the new life, but it always goes on. As God first created everything by the Word and after that preserves all things by the same Word, so the *vocatio interna* is also operative in the preservation and development of the spiritual life."

48. Warfield, *Inspiration and Authority of the Bible*, p. 83. The first mode is that of "external manifestation," comprising theophanies, miracles, and all God's other mighty works by which He makes Himself known.

and inspiration often coincide. Yet they should not be identified.

It is one of the merits of Charles Hodge that he has sharply defined the differences between inspiration and revelation. According to him they are twofold:

> They differ, first, as to their object. The object of revelation is communication of knowledge. The object or design of inspiration is to secure infallibility in teaching. Consequently, they differ, secondly, in their effect. The effect of revelation was to render its recipient wiser. The effect of inspiration was to preserve him from error in teaching.[49]

We have one objection against Hodge's formulation, which is that he concentrates inspiration one-sidedly upon the aspect of infallibility.[50] We wholeheartedly agree with him that this aspect belongs to the essence of inspiration. Yet we do not believe that it is the main aspect. For that purpose it is too formal. The main aspect is the material one, namely, that in the inspiration the Holy Spirit operates in, with, and through persons, selected by Himself, in such a way that what they say or write is *indeed the revelation of God*. What these men produce is not a collection of human ideas, however sublime, nor is it a human and fallible witness to revelation, but it is really what it claims to be: God's own, and therefore infallible, revelation.

It would be better, therefore, to formulate the difference between the two concepts as follows. In revelation we have to do with God's direct act of self-revelation in Jesus Christ. He Himself speaks *directly* to certain persons, either by deeds or words or internal suggestion. In inspiration we have to do with that special operation of the Holy Spirit by which He uses certain persons to communicate the knowledge received by revelation *to others,* and that in such a way that this com-

---

49. Cf. Ch. Hodge, *Systematic Theology,* 1883, I, 155. Cf. also A. Kuyper, *The Work of the Holy Spirit,* 1956, p. 76: " 'Revelation' is a communication of the thoughts of God given in extraordinary manner, by a miracle, to prophets and apostles. But 'inspiration,' wholly distinct from this, is that special and unique operation of the Holy Spirit whereby He directed the minds of the writers of the Scripture in the art of writing." It is unfortunate that Kuyper limits it here to "graphical" inspiration. Cf. also Bavinck, *op. cit.,* I, 397ff. On p. 397 he quotes Pesch: "Inspiratio non est revelatio," and "omnia inspirata sunt revelata."

50. This is also done by Warfield, cf. *op. cit.,* pp. 114f., 150f., 158f. Cf. also *Acts of the Reformed Ecumenical Synod of Potchefstroom,* p. 49.

munication is, once more, nothing less than God's own self-revelation in Jesus Christ.[51]

Particularly illustrative here is the well-known passage from II Peter 1. For one thing, it clearly shows that inspiration is much wider than graphical inspiration. Peter refers here to all the speaking of the prophets, whether inscripturated later on or not. "Men *spake* from God." Every time that men are called to communicate God's revelation to others, either orally or by writing, there is that special operation of the Holy Spirit which we call inspiration. Further, this passage also says explicitly that what these men communicate is indeed God's revelation. "They spake *from God.*" Finally, it is quite obvious from the context that this revelation is *God's self-revelation in Jesus Christ.* Revelation is never a mere communication of all kinds of facts, truths, or other things worth knowing, but revelation is always primarily and basically God's self-revelation in Jesus Christ.[52] Bavinck once stated this very pointedly in these words:

> Even if a book about geography, for example, was fully "inspired" and dictated in the most literal sense of the word, yet it would by that very fact not become "theopneust" in the sense of II Tim. 3:16. Holy Scripture is the Word of God, because in it the Holy Spirit witnesses to Christ, because the incarnate Logos is its material and content.[53]

Peter's argument bears this out fully. The whole chapter speaks of God's self-revelation in Jesus Christ. In the opening verses Peter speaks of the "knowledge of God and Jesus our Lord" (v. 2) and in verse 8 he repeats the last part of it: "the knowledge of our Lord Jesus Christ." In the verses immediately preceding verse 21 he also speaks of Jesus Christ. Emphatically he states that the content of his preaching was

---

51. Cf. Bavinck, *op. cit.*, I, 396. "Revelation and inspiration are distinct, the former is more a work of the Son, the Logos, the latter of the Holy Spirit." In this connection Bavinck also points out that there is a difference between John 14:26 and John 16:12-14. In the former text Jesus speaks of the operation of the Spirit, by which He will bring to the remembrance of the apostles all that Jesus has said to them. In this case the apostles did not need a new special revelation. In John 16 we read of new revelation. It is transmitted by the Spirit, but it comes from the Son. "He shall take of mine, and shall declare it unto you."
52. It is evident, of course, that we speak here of special revelation and not of general revelation.
53. Bavinck, *op. cit.*, I, 414.

not "cunningly devised fables," but "the power and coming of our Lord Jesus Christ" (v. 16). Was he himself not one of the eye- and ear-witnesses, when on the Mount of Transfiguration God the Father spoke these words: "This is my beloved Son, in whom I am well pleased" (vv. 17, 18)? And then, in the following verse, he immediately relates the "prophetical word" with this revelation of God in Jesus Christ. He calls this prophetical word "more sure," not because he could not trust his own ears, but because this prophetic word is "of wider and larger reference, embracing not only a single testimony to Christ as that divine voice did, but all the sufferings of Christ and the glory afterwards."[54]

Indeed, all this is basic for Peter's whole thinking. To him the Old Testament is nothing else than the testimony to Christ. In his first epistle he says about the same prophets, who prophesied of the grace in Jesus Christ, that they always searched diligently "what time or what manner of time the Spirit of Christ which was in them did point unto, when it testified beforehand the sufferings of Christ, and the glories that should follow them" (I Peter 1:10, 11). In other words, the same message is found in both the Old and New Testaments. "They [the Old Testament prophets] ministered these things which now have been announced unto you through them that preached the gospel unto you by the Holy Spirit sent forth from heaven" (1:12).[55] It is the same message: God's self-revelation in Jesus Christ.[56]

This is also the setting of Paul's statement about the "theopneustia" of "all scripture" (A.V.) or "every scripture" (R.V.) in II Timothy 3. We are not allowed to isolate the word "theopneustos" from its context. Paul does not give here an isolated statement about the divine origin of Scripture, but this origin is mentioned in immediate connection with the divine purpose of Scripture. This purpose is the hearing and receiving of God's self-revelation in Jesus Christ. In verse 15

---

54. Dean Alford, *ad locum*.
55. Cf. also Peter's addresses in the Acts of the Apostles. In all of them the Old Testament is interpreted christologically, whereby Christ is designated as the fulfillment of the Old Testament.
56. Cf. also John 20:21. What John says here of his own Gospel holds true of all Scriptures, of all that was spoken and written by God's messengers. "These are written that ye may believe that Jesus is the Christ, the Son of God; and that believing ye may have life in his name."

it is said of the "sacred writings" that "they are able to make thee wise unto salvation through faith which is in Christ Jesus." And the words about the "theopneustia" are immediately followed by the statement that this Scripture, because it is "theopneustos," is "profitable for teaching, for reproof, for correction, for instruction which is in righteousness, that the man of God may be complete, furnished completely unto every good work." In this context the use of the word "theopneustos" gives us much more than a piece of information about the divine origin of Scripture. It is tantamount to saying that this Scripture is fully God's own Word, His self-revelation to all who accept it in faith and obedience.[57]

At the same time Paul says in this passage that this Scripture is a *living* Word of God. That means that here, too, just as in the case of illumination, we are not allowed to isolate the original act of inspiration from the equally necessary and permanent activity of the Holy Spirit in and through this Scripture. For this reason Bavinck is fully correct when he says:

> Holy Scripture is still "theopneustos." The act of inspiration is not an isolated one. The Holy Spirit does not withdraw from Holy Scripture after the act of inspiration, and does not leave it to its own fate, but He sustains and animates it and brings its contents in all different ways to mankind, to its heart and conscience.[58]

In this connection we can also cite the beautiful statement about the finality of Scripture in the Westminster Confession:

> The supreme Judge by which all controversies of religion are to be determined, and all decrees of councils, opinions of ancient writers, doctrines of men, and private spirits, are to be examined, and on whose sentence we are to rest, can be no other but the Holy Spirit speaking in the Scriptures.[59]

---

57. Cf. also I Cor. 2:1-5 and especially I Thess. 2:13. In the latter text Paul roundly declares of his apostolic preaching, as it came *viva voce* to the Thessalonians, that it is the Word of God. Of course we have no right to make a contrast between his oral and written preaching. Of the latter it is also true to say: "as it is in truth the word of God," i.e., God's self-revelation.

58. Bavinck, *op. cit.*, pp. 410/11. Cf. also R. Bijlsma, *op. cit.*, p. 352: "The theopneustia has its origin in the inspiration as a work of the Spirit in the genesis of Scripture, just as it attains its goal and effect through the inspiration of the Spirit in the handling and application of Scripture."

59. Westminster Confession, I, X.

As Warfield has pointed out,[60] we should not understand this section of the Confession to say that there is a difference between the Scriptures and the Holy Spirit speaking in them. The phraseology is determined by the controversy with Rome, which distinguished between the Rule and the Judge, the former being found in Scripture, the latter in the Church. Over against this the Westminster Assembly maintains that Scripture is not an incomplete and lifeless rule, but that it is the living Word of God, for the Holy Spirit still speaks in it. "Whenever and wherever Scripture speaks, it is the Holy Ghost speaking."[61]

It may well be that orthodoxy has not always given due attention to this aspect of inspiration. Though it certainly has never been officially denied, yet in actual practice orthodoxy has often too one-sidedly concentrated the discussion of inspiration upon the origin of Scripture. This comes to the fore, among others, in the emphasis very common in evangelical circles on the inspiration of the so-called "autographa." According to Reid[62] this "hypothesis of a perfect original text" played a very important part already in seventeenth-century orthodoxy. So the Lutheran theologian Quenstedt held that as Scripture is inspired both as to its formal and material aspect, only the original text and not any of the versions is inspired. Inspiration applies to original manuscripts or autographa, not properly to the apographa.[63] But of course this immediately evokes the question: Do we then not have the inspired Word of God any more? What is the use of a literally inspired record if in its literal form it is lost in the vicissitudes of history? To solve this problem Quenstedt takes refuge in another hypothesis:

> We believe, as is our duty, that the providential care of God always watched over the original and primitive texts of the canonical Scriptures in such a way that we can be certain that the sacred codices which we now have in our hands are those which existed at the time of Jerome and Augustine, nay, at the time of Christ Himself and the apostles.[64]

60. Warfield, *The Westminster Assembly and its Work*, 1931, p. 254.
61. Warfield, *op. cit.*, p. 255
62. J.S.K. Reid, *op. cit.*, pp. 87ff.
63. Reid, *op. cit.*, p. 88.
64. Reid, *op. cit.*, pp. 88/89. Cf. also the expression "kept pure in all ages" in the Westminster Confession, I, VIII. As Warfield has convincingly

These hypotheses have often been ridiculed, and it is often thought possible to pass them off with a shrug of the shoulders by the simple remark that nobody has ever seen these errorless, infallible originals. Of course, this is true. But, as Carl F. H. Henry once observed, no one has seen the fallible originals either! "The one is as much a presupposition as the other."[65]

To every one who is willing to listen carefully to what others say, it must be clear that in all these "hypotheses" (the word "presuppositions" is much better here!) we have to do with an important and genuine aspect of faith in Scripture. Behind them there is a truly biblical motive which ought to be honored by every serious student of Scripture, namely, the refusal to dismiss the divine and inspired character of Scripture on account of the errors of copyists. Yet in a one-sided emphasis on the autographa, there is the real danger of creating and promoting the idea that inspiration has only to do with the origin of Scripture and that the Bible as a finished product is an inspired (pluperfect tense) thing. But in reality the Bible is the living Word of God which still communicates His revelation. Yes, it is itself His living revelation, for from moment to moment the Holy Spirit accompanies this Word. Within this context we would venture to say that, for example, Paul's Epistle to the Galatians in the Authorized Version is just as much the inspired Word of God as the original copy which was written by Paul's own hand and received by the Churches of Galatia. A manuscript with some textual errors, due to the mistakes of copyists or translators, does not in any way reduce the inspired character of Scripture. To say this would not only deprive us *all* from a really inspired Scripture, but it would first of all mean a derogation from the ever-real and living relation between the Spirit and the Bible.

---

proved (*op. cit.*, pp. 238ff.), the Westminster Divines did not mean to say that the precise text "immediately inspired by God" lies complete and entire, without the slightest corruption on the page of any extant copy. They only wanted to say that in the multitude of copies the inspired and infallible Scripture was still there, safe and accessible. Hence all their serious efforts in the field of textual criticism. All this is quite different from later exaggeration, in which it was asserted that (e.g.) in the manuscripts underlying the Authorized Version we have the real original text. Cf. Benjamin G. Wilkinson, *Our Authorized Bible Vindicated*, 1930.

65. Everett F. Harrison, in *Revelation and the Bible* (ed. C.F.H. Henry), p. 239.

The Bible is not only a record of former revelation but is itself revelation, "the final, complete, and only extant form of special revelation. Scripture is redemptive revelation and is therefore not simply a concomitant of God's redemptive acts and of the fulfillment of His redemptive designs; it is itself a substantial and indispensable element of the process by which God has wrought His redemptive work and by which He continues to bring to perfection His redemptive purposes."[66] This becomes particularly clear when we note the prominent place which the *category of fulfillment* has in Scripture, exactly with regard to Scripture itself. Reviewing all the passages where the New Testament speaks of fulfillment, Bijlsma comes to the conclusion that, although the category is applied to many widely diverging realities (such as the world, time, righteousness, law, Passover, works of God, joy, knowledge of God, etc.,[67]) yet the all-embracing aspect is the fulfillment of the Scriptures themselves.[68] For they witness to Christ in whom all the fullness (plerooma) of grace is (John 1:16), and in whom the whole fullness of God was pleased to dwell bodily (Col. 1:19, 2:9). With regard to Scripture this fulfillment has a twofold aspect: the first is the closing of the written word in the direction of the past, and the second is the opening of the written word in the direction of the future. We may not say that the one is only negative and the other is fully positive. "The fulfillment is a 'praesens' into which the 'futurum' of the prophecy passed. And this 'praesens' is a real 'praesens' in this respect that it has its own 'futurum' again."[69] Particularly important is the fact that Bijlsma relates all this to the act of *proclamation*. In the Bible we are not concerned with a mere book, a mere record, but the Bible is part of God's proclamation and has to be taken up in the living proclamation of the Church:

---

66. "Report on Inspiration," Reformed Ecumenical Synod of Potchefstroom, 49. In this formulation the Church proclamation, which is also a form of revelation, has not been taken into account. From that point of view the three adjectives "final, complete, and extant" have limited sense. However, in view of the fact that Church proclamation does not add any new element of truth to that revealed in Scripture, but is only exposition and application of the scriptural revelation, the three adjectives can also be used in an absolute sense.
67. R. Bijlsma, *op. cit.*, p. 335.
68. *Ibid.*, p. 336.
69. *Ibid.*, p. 337.

> In the category of fulfilment the closing and opening of Scripture coincide. That happens in Jesus Christ, who is the Lord of all Scripture. What stands written, is completed in Him and His work. But at the same time it begins to move again as proclamation about Him. It starts off towards His future, proclaiming the great work of God to all nations.[70]

All this means that we must qualify Scripture as an eschatological quantity:

> Its destiny is not to lie on the shelf as a mere book. Just as the proclamation, from which it proceeded, it strives forwards. It has a goal ("telos"), towards which it has to press; as the message of Gods works it has to contribute to the attainment of the goal set by God, namely that all nations shall share in the salvation of Israel. It has the very important task of helping to realize the fulness ("pleroooma") of the salvation in God's future. This is its function as instrument of the Holy Spirit.[71]

*   *   *

This emphasis on the continuing operation of the Holy Spirit in and through Scripture[72] may, however, never lead us to deny or neglect the inspired nature of the original writings. However much Barth may pour out his wrath on the concept of "inspiredness," the scriptural data compel us to maintain its legitimacy in a Christian theology of Scripture. In our opinion Barth has made a caricature of it, and to a great extent his fight is against his own self-constructed caricature. This comes clearly to the fore in the description which Reid, following Barth, gives of the orthodox position. According to Reid, it is a "deistic 'prison'" to which Protestant orthodoxy has consigned God.[73] The merit of Barth is that he has "effectively shut the door against all bibliolatry." Through Barth we know again that "the Bible can never take the place of God. On the contrary, God retains in His own hands the

---

70. *Ibid.*
71. *Ibid.,* p. 372.
72. Cf. also Francis I. Andersen, "We speak . . . in words . . . which the Holy Ghost Teacheth," *Westminster Theological Journal,* XXII, May 1960, 118/9. "We . . . maintain that a truly biblical doctrine of revelation will understand it as a dynamic, personal, existential, saving event in which God leads those whom He calls to a living faith into a knowledge of the truth by means of human language, i.e., plain words, and that the holy Scriptures are precisely the instrument of that instruction and the medium of that encounter, created by God specifically for that purpose, and perpetually wielded by the Holy Spirit to that end."
73. J.S.K. Reid, *op. cit.,* p. 202.

action, however regularly the Bible is taken by Him for His instrument."

We would like to ask here: But who among the orthodox Protestants has ever denied this? True, it was perhaps not always sufficiently realized. In that respect we can be grateful to Barth that he has so vigorously reminded us of this basic truth. But at the same time we also must say that Barth falls into the other extreme when his own emphasis of this basic truth leads him to reject the "inspiredness" of the sacred writings. Orthodoxy, with its emphasis on the ontic aspect, may sometimes not have given sufficient attention to the dynamic aspect. But in Barth we see the opposite, namely, that the ontic aspect is denied on account of the dynamic, resulting in a no less serious distortion of the doctrine of Scripture.

We will not deny, of course, that there are great dangers latent in speaking of inspiredness. But is that sufficient reason to reject it? It is rewarding to listen here to what G. W. Bromiley says:

> The doctrine of "inspiredness" is a dangerous one, for attention may easily come to be focused on a quasi-miraculous text instead of its ultimate Author and His act of inspiration. But the mere fact that a doctrine is dangerous does not mean that it is false. Almost all doctrines have been abused at one time or another. What is necessary is to prevent the abuse by relating this secondary doctrine clearly and strictly to the primary inspiring of the authors and the subsequent illumination of the hearers and readers.[74]

* * *

The same holds true to a great extent, perhaps even to a greater extent, of the doctrine of verbal inspiration. Orthodoxy has always seen it as a collateral of the doctrine of inspiration. And this is not surprising at all. Once the scriptural teaching of inspiration in its full compass has been accepted, this aspect is naturally included. Though Scripture does not give a clearcut dogma about this aspect, no more than about many other doctrines, it contains enough statements which clearly intimate it. We need only to recall Paul's words to the Corinthians: "Which things also we speak, not in words which man's wisdom teacheth, but which the Spirit teacheth" (I Cor. 2:13); and to the Thessalonians he writes: "and for

---

74. G. W. Bromiley, "Karl Barth's Doctrine of Inspiration," *Journal of the Transactions of the Victoria Institute*, LXXXVII (1955), 77.

this cause we also thank God without ceasing, that, when ye received from us the word of the message, even the word of God, ye accepted it not as the word of men, but, as it is in truth, the Word of God, which also worketh in you that believe" (I Thess. 2:13).

This, too, is a dangerous doctrine, and it is rather easy to pour ridicule upon it. This has been done so often that one could easily fill an entire volume with all the deriding words. In fairness we must immediately add that orthodoxy itself has too often given occasion for such derision. Sometimes it has gone to such extremes that they have justly evoked protest, and we can imagine that here ridicule was the only suitable weapon. One of the most notably extreme formulations occurs in the Helvetic Formula of Consensus, in which the Hebrew Text of the Old Testament is said to be "theopneustos regarding both the consonants and the vowels, whether the very points themselves or at least the power of the points."[75] It is certainly not correct, however, to identify the orthodox position with these extreme statements. The Formula of Consensus was never generally accepted by the Reformed Churches.[76] It is even criticized sharply by Reformed theologians for being far too quantitative-massive. It conceives of inspiration as purely mechanical. And once we have entered upon this level we cannot possibly stop, for then a comma is just as important as a text like John 3:16. In both cases we must accept the will of the Holy Spirit, who never expresses Himself at random.

It is obvious that such a conception of inspiration does grave injustice to the Bible as the Word of God. The secret of the Bible, namely, that it is God's self-revelation in Jesus Christ, fully disappears behind the formal aspect, and the

---

75. Cf. Bavinck, *op. cit.*, I, 385. Reid, *op. cit.*, pp. 87f. "In specie autem Hebraicus Veteris Testamenti Codex, quem ex traditione Ecclesiae Judaicae, cui olim Oracula Dei commissa sunt, accepimus hodieque retinemus, tum quoad consonas, tum quoad vocalia, sive puncta ipsa, sive punctorum saltem potestatem, et tum quoad res, tum quoad verba *theopneustos,* ut fidei et vitae nostrae, una cum Codice Novi Testamenti sit canon unicus et illibatus, ad cuius normam, ceu Lydium lapidem, universae, quae extant, Versiones, sive orientales, sive occidentales exigendae, et sicubi deflectunt, revocandae sunt." P. Schaff, *Creeds of Christendom,* I, 487.

76. Cf. Schaff, *op. cit.*, p. 486. "Its authority was confined to Switzerland, and even there it could not maintain itself longer than about half a century."

perspectives which the mountain landscape of the Bible offers, fade away in the monotony and shapelessness of an endless uniform plain. The only correct view is the *qualitative-organic* one. Not that there is a contrast here between the qualitative and quantitative. The former definitely includes the latter. But it is also true that the latter is fully qualified by the former. It is important only within the context of the qualitative-organic aspect. Thus Bavinck, on the one hand, says: "In the thoughts the words are included, and in the words the vowels."[77] Yet he immediately continues: "This does not at all mean that everything is full of divine wisdom, that every jot and tittle has an infinite content." Bavinck even does not hesitate to distinguish between the center and periphery. Of course he does not mean to say that one part is inspired and the other not. He only means that in his conception the quantitative aspect is fully determined by the qualitative, i.e., the revelatory aspect. For example, statements like "The Word became flesh" (John 1:14) and "Now there was much grass in the place" (John 6:10) are both inspired, they both belong to the Word of God and both have the task to convey God's message to His people, yet both have an entirely different function in the whole. Bavinck uses the metaphor of the organism of the human body. In this body nothing is accidental. Every part has its own place and function. Yet head and heart have a much more important place than hand and foot, which in turn again are more important than hairs and nails. Likewise, the soul is in the whole body and in every part of it, but not in all parts in the same way.[78]

In our opinion, therefore, it is better to speak of *plenary* than of verbal inspiration. Again we do not mean any contrast. The former includes the latter, but at the same time it avoids many of the misunderstandings which almost necessarily arise from the latter. We know it has been said that this substitution is not really helpful, because the adjective "plenary" requires as much explanation as the term "verbal." Even if this were true (which is only so to a certain extent), yet the word "plenary" involves a different approach. Although it also has a quantitative flavor — which cannot be avoided, as we are concerned with the question of the *extent*

---

77. Bavinck, *op. cit.*, I, 409.
78. *Ibid.*, 409/10.

of inspiration — yet it has a strongly qualitative connotation. It does not focus our attention on the formal aspect, nor on the isolated words, but it accentuates the inspired character of Scripture in its total structure. It keeps words and thoughts together in an inseparable unity and clearly intimates the organic oneness of Scripture in all its different parts and aspects.

The whole problem could perhaps be best summed up in this way. The *formal* aspect of Scripture (inspiration) may never, not even for a single moment, be detached from the *material* aspect (Scripture's being revelation, God's Word). The question of the extent of inspiration is indissolubly linked with that of the purpose of inspiration, namely, to communicate God's Word to the world. As soon as orthodoxy forgets this, its contention for plenary (or verbal) inspiration will become sterile. What John Mackay says of orthodoxy in general, also holds true of orthodox belief in Scripture:

> Now orthodoxy, that is, right and sound doctrine, is important. Yet we can *have* the truth in a purely intellectual sense without the truth having us. And Christian truth, let it never be forgotten, is personal truth; it centers in a Person and it must possess the lives of the persons who in the fullest sense become servants of the Truth. Christian truth must not only be believed, it must be obeyed. Men must *do* the truth. Here is the paradox. Loyalty to ideas about Christ can become a subtle substitute for loyalty to Christ himself. Ideas can become idols. The heresy of orthodoxy, that is, the heresy to which orthodoxy is everlastingly subject, can be the most soul-destroying, mind-shattering of all heresies.[79]

J. Overduin, who spent a great part of his ministry as a special minister for evangelism among the unchurched of Amsterdam, recounts the story of a man who for more than thirty years had been an avowed atheist. After his conversion the man told Mr. Overduin that one Sunday he had attended a church service. He did not believe at all, and could not understand how other sensible people could accept all those improbable stories in the Bible. His only reason for going to church was the kind invitation of good friends to whom he could not say no. During that service, however, something happened to him. The preacher hit one nail after another

---

79. John A. Mackay, "The Form of a Servant," *Theology Today*, XV, 312/13.

right on the head. As an avowed atheist he did not want to accept it, but all his arguments failed:

> The truth of the Gospel was too powerful. And since that day I have gone to Church every Sunday. And every time a very real world opens itself to me. There is no one who tells you the truth as Jesus does. The Bible gets increasingly more authority for me. I still have a lot of problems, especially in connection with the Old Testament, but my attitude has changed completely and I am sure that God will bring me, a novice, further. However many questions still may be open, I cannot get loose from Christ.[80]

Overduin then observes: How clearly do we see the imminent authority of the Truth! What really and finally matters is the *content* of the Gospel. "The early Christians were overwhelmed by the power of the Truth of the Gospel, without having a clear insight into a theory of inspiration."[81] Such a statement, of course, can easily be misinterpreted. It can easily be used for the construction of a contrast between the formal and the material aspect, as if the former would not really matter. Too often this is done in our day. But such a contrast is a far cry from Overduin's intention. He wants only to stress the primary character of the material aspect, and rightly so! The same holds true of what he further says: "It is possible that a man in his formal view of Holy Scripture has many erratic ideas and yet with his whole heart lives out of the content of the Gospel, while it is also possible that formally the infallibility of Scripture is very much stressed, without a real, spiritual assimilation of the content of Scripture."[82]

On our part, we believe that this emphasis on the imminent authority of Scripture is also one of the major reasons why the Reformers accorded comparatively little attention to the formal aspect.[83] What mainly concerned them was God speak-

---

80. J. Overduin, *Tact en Contact*, 1958, p. 105.
81. Overduin declares emphatically that it is of the utmost importance to have a view of the formal aspect as pure as possible because the formal and material aspects are closely interrelated (*ibid.*)
82. Cf. also R. Schippers, "Biblicisme en Fundamentalisme," *Bezinning*, Vol. XIV, No. 2 (1959), and C. F. H. Henry, *The Uneasy Conscience of Modern Fundamentalism*, 1947.
83. There were, of course, more reasons. E.g. the fact that there was little or no disagreement with the Roman Catholic Church as to the mode and extent of inspiration.

ing in and through Scripture. This is the only explanation for the rather easy and surprising way in which they sometimes tackled and dismissed textual difficulties. When Calvin, for example, comments on Acts 7:14, he starts with the remark: "Whereas he [i.e. Stephen] saith that Jacob came into Egypt with seventy-five souls, it agreeth not with the words of Moses; for Moses maketh mention of seventy only." He then goes on to mention several solutions suggested throughout the centuries. He even seriously considers the possibility that Luke, being a proselyte, had no knowledge of the Hebrew tongue, or that Luke wished to grant this to his Gentile readers, who used to read it thus in the Septuagint. Finally he winds up his argument with the casual remark: "If any man contend more stubbornly, let us suffer him to be wise without measure." Why does Calvin take this so lightly? Because that which really matters to him is the divine message.

> This, so small a number, is purposely expressed, to the end the power of God may the more plainly appear, in so great an enlarging of that kindred, which was of no long continuance. For such a small handful of men could not, by any human manner of engendering, grow to such an infinite multitude as is recorded in Exodus (XII. 37), within two hundred and fifty years. We ought rather to weigh the miracle which the Spirit commendeth unto us in this place, than to stand long about one letter, whereby the number is altered.[84]

In this respect we can agree with J.S.K. Reid when he says that Calvin's emphasis and interest is placed, not on the record as such, but on the content of the record.[85] When he goes on to say, however, that it is nowhere affirmed by Calvin that the record itself is inspired, and then quotes the following words of H. Heppe: "The authority of Scripture rests not upon the form of the recording, but upon its content, i.e., upon the reality of the revealed facts attested in the writing," he creates a contrast that is fully foreign to Calvin.[86] However much it is true that in Calvin's writings the main emphasis is placed on the content, yet this never takes place at the expense of the form. Calvin was too much aware of the Bible's

---

84. Calvin, *Commentary on Acts*, I, 264. Cf. R. Schippers, *Johannes Calvijn*, 1959, pp. 48ff.
85. J.S.K. Reid, *op. cit.*, p. 43.
86. Cf. Reid's own rendering of Calvin's view on pp. 34ff.!

clear testimony concerning its own inspiration. On the other hand, it is true that in the inseparable correlation between form and content, the latter is the determining aspect. In fact, this was always the deepest intention of orthodoxy. Its emphasis on the formal aspect had its basic motive in its concern for the material aspect.

This clearly appears, for example, in the Belgic Confession. This Confession time and again emphasizes the formal aspect, but it is always done in direct relation to the material aspect. In Article IV it frankly says: "We believe that the Holy Scriptures are contained in two books, namely the Old and New Testament . . . against which nothing can be alleged." There cannot be any doubt that the latter expression refers to the so-called formal aspect. But it is not an isolated interest in formal infallibility which prompts the Confession to make this statement, for these very same words are immediately preceded by the declaration "which are canonical," an expression which is through and through "material" as appears from Article V, where the word "canonical" is explained as "for the regulation, foundation, and confirmation of our faith." Again, we read in Article V that we believe "without any doubt all things contained in them," and that "not so much because the Church receives and approves them as such, but more especially because the Holy Spirit witnesses in our hearts that they are from God." Likewise the Confession states in Article VII that "we believe that those Holy Scriptures contain the will of God, and that whatsoever man ought to believe unto salvation is sufficiently taught therein."

If anything is evident, it is that the interest of the Reformation Churches in the formal aspect of Scripture had for its solid ground the unshakeable conviction that in the Bible we have to do with God's Word, with God Himself speaking to us through the medium of prophets and apostles. And this same conviction remained the deepest motive of orthodoxy in its tenacious clinging to the doctrine of an infallible Scripture. Its contention for this infallibility was never a fight for a merely abstract *theologoumenon*. As Alan Cole puts it:

> "Infallibility" may be predicated of the Bible in that it partakes in the infallibility of God, the Source: we may accept it, in reverent faith, as our infallible guide in faith and conduct. The Bible, rightly read, read as a whole, read Christocentrically,

and read humbly under the guidance of the Holy Spirit in the fellowship of the Church can never deceive us as to what God is like, or as to what man is like, or as to what God's word is like.[87]

87. Alan Cole, "Gabriel Hebert on 'Fundamentalism and the Church of God,'" *Reformed Theol. Review*, XVIII, 19/20.

CHAPTER VII

THE AUTHORITY OF THE BIBLE

Everyone who writes on the doctrine of Holy Scripture must also deal with the authority of the Bible. Barth is no exception to this rule; in fact, he devotes a separate paragraph of considerable length to this matter.

He takes his starting point in the plain fact that the Bible *has* authority in the Church. And that is no wonder, for the Bible is historically the *oldest extant record* of the origins and therefore of the basis and nature of the Church[1] In point of age no other written document can compete with the Bible as a "primitive authority." But of course this kind of authority is only indirect and relative and formal; so there is place for the question whether beside and even beyond Holy Scripture there are *other authorities* in the Church.

Two different groups say that there are: the *Church of Rome* and *Neo-Protestantism*. Though externally they differ considerably and even seem to be opposites, in fact they are *essentially the same*. According to Barth, the heresy of Neo-Protestantism, which broke out within the Evangelical (that is, the Reformation) Church, is in this matter "simply the extended arm of the errant Papist Church."[2] Actually we have here not two churches, but the "two poles between which the life of the one Church would have to swing in a highly unnecessary and dangerous tension, were it not that Holy Scripture is the Word of God."[3] Both Roman Catholicism and Neo-Protestantism do not understand the statement that the Bible is the Word of God exclusively, but *inclusively*. Not only

1. *C.D.*, I, 2, 540.
2. *Ibid.*, p. 546.
3. *Ibid.*, p. 545.

do they have place for another authority, but they even regard this as necessary. Both pervert the proper relationship of obedience by supposing that they can deal with God, Christ and the Holy Spirit on a basis of possession, knowledge, and power; they think that they can control instead of simply obeying. Barth formulates the distinction and the similarity between the two as follows:

> The distinction consists in the fact that the reality of the Church equated with revelation has in Catholicism, in the form of the Roman hierarchy, a theoretical and practical definiteness, which the Neo-Protestant "History" of Christianity, lacking any visible form, can never have. Yet the two are one in the fact that behind there stands the possibility to extend the long line of equations by another line, i.e. by identifying not only Christian history, but the history of religion, indeed all history or human reality generally, with revelation.[4]

The Church of Rome set foot on this road by accepting the oral tradition as of equal value with Holy Scripture. In a long excursus Barth gives a very interesting survey of the historical development from the Early Church Fathers (Irenaeus, Tertullian, Augustine, and others), via Vincent of Lerins' Commonitorium ("that we hold, what everywhere, always and by all has been believed") to the Council of Trent, which in its session of April 8, 1546 decided that "this truth and this discipline are contained in written books and in unwritten traditions," and that "this Synod receives and venerates, with equal pious affection and reverence, all the books both of the New and Old Testaments . . . together with the said Traditions." From Trent there is a straight line to the Vatican Council of 1870, which defined the infallibility of the Pope, when he speaks "ex cathedra, that is, when — fulfilling the office of Pastor and Teacher of all Christians — on his supreme Apostolical authority, he defines a doctrine concerning faith or morals to be held by the Universal Church."[5] It is clear that here the revelation has been fully placed under the authority of the Church. Holy Scripture no longer has absolute authority, but the Church, in the person of the Pope, has the last and deciding word.

The origins of Neo-Protestantism can be traced back to the

---

4. *Ibid.*, p. 546.
5. *Ibid.*, pp. 547ff., 559ff.

end of the sixteenth century, where we can already observe the rise of a new, overestimated Protestant tradition. Barth points, for example, to the magic exercised by the name of Luther and to a certain extent of Calvin, to the almost magical authority which the Augsburg Confession acquired for Lutheranism, etc.[6] In the seventeenth century men such as Hugo Grotius and George Calixt consciously accepted the oral tradition as in a sense necessary besides Scripture. Once on the road of a theology which says "and" (Scripture *and* Tradition), the "ands" appear everywhere: faith *and* works, nature *and* grace, reason *and* revelation.[7] The final result of this development is found in nineteenth century Neo-Protestantism, which, to be true, did not accept a tradition any more, neither did it accept a revelation which stands above the Church. It knew only old sacred books which spoke of a revelation that once took place long ago — a revelation that at bottom does not affect us because it cannot be revelation to us, but that always surprises and claims us from afar, not without a certain devotion and enjoyment in us. But the decisive factor is the pious man himself with his feelings and ideas which are the ultimate norm.

Barth emphasizes that in both cases the whole development is nothing else than a process which increasingly rejects the *free and sovereign grace of God*. According to him it is not surprising that Vincent of Lerins was a Semi-Pelagian and Hugo Grotius an Arminian: "The battle against the freedom of grace is the root of Neo-Protestantism as well as of Roman Catholicism."[8] In both cases it is nothing else than self-government. For obedience to its own authority is the very antithesis of obedience. In Catholicism, "the final decision rests with the teaching office of the Church which comprises both Scripture and tradition and expounds them with unchallenged authority, identifying itself with revelation." In Neo-Protestantism, "it rests with the less tangible but no less infallible authority of the self-consciousness and historical consciousness of man."[9] But essentially it is the same phenomenon: The wish for self-government. And that means that man, either

6. *Ibid.*, p. 554.
7. *Ibid.*, p. 557.
8. *Ibid.*, p. 554.
9. *Ibid.*, p. 575.

in the Church or individually, usurps the great prerogative of God! He lives in open disobedience against God, who is the only self-governing One.

Barth utterly rejects this. "The Evangelical, and with it the true Church, stands or falls by the fact that [apart, of course, from the revealed and proclaimed Word of God, which is identical with Scripture] it understands *exclusively* the statement that the Bible is the Word of God."[10] This does not mean that Barth rejects all authority of or in the Church. He emphatically maintains that there are fathers and brothers in faith and proclamation, to whom we ought to listen reverently.[11] There is also an authority of the Church in the present day, namely, when and where the Church witnesses in response to and in conformity with the original prophetic and apostolic witness.[12] But this authority of the Church is always founded in an authority which is beyond the Church. The Church has authority only when it submits itself to this higher authority. This higher authority is that of Jesus Christ. "Its Lord is Jesus Christ."[13] He alone is the immediate, absolute, and material authority.

So it was in the original act of revelation. The prophets and apostles were "recipients of revelation in the sense that revelation meets them as the master and they become obedient to it. It is because they are obedient that they are prophets and apostles. It is because they are obedient that they have the Holy Spirit."[14] And likewise Jesus Christ is now the authority in and through the witness of the prophets and apostles. This witness, which comes to us in the Bible, confronts us "commandingly" as Holy Scripture.

This understanding of Scripture was the *great rediscovery of the Reformation,* both in its Lutheran and Reformed form. It may be that the Lutheran confessions do not speak of it as explicitly as the Reformed symbols,[15] yet it was *the* great prin-

---

10. *Ibid.,* p. 546 (italics mine, K.R.).
11. *Ibid.,* p. 573.
12. *Ibid.,* pp. 573/74.
13. *Ibid.,* p. 576.
14. *Ibid.,* p. 543.
15. Among the Reformed confessions there are some that hardly speak of this matter. Barth mentions the Confession of the Berne Synod of 1532, the Basel Confession of 1543, and especially the Heidelberg Catechism "in which we need a microscope to find the Scripture principle, as we do in the older Lutheran documents."

ciple of the whole Reformation. As an example Barth quotes Luther's words in the Articles of Schmalkald: "We must not make the work or words of the holy Fathers into articles of faith. . . . We are told that the Word of God must constitute articles of faith, and no one else, not even an angel." On the Reformed side there is, for instance, the French Confession of 1559, which in Article 5 states without any ambiguity:

> We believe that the Word contained in these books has proceeded from God, and receives its authority from him alone, and not from men. And inasmuch as it is the rule of all truth, containing all that is necessary for the service of God and for our salvation, it is not lawful for men, nor even for angels, to add to it, to take away from it or to change it. Whence it follows that no authority, whether of antiquity, or custom, or numbers, or human wisdom, or judgments, or proclamations, or edicts, or decrees, or councils, or visions, or miracles, should be opposed to these Holy Scriptures, but, on the contrary, all things should be examined, regulated and reformed according to them.

* * *

All this does not mean that Barth in his opposition to Rome and Neo-Protestantism gives up his own basic principles, and acribes to the Bible the nature of being God's Word in a direct sense. Time and again he emphasizes that the Bible and God's Word are not directly identical. The Church never *has* the Word of God. She may expect the miracle of revelation to happen, but that it really does happen is always the act and truth of Jesus Christ in the power and mystery of the Holy Spirit. It is not the book as book, nor the letter as letter that contains the authority of Jesus Christ. The book has no "godlike value" in itself.[16]

Yet at the same time it must be stressed that God Himself has willed that the primary sign of revelation, the reality of the prophets and apostles, has this concrete form of *a book* and *a letter*. "And we need not blush to say this, it is not contrary to spirit and power and life but it is the strait gate which we will not pass by, if we do not want to miss the reality of the spirit and power and life of God."[17] In fact, this very concrete form of the primary witness is its protection against

---

16. *Ibid.*, p. 581.
17. *Ibid.*, p. 581.

the self-will and chance to which it otherwise would be exposed. It is therefore unalterable over against all misunderstandings and misinterpretations, and it sets itself continuously before the Church. The Church may attempt to interpret it away, but in its concrete form of a written record it forces itself constantly upon the Church. This is why the Reformation of the sixteenth century could take place. The Word in its written form broke through erroneous human interpretations and brought the Church back under the absolute authority of Jesus Christ, at the same time restoring the Church's own authority — for the Church has real authority only when her own glory and authority is a predicate of Jesus Christ's divine glory and authority, as in the incarnation Christ's human nature was a predicate of His eternal deity.[18] Here is no place for boasting. Here is a place only for thankful receiving.

* * *

Apart from the characteristic Barthian distinction between the Bible and the Word of God, a distinction which again and again comes to the fore, we gratefully acknowledge that Barth presents the great principle of the authority (and sufficiency) of the Bible in a clear and convincing way. The Roman Catholic system and the "systemless system" of Neo-Protestantism are attacked at their core, and the line of the Reformation is continued with a firm hand.

And yet, many of our questions regarding the authority of Holy Scripture have not been answered by Barth — especially not the questions which are raised by his own distinction between the Bible and the Word of God. We remember that Barth calls the Bible the human and fallible witness to revelation, and that according to him only in the divine act of revelation does this witness become the vehicle of the infallible speaking of God. At this point many questions suggest themselves. How is this possible? What *does* happen to the fallible witness when God in His divine act of revelation takes it into His service? What, then, at that very moment, is the authority of this fallible record?

Barth gives no answer to these questions. He even does not touch them. In our opinion there is only one explanation of this silence: To Barth these questions are wholly irrelevant

18. *Ibid.*, p. 577.

because in the divine act of revelation all our problems cease to exist. When this divine act of revelation takes place, God Almighty speaks to us, and His authority is factual in spite of the defective medium. The final authority of His speaking is there, and we can only submit. To say it in other words, revelation is a miracle and therefore is beyond our understanding. It simply takes place, and in it the fallible witness does what pleases God, namely, it does reveal Him in spite of its fallibility.

We wonder, however, whether it is permissible so to dismiss all these questions. The fallible witness, as we have it in the Bible, is a concrete thing and it is before us. Besides, Barth himself has emphatically declared that we must seek for and will find the revelation only in the texts, as they lie before us! But is it not our task then to assess their value as a witness? Does their fallibility not restrict somewhat their value as a vehicle for the act of revelation? What is the influence of the fallible aspects (and Barth has said that they are fallible in all their aspects!) on the miracle of the revelation? Is the fallibility taken up into the infallibility and transformed into infallibility? Or does the infallible revelation break through the fallible witness? Or does the revelation use certain elements of the record only? If the prophet or the apostle has made a mistake in his witness (and according to Barth they were liable to and even guilty of errors), what then is the place of this mistake or error in the revelation?

As far as we know, Barth has never dealt explicitly with all these questions. We can hardly understand this, for they force themselves upon everyone who studies his doctrine of Holy Scripture. Some scholars who are deeply influenced by him seem to have realized this and have attempted to answer, but these attempts show clearly that the Barthian solution is *basically untenable*. However attractive at first glance, it does not really solve the problems but returns us again, this time from a different side, into the old horizontal dualism.

* * *

A good example is the discussion of the problem by J. S. K. Reid in his study *The Authority of Scripture*. Reid fully accepts the Barthian distinction between the Bible as a witness and the Word of God.[19] The Bible in itself, as it lies before us, is only a witness which is used by God to reveal Himself.

> The power of the gospel lies in the fact that the Word of God identifies Himself with the gospel when it is proclaimed, so that where the Word is spoken and witness borne, He recognizes what is there accomplished, and is present in person and power. Once again the distinction between the witness to the Word of God and the presence of that Word collapses. He is present when He is proclaimed.[20]

As a witness the Bible is not infallible. Emphatically Reid says of the Old Testament (but *mutatis mutandis* it applies to the New Testament as well): "This witness is not *ipso facto* infallible. Where this witness, incorrect and distorted though it may be, is borne, He to whom it is witness is present."[21]

Reid full well realizes that this view carries a host of difficulties with it. He attempts to solve them by concentrating everything upon Christ, who is the unity of the Old and New Testaments. "There is, of course a difference between the Old and New Testaments; yet the story is one, as Christ pre-existent, Christ incarnate, and Christ risen and regnant, is one."[22] But even this christological concentration does not solve all the problems. Reid himself asks: What should be our attitude to the witness when at certain points it appears not to be up to the standard? As examples he mentions I Corinthians 7:9, where Paul is "not so good" in commending marriage on the ground that "it is better to marry than to burn," and Psalm 68:21-23, which verses the congregation is directed "to omit" in the singing on Whit-Sunday.[23] The general solution offered is: "The authority of the Bible reposes in the fact that, in statements some right and some wrong, and in practical application some of which is disputable and some even more dubious, a unified witness is borne to Him who is at the center of the Gospel."[24] It might be observed that this speaks only of the witness as witness. But what does happen in the

---

19. As we have seen in Chapter II, he finds this distinction also in Calvin. In fact, it *is*, according to him, characteristic of the whole Reformation, both Reformed and Lutheran. Cf. for Luther, *op. cit.*, pp. 56ff.
20. *Op. cit.*, p. 274.
21. *Ibid.*, p. 272.
22. *Ibid.*, p. 266.
23. *Ibid.*, p. 267.
24. *Ibid.*, p. 267.

act of revelation? According to Reid, in the act of revelation God breaks through this defective witness and makes Himself known to us through this witness. "The very character of God makes itself known to us through the opacity and even distortion of the human witness."[25]

All this, however, in fact means that there is an unbearable tension between the actual words of the witness and the presence of God. Reid fully acknowledges this, but thinks that it can be solved by putting heavy emphasis on the primacy of God's presence. Writes he: "'If primacy is rightly accorded to the presence of God when the prophet addresses his people in God's name, it is withdrawn from the actual words which were used."[26] From this very statement he draws three important conclusions. (a) First importance no longer attaches to the accuracy of what is said, as though it were needful that the very words of God be reported. (b) There is therefore no need to suppose the complete suppression of the personality and the individuality of the spokesman God has chosen. (c) There is thus room for distortion and misrepresentation of God's intention.

No one, of course, has any objection to the second conclusion. Only advocates of a purely mechanical conception of inspiration would take offense here. But apparently Reid fails to recognize that conclusion (b) is of quite a different nature from conclusions (a) and (c). For what do the latter in actual fact mean? They mean that God reveals Himself through a witness that in fact speaks quite differently from what it ought to say! In other words, the propositional aspect of the revelation (which is inherent in the scriptural idea of revelation) is here sacrificed to the personal, existential aspect of the meeting with God. But these two aspects can never be separated. God reveals Himself in no other place than in this witness and in the actual words of this witness. As soon as we give this up, we are back in the morass of *subjectivism*.

As a matter of fact, this is so with Reid. The whole thing becomes a matter of "due explanation and exposition."[27] Of course we do not want to deny the right and necessity of

---

25. *Ibid.,* p. 268.
26. *Ibid.,* p. 272.
27. *Ibid.,* p. 268.

exegesis; no one can read the Bible without being engaged in it. From this point of view all our reading and understanding of the Bible is personal and subjective. But Reid applies this expression to the so-called "wrong statements" and "dubious applications" mentioned above. Through such explanation and exposition we would be able to hear even such "rough sentiments" as in Psalm 68 as rightful and important aspects of the witness to the God and Father of our Lord Jesus Christ. We cannot see this otherwise than as a return to the old horizontal dualism. True, exaggeration of this dualism is checked by the statement that the difficulties are only found in isolated texts and that as a whole the Bible is reliable and unified in its witness,[28] but such a statement does not alter the fact of a return-in-principle to the old horizontal dualism.[29]

As far as we can see, this return cannot be avoided here. Once the Barthian distinction between the witness and the Word is accepted, dualism in some form or another is the inescapable result. We realize, of course, that Reid is not Barth and that Barth may not be charged with the deficiencies of Reid's solution. But the latter is certainly illustrative of how impossible it is to solve the problems created by Barth's thesis of "indirect identity" without landing in the dualism that at first was rightly rejected.

28. *Ibid.*, pp. 267, 268. Cf.: "There is no need — nor is it possible — to give an absolute guarantee of the historical accuracy of every detail recorded in the Old Testament. History never achieves demonstrable certainty, but it may be modestly stated, with the assurance which the subject matter allows, that the Bible records the events of the story of Israel with sufficient accuracy" (p. 254), and "The Bible is not authoritative because it is verse by verse immediately employable. The example of our Lord in matters of hygiene is not authoritative, yet this does nothing to impair the authority of the incarnation. It is rather to be expected that the authority of the Bible will consist in the intrinsic quality of the whole (pp. 235/36; for an example of Jesus' attitude to hygiene he refers to John 9:6).

29. How much the whole picture becomes confused appears from the following statement taken from the next to last page of Reid's book: "God who is truth communicates Himself not through silence or untruth or nonsense, but through the veracious record of His saving deeds" (p. 278). In our opinion such a statement cannot be maintained in its absolute sense in the light of the foregoing. The adjective "veracious" appears to be subject to so many restrictions that in its literal meaning it cannot serve its purpose here.

* * *

Similar tensions are found in the dogmatics of the Dutch theologian G. C. Van Niftrik.[30] He is even more illustrative, because he is much more of an avowed Barthian than Reid.

Van Niftrik fully adopts the "indirect identity" between the fallible witness and the infallible Word of God.[31] At the same time he repeats again and again that it is not our task to sift the human element from the divine. We have no norm to say that this is human insight and that is God's Word. If we try to do this we fall into a kind of natural theology. "In and through the fallible word of man God's Word comes authoritatively to us in the economy of the Spirit."[32]

But this sort of statement does not solve the problems. In a sense, it only serves to raise them. This appears clearly when Van Niftrik works out the infallibility of the witness in further detail. In his opinion, for example, we can scienitfically criticize the witness with regard to its world view, its conception of history, its religious and theological contents from a phenomenological point of view, its terminology, and the like.[33] It is even possible to exercise an internal criticism of the witness with regard to its view of reality, its moral and historical contents, even its religious and theological contents.[34] "There are considerably great contrasts between the Law and the Prophets, between the Synoptic Gospels and that of John, between Paul and James."[35]

How much tension this view creates becomes apparent especially in Van Niftrik's discussion of the *historical aspect*. It is not surprising that he stresses this aspect, for, as he himself says: "the Christian faith lives on *facts* and not on ideas."[36] Yet he holds the orthodox criterion, namely, that "the Bible in all its parts is historically reliable," to be completely wrong. "The statement means that it really did happen this way. But how uncritically one thinks and speaks. Of course, it did really happen. If only this is understood *spiritually!* How would it be possible to preach the content of the Bible as the

---

30. G. C. Van Niftrik, *Kleine Dogmatiek*, 4th ed., 1953.
31. *Ibid.*, p. 257.
32. *Ibid.*, p. 258, cf. p. 265.
33. *Ibid.*, p. 260.
34. *Ibid.*, p. 259.
35. *Ibid.*, p. 260.
36. *Ibid.*, p. 261.

Word of God, if it did not really happen!"[37] One can only wonder whether this is not a mere playing with words. What does "spiritually" mean here? That after all things may have happened quite differently from the way that they have been recorded?[38] But what then is the meaning of the word "really," twice repeated by Van Niftrik? Does the one not neutralize the other?

Van Niftrik immediately continues to speak of the problem whether the description of the facts in the Bible is historically "adequate," that is, whether it is in conformity with the norms of the modern science of history. With great emphasis he says: "This we deny!" But this, of course, is not the real problem. Hardly any one nowadays maintains that the Bible gives a description which is "adequate" in the light of modern standards of history. Nor is it relevant to say that the Bible does not give us history alone, but history plus interpretation, that is, kerygmatic historiography.[39] This, too, is generally accepted by all. The *real* point at issue is, did that which is described here (in all its "inadequacy" according to modern standards), indeed happen, and did it happen in the way in which it is described? If not, then we are again up against the old dualism, be it in a different form. As we have seen, Van Niftrik rejects such a dualism utterly. But the question must be asked whether such a rejection is in fact possible from his point of view. In our opinion the answer is negative. Even if one hesitates to apply it, even if one realizes the impossibility of applying it, yet in fact a sifting cannot be prevented. And this holds true not only of the historical parts of Scripture, but of the doctrinal and hortatory passages as well. If what Paul, for example, says in the text (and we must never read behind the words or between the lines, says Van Niftrik; God speaks to us in and through *these* words[40]) is fallible, yes factually contains errors, then I can no longer accept the statement as it is before me. Then I can do only one of two things: either *reject* it or *re-interpret* it. In fact, Barthian theology usually takes the second way. As we have already pointed out before, Barth (and this also applies to many of

---

37. *Ibid.*, p. 258.
38. Van Niftrik also accepts sagas and legends in the Bible (*op. cit.*, p. 260).
39. Cf. *op. cit.*, p. 262.
40. *Ibid.*, p. 265.

his followers, at least among the dogmaticians) hardly ever exercises "higher" criticism. But *re-interpretation* is often no better than criticism. In fact, it is often nothing else than a *camouflaged form of dualistic criticism!*

* * *

The foregoing does not mean that there are no difficulties for Reformed theology regarding the authority of Scripture. On the contrary, from the very beginning of the Reformation there was an awareness of the difficulty of this problem. From a certain point of view one may say that the problem actually arose with the Reformation itself. When the Church lost its function as the authority behind Scripture, as the power which defines decisively what is to be believed, the problem of the authority of Scripture presented itself anew in all its force to the Reformation churches. At one point there was full agreement. Holy Scripture *has divine authority*. As Calvin said: "The full authority which the Scriptures ought to possess with the faithful is not recognized, unless they are believed to have come from heaven, as directly as if God had been heard giving utterance to them."[41] Immediately, however, the question came up; what exactly do we mean when we speak of *divine* authority? How do we understand this *in concreto*, when a certain communication is made in a certain text?

One of the attempts to solve this problem is found in the distinction between the *historical* and *normative* authority of Scripture. Basically this distinction is already present in the theology of Zwingli, as appears from the following statement:

> When you see one person quote a word of God which is clear and plain in a certain sense, while another brings forward a second one equally clear, which openly contradicts the first, observe which is the passage that honours God and that which glorifies man. Hold fast that which gives God the glory and which ascribes to Him all the work, all the glory and all the honour.[42]

41. Calvin, *Instit.* I, vii, 1.
42. Quoted from A. Lecerf, *An Introduction to Reformed Dogmatics*, p. 316. Cf. Calvin on John 7:18: "For everything that displays the glory of God is holy and divine; but everything that contributes to the ambition of men, and, by exalting them, obscures the glory of God, not only has no claim to be believed, but ought to be vehemently rejected."

Especially in the Post-Reformation period the distinction between the *auctoritas historiae* and *normae* was much emphasized. A good example is G. Voetius. According to him *authentia historica* is that attribute of Holy Scripture "by which Holy Scripture is understood to be infallibly true with a *veritas Theopneustos,* so far as the historical writers, in setting forth historically all the dogmas, decrees, words, deeds, good or bad, which are contained in the Bible, are believed to have received them from the mouth and by the direct revelation of God and to have shown them to us without any error." *Authentia normalis* is the attribute of Holy Scriptures "by which the actual matter of the things contained in the Scriptures (e.g., decrees, sayings, doings), apart from the knowledge of them, oblige and constrain our consciences to faith in, observance and imitation of the things which are there said to be necessary to believe, observe and initiate."[43]

Although we do not wish to deny the relative right of this and similar distinctions,[44] yet there is a serious danger looming here which already became a reality in Voetius' formulations. We mean the danger of approaching the Bible as if it were an ordinary book of history. In Voetius' formulation the historical aspect becomes too "massive." There is no indication of the fact that the Bible is an historical book *sui generis*. No doubt this is closely linked with Voetius' mechanical conception of inspiration,[45] in which even the "puncta vocalia" of the Old Testament are inspired and the stylistic peculiarities of the biblical writings are attributed to the Holy Spirit.[46]

43. Cf. H. Heppe, *Reformed Dogmatics,* 1950, p. 27. Voetius even worked the whole thing out in elaborate details. Absolute normative significance must be ascribed to the words and works of God, Christ as God and man, and the angels. Those words of the prophets and apostles are normative in which they as public teachers, orally or in writing, edify the Church. Their deeds are authoritative only when they are approved by Scripture. Further, he does not regard all the words of Job as normative, nor the words of the friends of Job. Cf. also Berkhof, *Intro. Vol. to Syst. Theol.,* pp. 164f.

44. Cf. the very balanced article of N. H. Ridderbos, "Schriftbeschouwing en Schriftgezag," *Vox Theologica,* Vol. 24, No. 4. Cf. A. J. Bandstra, "Infallible in What It Intends To Teach," *Reformed Journal,* October, 1959.

45. H. Heppe, *op. cit.,* 27.

46. Against this background it is understandable that the charge of a "paper Pope" was advanced by certain critics against the orthodox position — although we must immediately add that the spirit behind this charge was often much farther removed from the Spirit of the Bible than that of

Nowadays it is generally recognized in Reformed circles that we are never allowed to handle the Bible as an ordinary history book. If we do this, we will miss the real secret of the Bible. What holds true of our concept of inspiration also applies to the authority of Holy Scripture: it must be derived from Scripture itself. In other words, Scripture has *its own peculiar authority*. One of the most recent and fruitful attempts to define this peculiar authority is that of R. Bijlsma.[47] He begins by placing it emphatically first in the series of attributes of Scripture. The authority of Scripture is the presupposition of its necessity, perspicuity and sufficiency.[48] Further, it is fully determined by the peculiar character of Scripture.

> The structure of Scripture is that of the saving acts of God. Every part is included in this structure. And so every word of Scripture has authority. It carries with itself the relationship to God's dealing with mankind. There is no question of a more or less of authority. It is the one revelatory authority which makes itself felt in every separate passage.[49]

This does not mean that there is only rigid uniformity and no *differentiation* whatsoever in the authority of Scripture. According to Bijlsma there is a "hierarchy of accents." The first accent is that of salvation, the second of history, the third of commandment.[50] The Bible has first of all "auctoritas salutis," because it is primarily concerned with God's saving acts, and the center of these acts is Jesus Christ. "The pleroma of God's saving work has appeared in Christ. The whole Bible in its totality groups itself around Him." Immediately connected with this is the "auctoritas historiae," for God's saving acts took place in our human history. God's saving truths are not abstract ideas, but they happen. The tertiary layer in the

---

the accused! It is, however, an indication of gross misunderstanding, when even today this charge is levelled against the evangelical position. When, e.g., Theo Preiss writes: "In opposition to the doctrine of Calvin (sic!), the conception of the verbal inspiration of the Bible petrified its authority, and we acquire a paper Pope, a Word of God, which a man can stick in his pocket and whose master he himself fundamentally is" (*Das innere Zeugnis des Heiligen Geistes*, pp. 13f., quoted by J.S.K. Reid, *The Authority of Scripture*, pp. 49/50), then this is nothing else than a caricature. Cf. also Reid's own charge of "bibliolatry."

47. In his doctoral thesis, *Schriftuurlijk Schriftgezag*, 1959.
48. *Ibid.*, pp. 286f.
49. *Ibid.*, p. 297.
50. *Ibid.*, pp. 390f.

authority of Scripture is its "paraenetical" (hortatory) authority. The Bible contains a great number of precepts and rules, commandments and admonitions, and they too have their background in the saving acts of God. In Scripture the "paraenesis" (exhortation) arises from the "anamnesis" (the believing recollection). To say it otherwise, the imperative (the call to do good works) is founded on the indicative (the proclamation of the good works God has done for us).

* * *

There can be no doubt that Bijlsma gives us the correct *starting point* to find the solution of our problems. The authority which belongs to Scripture is a *revelatory authority*. In Scripture we have to do with the revelation of God and His great saving acts in Jesus Christ. Scripture is "a kerygma and not a history lesson; a message calling to faith and conversion and not only a proclamation communicating certain historical facts."[51] Of course this must not be interpreted to mean that in the Bible historical facts are unimportant, or that there is a contrast between the kerygma and the historical facts. If one thing is clear from the Bible, it is that the kerygma stands and falls with the factual reality of the historical events of which it is the proclamation. The above-mentioned distinctions intend only to say that history has its place and function *in* the kerygma. It finds its correct accent only within the structure of the kerygma. In all its necessity and indispensability the history is "subordinate" to the proclamation of salvation, and serves the proclamation in its own peculiar way. And only in this light we can understand it correctly.

This was also meant by Bavinck when he said that we must read the Bible "theologically."[52] Bavinck did not mean that we ought to impose our own theological views upon the Bible, or that the Bible is a book for theologians only, but he meant that in all our study of Scripture we should be concerned with the "saving knowledge of God." And in this respect the Bible is indeed "sufficient and perfect," for it gives us all the necessary data for such a knowledge. We could also say we must read the Bible "heilsgeschichtlich," that is, from the viewpoint of the history of salvation. This viewpoint explains most of the characteristic features of the biblical historiography, which

---

51. H. N. Ridderbos, *Heilsgeschiedenis en Heilige Schrift*, p. 128.
52. H. Bavinck, *Gereformeerde Dogmatiek*, I, 415.

from the point of our modern scientific historiography seems to be highly inadequate, to say the least.[53]

None of this derogates in any way from the authority of Scripture. On the contrary, exactly here we meet with its peculiar and absolute authority. And in this way, too, we are fully in line with the *attitude of Jesus and the apostles*. For them, too, Scripture had an absolute, divine authority, but it was clearly a revelatory, "heilsgeschichtliche" authority. Their appeal to the Old Testament was never in the abstract, as to a kind of divine oracle-book, but always to the divine record of God's saving acts in the past, to the divinely given proclamation of the history of salvation, to the Old Testament as the book of the prophecy of Christ. Unfortunately this has been too often neglected by orthodoxy. The attitude of Jesus and the apostles has sometimes been described as a more or less mechanical, undifferentiated appeal to a book which in all possible respects is sacred and infallible. When, for example, Warfield in his defense of the doctrine of verbal inspiration (which we also hold) says that Jesus in John 10 appeals to one of the "most casual clauses" of Psalm 82, "more than that, the very form of its expression in one of its most casual clauses,"[54] then this is a serious misrepresentation of Jesus' attitude. It is without doubt incorrect to say that the expression "Ye are gods" is "one of the most casual clauses" in Psalm 82. On the contrary, the word "gods" is no less than the key word in this Psalm. Without it the Psalm not only wholly loses its point, but one of the most decisive indications of the very special place and function of the magistrates has disappeared from Scripture. No, Jesus does not use the Scriptures indiscriminately. He does not juggle with them as the Jewish rabbis often did in their rather arbitrary exegesis, but He deliberately appeals to them as the divine revelation in the past, a revelation which is "heilsgeschichtlich" understood, which has its center in Himself as the promised Savior. Bijlsma rightly points to Matthew 12:1-8,[55] where Jesus defends His disciples against the Pharisees who charge them with breaking the sabbath by plucking ears of corn. Jesus appeals to the story of David, who

---

53. Cf. H. N. Ridderbos, *op. cit.*, pp. 129f.; also, *When the Time Had Fully Come*, p. 91.
54. B. B. Warfield, *Inspiration and Authority of the Bible*, p. 140.
55. Bijlsma, *op. cit.*, pp. 389f.

with his men ate the shewbread from the tabernacle. David, too, transgressed a commandment, but this was a ceremonial law, not the sabbath law. Two quite different laws are related here, and moreover, the circumstances were quite different. And yet there is a definite point of contact, for David is the messianic King and Jesus is the Messiah Himself.

> Jesus' use of Scripture pushes the commandment (in casu the transgression of the commandment) through the historical connection to the messianic line of Scripture, where David (as the prophetic type) and Jesus (as the Fulfiller) meet one another. This last aspect is the decisive one, including and comprising all the other aspects. God's salvation is the dominating aspect in the authority of Scripture. It surpasses the other elements and subordinates them to itself.[56]

The same is true of the apostolic use of the Old Testament. It is all read from the center of the "Heilsgeschichte," that is, from Christ. This was the way Jesus Himself had taught them to read the Scriptures (Luke 24:27, 44f.), and all their writings are proof how deeply this instruction had penetrated into their hearts and minds.[57] They have no independent interest in the religious and political history of their forefathers, but to them the Old Testament is the book of the *coming* Christ. And their own writings, later on collected in the New Testament, enter into this one kerygma as the writings about the Christ who *did come*. As such the authority of this unified witness is *total*.

> It concerns all spheres of human life and knowledge; for the salvation of which it speaks is total. But it is as such "suo modo," that is, it throws light on man and world, history and future, church and nation, science and art, from *one* point, namely, from the coming, the death, the resurrection and the return of Christ.[58]

* * *

From here we also get a better and clearer view of the infallibility of Scripture. Authority and infallibility are interrelated as the material and formal aspect of the same kerygma. In other words, the Bible is infallible in the same way in which

---

56. *Ibid.*, p. 390.
57. Cf. Earle Ellis, *Paul's Use of the Old Testament*, 1957, pp. 85f., esp. 112f.
58. H. N. Ridderbos, *Heilsgeschiedenis en Heilige Schrift*, p. 116.

it is divinely authoritative, and both extend equally far. Infallibility, too, must be seen in "heilsgeschichlich" light. This is by no means a limitation. On the contrary, it is the greatest possible extension of infallibility.[59] We do fully agree with Dr. Sasse's statement: "Whatever the answer to these questions [viz.: the historical questions presented by Scripture], one thing Christian theology can never admit, namely, the presence of 'errors' in the sense of false statements in Holy Scripture."[60] But he is no less right in saying that "what we have to learn again is to measure Biblical history by its own standards."[61]

This was also the attitude of Bavinck. He utterly rejects the "secundum apparitiam" idea, that is, the idea that the biblical writers would have written their historical records according to subjective apparition and not objective reality. Such a method of procedure may be defensible where natural phenomena are concerned, but it is entirely wrong in the sphere of history, for there it would mean that the writers give us a false representation of the actual facts. And yet Bavinck does not want to read our modern conceptions of history into Scripture:

> The historiography of Holy Scripture has its own character. It is not its intention that we should know precisely what happened with mankind and Israel in past times, but it narrates the history of God's revelation, records only that which is connected with this, and intends by its history to make us know God in His search for and coming to humanity. The sacred history is a "historia religiosa."[62]

Bavinck works this out further in the following three points.[63] First, in the definition of place and time, in the sequence of events, and in the grouping of circumstances there is certainly not the accuracy which we often would like to see. Second,

---

59. Cf. Ridderbos, *When the Time Had Fully Come*, p. 93. "The Spirit has inspired men, has inspired the apostles, according to the promises of Jesus Himself, in order to be the foundation of the Church. And the Spirit has guided them in such a way that their words and writings are the foundations of the Church. This is the infallibility of the Word of the Scriptures as the Word of God."
60. H. Sasse, "Inspiration and Inerrancy," *Reformed Theol. Review*, XIX, 47.
61. *Ibid.*, p. 46.
62. H. Bavinck, *op. cit.*, p. 418.
63. *Ibid.*, p. 419.

there is room for the distinction between historical and normative authority. Third, Scripture is indeed true in everything, but this truth is certainly not of the same nature in all parts. There are the different genres of literature. There can even be a difference of opinion about the question whether and to what extent we have to do with history or historical appearance in cases like Job, Ecclesiastes, and the Song of Songs in the Old Testament, and for the New Testament in the case of Lazarus and Dives. Even in historical reports there is sometimes a distinction between the fact itself and the form in which it is represented. Bavinck refers here to the marginal notes of the Dutch State Bible on Genesis 1:3 and 11:5. And then he concludes the whole discussion with these profound words:

> Holy Scripture always speaks in human fashion of the highest and holiest, the eternal and invisible things. Just like Christ, it deems nothing human strange to itself. But therefore it is a book for mankind and lasts until the end of the ages. It is old without ever becoming obsolete. It remains always young and fresh; it is the Word of Life. *Verbum Dei manet in eternum.*[64]

For Bavinck these were not pious words to cover up his embarrassment or perplexity, but a *confession of faith* which came from the very bottom of his heart. And indeed our last word concerning the Bible can only be a word of confession. As Calvin put it:

> Scripture carrying its own evidence along with it, deigns not to submit to proofs and arguments, but owes the full conviction with which we ought to receive it to the testimony of the Spirit. Enlightened by Him, we no longer believe, either on our own judgment or that of others, that the Scriptures are from God; but in a way superior to human judgment, feel perfectly assured — as much so as if we beheld the divine image visibly impressed on it — that it came to us by the instrumentality of men, from the very mouth of God. We ask not for proofs or probabilities on which to rest our judgment, but we subject our intellect and judgment to it as too transcendent for us to estimate.[65]

64. *Ibid.*, p. 420.
65. *Instit.* I, vii, 5.

CHAPTER VIII

BASIC MOTIFS

When in this last chapter we try to summarize the results of our study, we cannot do better than to point out the basic motifs which dominate Barth's entire view of Scripture. As a matter of fact, they have already come to the fore repeatedly in our discussion.

We can state Barth's view very briefly as follows. God is the *Sovereign* and *Gracious One,* who in sovereignty speaks His Word of grace to us through the medium of the Bible, the unique witness to the unique revelation of God in Jesus Christ. In His gracious speaking God remains fully sovereign. His gracious Word is never a static deposit which man can *control.* It is always His. God remains free, even in His gracious gifts to man. These gifts are not "data" but "danda." They must be given to man again and again.

> In this equation [viz. the Bible *is* the Word of God] we have to do with the *free grace* and the *gracious freedom* of God. That the Bible is the Word of God cannot mean that with other attributes the Bible has the attribute of being the Word of God. To say that would be to violate the Word of God which is God Himself — to violate the *freedom* and *sovereignty of God.*
> . . . If the church lives by the Bible because it is the Word of God, that means that it lives by the fact that Christ is revealed in the Bible by the work of the Holy Spirit. That means it has *no power* or *control* over this work.[1]

In other words, we find *two basic motifs* side by side. The one concerns God — His sovereign freedom; the other concerns man — he has no control. When we consider them more care-

---

1. *C.D.,* I, 2, 513 (italics mine, K.R.).

fully, however, we discover that in actual fact the two are *fundamentally one*. Both express the same truth, the one in a positive way (God is free), the other in a negative way (man has no control). Undoubtedly the former is the main aspect. Yet in the discussion the latter sometimes receives the whole emphasis.[2]

This becomes particularly apparent in Barth's historical survey of the doctrine of inspiration throughout the centuries. The Early Church soon displayed a striking inclination to concentrate upon the work of the Spirit in the emergence of the prophetic and apostolic word. While Paul (in II Tim. 3) and Peter (in II Peter 1) were speaking of a free act of the grace of God, the Early Church wanted "a conclusion and a datum which we can grasp."[3] So they came to the doctrine of "verbal inspiredness." That means, the inspiration was "no longer understood as grace but as a bit of higher nature";[4] it became the nature of the book itself. Obviously the aim was to stabilize the word of man as the Word of God. They wanted to be sure of the presence of the Word of God. But in this way "the mystery of the freedom of its presence both in the mouths of the biblical witnesses and also in our ears and hearts" was lost.

In the days of the Reformation the authority and lordship of the Bible in the Church are restored, and accordingly a new reading and understanding and expounding of Scripture arises. True, both Luther and Calvin speak of "dictation" and "verbal inspiredness," but these conceptions are set in a con-

---

2. It is the mistake of G. Wingren in his *Theology in Conflict* (1958), pp. 25ff., that he concludes from this emphasis that Barth actually remains within the framework of Schleiermacher's theology. According to Wingren, Barth merely turns liberal theology upside down. His dogmatics is only a free rearrangement within the old frame, so that God's freedom and superiority become clearly expressed. "One only reacts, expresses the opposite, turns something upside down. Such a procedure always implies that one remains within the frame of reference of one's opponent." In our opinion this is a serious misunderstanding of the deepest intentions of Barth's theology. However much criticism one may have, it cannot be denied that Barth's emphasis on divine sovereignty and on grace means a mortal blow to the anthropocentric liberalism of Schleiermacher and his followers. Perhaps this did not always become entirely clear in the first reactive period of the *Römerbrief*, but the more positive views of the *Church Dogmatics* do not leave any room for doubt in this respect.

3. *C.D.*, I, 2, 517: "Ein griffbereites Resultat und Datum" (German Edition).

4. *Ibid.*, p. 518.

text which in fact makes them innocuous. In spite of the use of these concepts there is neither a mantico-mechanical nor a docetic conception of biblical inspiration. All their attention is concentrated on the content of the biblical witness, that is, on Christ, and it is this content which inspires the biblical witnesses and makes their writing Holy Scripture. Besides, they continuously insist that "the word of Scripture given by the Spirit can be recognized as God's Word only because the work of the Spirit, which has taken place in it, takes place again and goes a step further, that is, becomes an event for its hearers or readers."[5] The only conclusion possible is: "The Reformers' doctrine of inspiration is an honoring of God and of the free grace of God."[6]

In the post-Reformation period, however, the new understanding is lost sight of again. The statement that the Bible is the Word of God is now "transformed from a statement about the free grace of God into a statement about the nature of the Bible as exposed to human inquiry, brought under human control." Now man can have knowledge of God "without the free grace of God, by his own power, and with direct assurance."[7] Orthodoxy is no longer contented with an attitude of mere receiving, but it seeks — under the disguise of a highly supernaturalistic form — "the understanding and use of the Bible as instrument separated from the free grace of God and put into the hands of man."[8] It wants "a tangible certainty, not one that is given and has constantly to be given again." It wants "a human certainty and not a divine, a certainty of work and not solely of faith."[9]

All this, according to Barth, is the greatest sin. It means

---

5. *Ibid.*, p. 521.
6. *Ibid.*, p. 522.
7. *Ibid.*, pp. 522/23. This, of course, is nothing but a caricature. All the theologians of this period stressed the absolute need of the illumination by the Holy Spirit. Admittedly, there were tendencies towards a natural theology (cf. their emphasis on an innate knowledge of God, *cognitio Dei innata,* and on the seed of religion, *semen religionis*), and also a tendency towards subjectivism (cf. their one-sided attention to the work of the Spirit in man). But it certainly goes too far to say with Barth that with regard to the Bible they no longer recognized the freedom of God's grace. Words like "by his own power" would have been utterly rejected by them all.
8. *Ibid.*, p. 523.
9. *Ibid.*, p. 524.

the violation of God's sovereign freedom. Man tries to master God in His Word. Man tries to control God's revelation. Man thinks he *has* God's revelation as a deposit and can dispose of it at will. He does not need God's grace any more in order to hear God's revelation, that is, the revealing God Himself, for he "has" God's revelation in a stabilized form in the Bible. In the human words the Bible speaks to us "the Word of God in such a way that we can at once hear and read it as such with the same obviousness and directness with which we can hear and read other human words."[10] Barth has but one word for this: it is pure "naturalism," in spite of the highly supernaturalistic form. And the purely rationalistic approach of the enlightenment was nothing but a natural consequence. It only disclosed what had secretly been present for a long time, that is, that "the knowledge of the free grace of God as the unity of Scripture and revelation had been lost."[11]

* * *

How much the two above-mentioned basic motifs dominate Barth's view, how much they are the all-decisive starting point in his doctrine of Scripture, also clearly appears from his view of the Canon. On the one hand, he fully recognizes the idea of the Canon; on the other hand, he strongly rejects the idea of the so-called "closed" Canon. And both views have the very same background.

As to the *recognition* of the Canon, Barth fully defends the Reformation view. The Church does not "create" the Canon. "The Church can only confirm or establish it as something which has already been formed or given."[12] True, the establishment of the Canon took place in a long and complicated history, a really human history. From this point of view the fixation of the Canon is human judgment, it is a "dogma" like all other human dogmas. Yet there is another aspect. It was not so that the Church by its decision made these writings canonical, but we must say that these writings, by the very fact that they were canonical, saw to it that they in particular were later recognized and proclaimed to be canonical:

> Therefore we hear the judgment of the Church, but we do not obey its judgment, when we accept the settlement which

10. *Ibid.*, p. 525.
11. *Ibid.*, p. 526.
12. *Ibid.*, p. 473.

the Church has, of course, made. In and with the Church we obey the judgment which was already pronounced, before the Church could pronounce its judgment and which the Church's judgment could only confirm.[13]

In other words, not we individually, nor the Church collectively, decides this matter, but it is *God's decision*. He is *Lord of the Canon* and we can only obey in the act of faith.

But then Barth immediately continues: God also *remains* the Lord of the Canon. Because the answer of the Church about the Canon is an entirely human answer (be it in faith), it is also relative. There is, therefore, no absolute guarantee that the history of the Canon is closed and also that what we know as Canon (the sixty-six books of our Authorized Version) is closed. "The insight that the concrete form of the Canon is not closed absolutely, but only very relatively, cannot be denied even with a view to the future."[14] Barth points to the fact that there once existed an unknown letter of Paul to the Laodiceans, and two letters of Paul to the Corinthians, which are no longer extant. There are also known to be some "unrecorded" sayings of Jesus which did not find a place in our present Gospels. Besides, the many discoveries of recent days should warn us that there may be things awaiting us in the sands of Egypt. Perhaps even Rome would then drop the concept of a closed Canon! But all these — so far merely hypothetical — possibilities are not the main reason why Barth rejects the closed Canon. "It is the basic consideration of the positive nature and meaning of the Canon which forces us to reaccustom ourselves to the thought that the Canon is not closed

---

13. *Ibid.,* p. 474. It is obvious that Barth here opposes certain views held by the Roman Catholic Church, which also in this respect tends to place the Church more or less above Scripture. However, not all Roman Catholic theologians go so far. Barth quotes (among others) Bartmann, who says: "The books are canonical *in actu primo* and *quoad se* because they are inspired; *in actu secundo* and *quoad nos*, because they were adopted into the canon as inspired. By the divine act they were adapted to canonicity, by the Church's act this was formally accorded to them." Here the Church's only function seems to be that of recognition. But there are also other statements, like that of John Eck, one of the great opponents of Luther, who boldly declared that "Scriptura non est authentica sine auctoritate ecclesiae." It is not entirely clear which of the two is the official view of Rome. The Vatican Council seems to agree with Bartmann rather than with Eck. Yet even so the authority of the Church is strongly emphasized.

14. *Ibid.,* p. 476.

absolutely."[15] Here, too, there is no place for any disposal or control on man's side. If the Church takes the Word of God seriously as *God's* Word, it cannot speak of its Canon, as if in its own decision it had made the decision for the Holy Spirit Himself and therefore the decision for all ages and for all individuals in the Church.[16]

It is evident that here the *same* motifs which we observed before are present and play the decisive part. God is the free and sovereign One. Man has no control whatsoever of God or His revelation.

The all-important question is: Are these motifs indeed *fully scriptural?* Or are they a Barthian *construction,* only seemingly derived from Scripture but in reality imposed upon Scripture?

* * *

Starting with the statement that man can never have any control over God's revelation, nor can dispose of it at will, we fully admit that in itself this statement is entirely scriptural. When sinful man in the folly of his wickedness goes so far as to think or even say: "I can 'have' God in my power; I can compel Him to do what I like Him to do," he is utterly condemned by the Bible. The Bible regards such an attitude not only as blasphemy and *lese majesty,* but also calls it a foolish mistake.

There is hardly a clearer illustration of this than the story described in I Samuel 4. Israel has been defeated by the Philistines, and now it thinks it can compel God to give it the victory by bringing the ark into the battle. Is it not "the ark of the covenant of the Lord of hosts, which sitteth upon the cherubim" (v. 4)? Had God not promised to be there and "to commune with thee [Israel] from above the mercy-seat, from between the two cherubim" (Exod. 25:22)? In its unbelief Israel now identifies God Himself with the sign of His presence and thinks to have "caught" God in the sign. In doing this Israel places itself on the level of the Philistines, who as heathen perform the same magic identification (vv. 7, 8). But God, the Lord of hosts, does not suffer Himself to be forced by man. When faith is lacking on the side of the people, who received the ark as His gracious gift, this very same gift becomes a dead thing. Then God dissociates Him-

15. *Ibid.,* p. 478.
16. *Ibid.,* p. 480.

self from it and it is without effect. God even hands it over to the enemies. The narrator states it very briefly: "And the ark of God was taken" (v. 11; note: it is still the ark "of God"!). No pen can describe how terrible this must have been for the true believers in Israel. God's ark in the hands of the uncircumcised! It is so terrible that the old high priest Eli, on hearing it, falls from his seat, breaks his neck and dies, and his daughter-in-law in her last complaining words records it in the name of her son, born on this black day: "Ichabod" — "the glory is departed from Israel; for the ark of God is taken." Of course this story is but an illustration for our present discussion. We must not overlook the differences between the ark, the (in itself) mute sign of God's presence among Old Testament Israel, and the Bible, the Word of God, in which He communicates Himself to us in clear words. Yet the story is very instructive for the doctrine of Scripture.

It is true that man can adopt a wrong attitude with regard to the Bible. Every Bible reader — especially the regular reader, and even more specifically the theologian, for whom the Bible is the object of daily study — is permanently in danger of forgetting that he is dealing with *God's* Word. Man can grow so accustomed to it that he does not realize any more that God is speaking to him, requiring a complete subjection of all his thoughts. No, man begins to impose his own ideas upon the Bible, subjecting the Bible to his own personal schemes and systems. Usually this will happen without intention. It is a very subtle process of which the person concerned is not aware at all. "The heart is deceitful above all things, and it is exceedingly corrupt: who can know it?" (Jer. 17:9). The history of theology is full of examples. How often has it not happened that the authors of a theological system have been fully convinced that they have not given anything else than the pure teaching of Scripture, and yet, afterwards, it has clearly appeared that they have fitted Scripture into their own preconceived system, that they have made Scripture the cappingstone of the pyramid of their own reflections?

A striking example is found in the discussion between Jesus and the Sadducees, as recorded in Matthew 22. The Sadducees had their own theological system, in which they had no room for the resurrection-idea. According to them this was also the teaching of Scripture. When they come to Jesus to discuss the matter (and in that way to catch Jesus!), they indeed take their starting point in Scripture. They appeal to Deuteronomy 25 (the law of the levirate marriage), but they incorporate this starting point completely into their own system by making it a part of the story of the one woman and the seven husbands, and thus they consider the whole problem finished. Is their system not entirely water-tight? Does not their system, supported by Holy Scripture, conclusively prove the utter impossibility of a resurrection? Of course, in reality they have not listened to Scripture but only use it to defend their own pet ideas. It is, therefore, no wonder that Jesus starts at this very point. Jesus' first words are: "Ye do err, not knowing the Scriptures, nor the power of God" (v. 29). In spite of their learning and their priestly aristocracy they do not know the Scriptures. They have silenced them by their own preconceived ideas. And then, all of a sudden, Jesus Himself opens the immeasurable depths of Scripture by appealing to God's self-revelation in the burning bush: "Have ye not read that which was spoken to you (!) by God, saying, I am the God of Abraham, and the God of Isaac, and the God of Jacob? God is not the God of the dead, but of the living" (vv. 31, 32). In Jesus' words the Scriptures thus silenced suddenly prove to be the living Word of God, and they completely shatter the rationalistic system which has been imposed upon them.

Indeed, we cannot bind God's Word nor deal with it as if it were our possession. From that point of view, both Liberals and Evangelicals will do well to give heed to Barth's continually repeated warning that man can never dispose of God's revelation nor control it. Every Church, every Christian, and in particular every theologian should remember this constantly!

Yet we think Barth himself is going too far when he, in reaction, makes the rejection of this misuse one of the keywords of his doctrine of Holy Scripture. The fatal result of *reaction-theology* is always that the pendulum of thought now swings to the other extreme, and again the picture is distorted, this time from the other side. In Barth's opinion the above-mentioned misuse of God's revelation cannot be avoided if one accepts a direct identity between the Bible as a human book and the Word of God. Yes, the very idea of such a direct identity is in itself already a symptom of this misuse. There is therefore but one solution, namely, that of an *actualistic* conception of revelation. The Bible has again and again to become the Word of God. The miracle of identification must continually be repeated from God's side.

It is noteworthy, however, that the Bible itself nowhere teaches or even hints at such an "actualism." Although the Bible repeatedly warns against overstepping the limit on man's side, yet at the same time it also speaks very clearly of the real presence of God's Word in the written word. Yes, it even simply identifies the two. We are thinking here in particular of the attitude of Jesus and the apostles towards the Old Testament. In the temptation, for example, Jesus three times rejects the suggestion of Satan by a straightforward appeal to Scripture: "It is written . . ." (Matt. 4:4, 7, 10). In the Sermon on the Mount He says of the Old Testament law: "Till heaven and earth pass away, one jot or one tittle shall in no way pass away from the law, till all things be accomplished" (Matt. 5:18). In His many discussions with the Pharisees and Sadducees He again and again appeals to the Old Testament Scriptures as the final authority. They do not become authoritative because He appeals to them, but He appeals to them because they are authoritative. And the same holds true of the apostles, who openly say that the Old Testament is the inspired Word of God (cf. Rom. 10:8; II Tim. 3:15-17; II Peter 1:19-21; etc.).[17] And likewise the New Testament itself *is* the Word of God. Ridderbos rightly says of the word

---

17. Cf. also the passages where God (or the Holy Spirit) is mentioned as the real author, the *auctor primarius* (e.g. Matt. 1:22; 2:15; 15:4; [19:5?]; Luke 1:70, Acts 1:16; 3:18; 4:25; 28:25, and in particular also the Epistle to the Hebrews, where this is the usual introductory formula: 1:5f.; 3:7; 4:3, 5:5, 6; etc.). Westcott (*The Epistle to the Hebrews*, The Greek Text with Notes and Essays, pp. 474f.) points out that in some cases the words spoken by the prophet in his own person are treated as divine words, are assigned to God Himself, e.g. 1:6 (the poet of Ps. 97); 2:13 (Isaiah); 4:4 (the author of Gen. 2:2); 10:30 (Moses). Westcott then continues: "Generally it must be observed that no difference is made between the word spoken and the word written. For us and for all ages the record is the voice of God. The record is the voice of God; and as a necessary consequence the record itself is living. It is not a book merely. It has a vital connection with our circumstances and must be considered in connection with them. The constant use of the present tense in quotations emphasizes this truth" (p. 475). We would underline these last words about "the constant use of the present tense." The Old Testament need not become the Word of God, but it *is* the living Word of God and can be quoted as such! Cf. also B. B. Warfield's article on "It Says," "Scripture Says," "God Says," in *The Inspiration and Authority of the Bible*, pp. 299-350.

of the apostles that, seen as a witness (*marturia*), it is included in the reality of the revelation and participates in the divine work of salvation in Jesus Christ through the Holy Spirit.[18] Seen as a tradition (*paradosis*), we must say that Christ Himself stands behind it. It is He who, not only as the earthly Jesus but also as the exalted Lord, supports the tradition of the apostles by His authority. Therefore Paul can praise the Thessalonians because, when they received the apostolic word, that is, the apostolic tradition, they accepted it not as the word of men, but, as it is in truth, the word of God (I Thess. 2:13)[19]. And in the same connection Ridderbos does not hesitate to say that perhaps nothing is more in conflict with the "heilsgeschichtliche" idea of the Canon (as this is given by the New Testament itself) than the actualistic conception of the historical Canon as the confines within which the real divine Canon would manifest itself again and again.[20]

* * *

But what about the other positive motif, that of *God's freedom*? Is not that a genuinely scriptural motif? Does the Bible not continuously emphasize God's sovereignty and freedom? The answer can only be Yes. But again we must ask the question: Does Barth's concept of freedom coincide with that of the Bible?

According to Barth, God's freedom, as applied to the sphere of revelation, means that God always is and remains the acting *subject* in His revelation. This does not mean that God is not and never can be the object of revelation. If that were the case, there would be no divine revelation! For God's revelation is basically and primarily *self*-revelation. It is clear that the word "self" here means that God is indeed the object of revelation. But — and this is decisive — He is object of revelation only when at the same time He is the subject of this revelation. Briefly, *God reveals God!* The subject and the object of this sentence are identical, and that, according to Barth, is the freedom of God's revelation. God is never object in the sense of revealed-ness. If that should happen, God would not be free any more. He would be *only* an object,

---

18. H. N. Ridderbos, "De Canon van het Nieuwe Testament," in *Kerk en Theologie*, IX, 87.
19. *Ibid.*, p. 88.
20. *Ibid.*, p. 90.

imprisoned in this revealed-ness. The God of the revelation is the revealing God Himself who as the divine "I" (subject) makes Himself (object) known to the human "thou" (indirect object).

We even may go further. In the act of faith, which corresponds to God's act of revelation, God is also the divine "Thou" over against the human "I." But we may never go so far as to make Him an "it," a mere object of pure revealedness. Then we violate His divine freedom, which means that He always is and remains the subject in the act of revelation.

How basic this is for Barth's thinking appears from the fact that he applies it also to the *Word that became flesh.* Says he: "When it is said that the Word became flesh, even in this state of becoming and having become, the Word is still the free sovereign Word of God."[21] In this somewhat cryptic statement we are confronted with the same concept of freedom that we discussed above. Barth means to say that the subject in the incarnate Christ is and remains the divine Logos. "Strictly speaking the Logos can never become predicate or object in a sentence, the subject of which is different from God." In other words, strictly speaking I cannot say that the human nature of Christ revealed God or revealed the Logos, but only that God or the Logos revealed Himself through the human nature. Says Barth again:

> The statement "very God and very man" signifies an equation. But strictly speaking this equation is irreversible. . . . The Word became flesh, and it is only in virtue of this becoming, which was quite freely and exclusively the becoming of the Word, that the flesh became Word. The Word speaks, the Word acts, the Word prevails, the Word reveals, the Word reconciles. True enough, He is the incarnate Word, that is, the word not without the flesh, but the Word in the flesh and through the flesh — but nevertheless the Word and not the flesh.[22]

Elsewhere Barth says that the humanity of Christ as such *is not* the revelation.[23] If that were so, then the Logos would have become an object of revelation without being at the same time the subject of revelation. Strictly speaking we should say that the humanity of Christ revealed the Logos only when the Logos revealed Himself through this humanity.

21. *C.D.,* I, 2, 136.
22. *Ibid.*
23. *C.D.,* I, 1, 371f.

If all this holds true of *Christ,* who had the two natures in the inseparable unity of the divine person, how much more does it hold true of the *Bible,* where there is no "unio personalis" between the human witness and the Word of God. If God is the object of revelation here (and where true revelation takes place God is the object) then the subject can never be this human witness in itself. Strictly speaking we cannot say that the Bible reveals God, but that God (subject) reveals Himself (object) through this witness to the original revelation in Christ. God indeed wants to use this witness. That is His sovereign and free choice. But throughout He remains the Lord, the free and sovereign One, who reveals Himself when and where it pleases Him.

> Revelation always means to reveal, even in the form, even in the means of revelation. The form as such, the means, does not take the place of God. It is not the form that reveals, speaks, comforts, works, helps, but God in the form. . . . God's presence is always God's decision to be present. The divine Word is the divine speaking, the divine gift is the divine giving. God's self-unveiling remains the act of sovereign divine freedom. Here it may be for one man what the Word says, there for the next only the veiling of God. For the same man it may be the first thing today, and the second tomorrow. In it God cannot be grasped by man or attacked by sequestration, or caught at work . . . God is ever and again a mystery. Revelation is ever and again revelation in the full sense of the word, or it is not revelation, at all events not what is so called in the Bible.[24]

In other words, revelation can never have the form of a permanent and stabilized relationship, but it can take place (event! *Ereigniss!*) only in the *existential-historical* relation, in which the revealing God in His sovereign freedom comes and speaks to us.[25]

Our use of "existential" must *not* simply be interpreted in the terms of modern Existentialism. It will not do to make Barth an existentialist in theological disguise and to explain his theology from the basic ideas and categories of this modern philosophy. Admittedly, in his first period, especially in his *Commentary on Romans* and to a certain extent also in the

---

24. *Ibid.,* p. 369.
25. Cf. also M. P. Van Dijk, *Existentie en Genade, Grondgedachten en Samenhangen in de Kirchliche Dogmatik van Karl Barth,* 1952, pp. 29f.; and Jerome Hamer, O.P., *Karl Barth, l' Occasionalisme theologique de Karl Barth,* Etude sur sa methode dogmatique, 1949, pp. 25ff.

first design of his dogmatics (*Die Christliche Dogmatik, Prolegomena*, 1927), he frequently used a terminology either derived from or cognate with existentialism. But later on he has emphatically dissociated himself from it. In the preface of Volume I of his *Church Dogmatics* he says: "To the best of my ability I have cut out in this second issue of the book everything that in the first issue might give the slightest appearance of giving to theology a basis, support, or even a mere justification in the way of existential philosophy."[26] And this is still his attitude today, as increasingly he has criticized those theologians who interpret Scripture in terms of a philosophical "pre-understanding" (*Vorverständnis*).[27]

This does not mean that Barth rejects all philosophy as sinful or useless. He fully realizes that it is impossible to engage in biblical exegesis without using a certain scheme or system of thought, that is, some philosophy or other. Whether it is of a more professional or a more amateurish type, in both cases we bring some sort of conceptual scheme to the Bible. This cannot be prevented if our theology is not to be a mere copying of verses out of the Bible. But we ought to be permanently aware of the danger involved in this enterprise, and examine ourselves whether we are not forcing the Scriptures into the patterns of our scheme of thought. "No conceptual schemes may have priority over Scripture. All our conceptual schemes are in turn to be examined by Scripture and discarded, altered, or refashioned in the light of Scripture."[28]

From these summary remarks it is quite clear that Barth does not want to be dominated by any philosophy, nor build his

---

26. *C.D.*, I, 1, IX. Cf. also *K.D.*, III, 4, VIII.
27. Cf. Barth's criticism of R. Bultmann in K. Barth, "R. Bultmann, Ein Versuch ihn zu verstehen," *Theologische Studien*, Heft 34, 1952. Cf. also B. Ramm, "The Battle of Barth with Bultmann," *Christianity Today*, March 30, 1959.
28. Cf. Ramm, *op. cit.* In *C.D.*, 1, 2, 730ff. Barth mentions five conditions which should be met in order to limit the dangers involved in the use of a scheme of thought to the bare minimum. They are: (1) The theologian must be aware of the fact that his scheme of thought is not identical with Scripture; (2) All our philosophy can have only the character of a hypothesis; (3) Our mode of thought can claim no independent interest in itself; (4) Although we have to use some scheme, there is no essential reason for preferring one of these schemes to another; (5) The use of a scheme of thought is legitimate and fruitful only when it is determined and controlled by the text and the object mirrored in the text.

theology on any preliminary philosophical understanding. He wants to be "a theologian of the Word of God," and we ought to take this intention of his very seriously. On the other hand it is, of course, quite possible that in spite of all good intentions there are more philosophical presuppositions in a theology than the theologian himself realizes. "In the history of theology we time and again discover clearly evident presuppositions that have decisively influenced theological thought. Consciously or unconsciously — all kinds of presuppositions or factors play an important role in moulding theological conceptions."[29]

We do believe that this also happens in Barth's theology and that it applies in particular to his conception of revelation. Although we find many genuinely scriptural elements in this conception, yet there are undoubtedly also elements which have not been derived from the Bible, but have their origin in the *present-day existentialistic-personalistic way of thinking*.[30] We know, of course, that the latter has often been claimed to have much in common with the biblical way of thinking.[31] To a certain extent we can agree. We believe that the existentialistic approach has much more affinity with the Bible than, for example, the idealistic approach of the preceding period and the rationalism of the Enlightenment. Yet no one may identify the modern with the biblical way of thinking. We claim that the latter contains elements which are lacking in the former. For example, the modern emphasis on the dynamic and personal character of revelation is indeed truly scriptural, but it does not exhaust the biblical concept of revelation. Alongside this dynamic aspect and inseparably linked with it there is also the static, that is, revelation in the sense of revealedness. The Bible knows nothing of a fundamental contrast between the dynamic and the static, between the existential and the ontological, between the personal and the conceptual. What Barth once wrote about Kohlbrugge and Calvin with regard to their view of justification and sanctification, namely, "that where in Kohlbrugge we hear only one or almost

---

29. G. C. Berkouwer, *The Triumph of Grace in the Theology of Karl Barth*, 1956, p. 19.

30. Cf. Francis Andersen, "We speak . . . in the words . . . which the Holy Ghost teacheth," *Westminster Theol. Journal*, XXII, 113ff. M. P. Van Dijk, *op. cit.*, pp. 37f., 43f.

31. Cf. G. Vander Leeuw, *Sacramentstheologie*, 1949, p. 6. G. C. Van Niftrik, *De Boodschap van Sartre*, 1953, pp. 135ff.

only one word, in Calvin we regularly hear two,"[32] could, *mutatis mutandis*, be applied to Barth's own conception of revelation and that of Scripture itself.

According to Barth God is the free and sovereign One in His revelation. He is always the subject of His revelation. The latter can therefore never be objectivized in a written revelation, for in that case revelation would no longer be God's act. So Barth knows only *one word* here: the free *act* of revelation. But in the Bible we find *two words*. Surely, revelation is primarily an *act* of God. It is God Himself who reveals Himself. Man does not climb up to God and "discover" God, but God condescends to man in the free act of His infinite love and grace. But at the same time the Bible also speaks of an *inscripturated revelation*, that is, a revelation which has a written and therefore solidified form, and yet is fully revelation of God. For what the biblical writers have written, they have written through the inspiration of the Holy Spirit, and therefore it is no less than God's own Word. In other words, the Bible knows about *revelation* and *revealedness*. It knows about the dandum and the datum, and the two do not exclude each other, but rather presuppose and complement each other.

The problem in Barth's entire doctrine of revelation and Holy Scripture is the *tension*, yes the *contrast*, between freedom and continuity, between the dynamic and the static, the existential and the ontological. In our opinion such a contrast is entirely foreign to the Bible. In the Bible freedom and continuity never exclude one another, nor does the one endanger the other. In particular, this comes to the fore in the scriptural covenant-idea. In the covenant God binds Himself to His people. He gives Himself fully to His people, even calls Himself the husband and the people His bride or wife. And yet at the same time He is fully free and sovereign. He is never imprisoned in His covenant. When in Exodus 33:18 Moses asks the Lord to reveal Himself to him: "Show me, I pray thee, thy glory," then the answer of God, who just a while ago has promised that His presence shall go with the people (v. 10), is: "I will make all my goodness pass before thee, and will proclaim the name of the Lord before thee; and I will be gracious to whom I will be gracious, and will show

---

32. K. Barth, *Die Protestantische Theologie im 19. Jahrhundert*, 1947, p. 586.

mercy on whom I will show mercy" (v. 18). Indeed, God's grace is infinitely great, but He Himself decides to whom it will be given. Man should never think that he "has" God, the God of the covenant, in his grasp, precisely on the ground of that covenant. As soon as man in his sinful pride detaches the promise from the correlation with faith, the promise retreats and man himself stands in the fire of God's judgment, which as a negative aspect is related to the promise. As soon as man thinks that he "has" the God of the covenant in the ark of the covenant, God abandons His ark and gives it into the hands of the Philistines (I Sam. 4). Of course that does not mean that it is no longer His ark. On the contrary! The Philistines have noticed it too well! Their idol, Dagon, breaks his neck before this same ark! (I Sam. 5).

The same holds true of the Bible. In spite of all Barth's assertions that the Bible is not the Word of God in the sense of direct identity, in spite of his utter rejection of an objective revelation in Scripture apart from faith (Barth calls this an idol, "perhaps the worst of all idols"[33]), in spite of all this we maintain that the Bible *is* the Word of God in such an objective sense. For the Bible presents itself to us as such. Of course this does not at all mean that man now can rule over this Word of God, that he can have God's Word "in his pocket" and do with it what pleases him. As soon as man gets such ideas, God, as it were, abandons His own Word, and all that is left are mere "words."[34] This does not mean that it is no longer God's Word, that it is not God's Truth and the Truth about God! It certainly is, for all our unbelief can take away nothing from Scripture. But in such a case we personally do not hear the voice of Him, whose Word it is. For us, personally, it has become a lifeless record that provides no real encounter with the God of the Word.

---

33. *C.D.*, I, 2, 237.
34. We could also point here to the attitude of the prophets over against the cult. Cf. Amos 5:21-25; Hosea 6:6; Micah 6:8; Isa. 1:11-14; Jer. 7:21-23. Everyone who concludes with the "critics" that apparently the O.T. cult as prescribed in the Pentateuch was not instituted by the Lord in the days of the exodus, shows only that he has not understood the real problem behind this prophetic "rejection" of the cult. Not the cult is wrong, but the people that "uses" and "misuses" the cult, that thinks it "has" God and His grace in the cult. Then God in sovereign freedom disassociates Himself from His own cult and even disowns it publicly.

It is quite obvious from all this that the objective character of the revelation in the Bible (i.e., the identity between the Bible and the Word of God) does not in any way jeopardize *God's sovereign freedom*. Because the Bible functions as the Word of God only when it is read and heard in faith, God's sovereignty and freedom are fully maintained. Faith means utter dependence upon God, recognition of God's sovereign freedom. Faith is the opposite of control or disposal. Faith never transgresses the limits of God's freedom, but fully respects God's sovereignty, knowing that God's Word is and remains *His* and *never* becomes *ours*.[35]

At the same time, however, there is in faith a *strong assurance* that here God does speak to us. This assurance is not built upon faith itself, neither upon its quality nor its quantity. The only ground of this assurance is the *promise*: "He that heareth you, heareth me" (Luke 10:16, cf. Matt. 10:40). This promise is a fountain of constant joy. No, we need not wonder "with fear and trembling" whether and when it will please God to speak to us. In faith we may be sure: "In these very words God speaks His Word. It is His voice which I hear. It is His message that is proclaimed to me. Yes, He Himself comes to me through these words and communicates Himself to me." This wonderful assurance has nothing to do with idolatry or bibliolatry.[36] It only means that we receive the Bible as it presents itself to us, namely, as the inspired Word of God able to make men wise unto salvation through faith which is in Christ Jesus, and also profitable for teaching, for reproof, for correction, for instruction which is in righteousness: that the man of God may be complete, furnished completely unto every good work (II Tim. 3:15-17).

* * *

There is one important question left that must be discussed here. It is this question: Would Barth today still defend this same position with regard to Scripture? The position which

---

35. Cf. the beautiful things Calvin says about the necessity of a reverent approach to Scripture. R. S. Wallace, *Calvin's Doctrine of the Word and Sacrament*, 1957, pp. 102ff.: "This is the true reverence of the Scripture, when we acknowledge that there is wisdom laid up there which surpasses all our senses, and yet nothwithstanding we do not loathe it, but, reading diligently, we depend upon the revelation of the Spirit, and desire an interpreter given us" (*op. cit.*, p. 103; Comm. on Acts 8:31).

36. Cf. J.S.K. Reid, *The Authority of Scripture*, 202, 211.

we have discussed in this study was that of the years 1932 and 1938, when *C.D.* I, 1 and 2 respectively appeared. But have there not been *important changes* in Barth's theology since those years, changes which would also effect his view of Scripture?

Quite a few scholars are of the opinion that the Barth of "today" certainly would modify the presentation given by the Barth of "yesterday." G. W. Bromiley, for example, says: "To judge from the recent trend of his writing, it seems certain that he himself would not now be ready to give quite the prominence that he then did to the act of the Holy Spirit in the reader."[37] Previously, because of Barth's excessive emphasis on the dynamic view, there was no place for an objective revelation. But now, in the doctrine of the atonement, he strongly emphasizes the objective character of the reconciling work of Christ, for this reconciliation took place once and for all. "There can be little doubt that, faced with a thoroughgoing subjectivization, Barth himself would admit the inadequacy of his earlier safeguards and be prepared drastically to alter the balance of his presentation."[38]

Is this true? Have Barth's views indeed changed to such an extent that, if his doctrine of Scripture had to be written again, it would be a "new" one? For our part, we are inclined to deny this. Admittedly, there have been important changes in Barth's thinking since the thirties. Yet we do not believe that these changes fundamentally affect his doctrine of revelation or Holy Scripture. This is already proved by the mere fact that in 1947 and 1948 Barth himself published two papers on this very same subject[39] and in both he still fully defended his views of *C.D.* I, 1 and 2. The two above-men-

---

37. G. W. Bromiley, "Karl Barth's Doctrine of Inspiration," *Journal of the Transactions of the Victoria Institute*, LXXXVII, 80.

38. *Ibid.* Cf. also James Barr in a lengthy review of J.S.K. Reid's book in *Scott. Journal of Theology*, XI, 86ff. According to Barr there is in Barth's original exposition a neglect or underemphasis of the element of human response behind Scripture (p. 87). "Would we not expect that one like Karl Barth, who is becoming known now not only as the theologian of the Word but as the theologian of the human obedience of Christ, would give a greater place to the word of response, if he were writing his doctrine of Scripture today?" (p. 89).

39. In 1947: "The Authority and Significance of the Bible," a paper read for the Ecumenical Institute in Boissey, and later on published in *In de Waagschaal*, Vol. II, Nos. 38-42. In 1948: "Das Christliche Verständnis der Offenbarung," *Theologische Existenz Heute*, Neue Folge, Heft 12.

tioned dates are very important indeed. The year 1947 was two years after the publication of the first volume on Creation (*C.D.* III, 1), the volume in which the "changes" already became clearly visible. The year 1948 was the year in which *C.D.* III, 2, the volume on Anthropology, was published. This volume in particular led some to speak of a "new" Barth. And yet in this very same year Barth himself gives a short and clear paper on the Christian concept of revelation, in which all the former elements and emphases are still present. These historical facts alone seem to be sufficient proof that Barth still holds his former views.

But there is more. In our opinion the "changes" themselves are not of such a nature that one should expect really drastic alterations in the doctrine of Scripture. G. C. Berkouwer has pointed out clearly that there is no fundamental difference between the younger and the older Barth.[40] Admittedly, in the first period the emphases were sometimes too much of a negative nature, yet we would make a great mistake if we saw only those negative aspects and forgot that even then the "yes" prevailed over the "no." "Barth's theology must *from its inception* be characterized as triumphant theology which aims to testify to the overcoming power of grace. We do not find in it a transition from crisis to grace, or from disjunction between God and man to fellowship between them, but rather a relationship between these polarities which Barth was concerned to set forth in varying emphases and accents."[41]

Particularly clarifying is what Barth himself writes about the development of his theology in one of his recent publications, namely, the lecture on "The Humanity of God," which he delivered in 1956 at the meeting of the Swiss Reformed Ministerial Fraternal in Aarau.[42] Barth begins by stating that forty years ago the "Godness" of God forced itself upon him and his friends. This expression means that property of God which in relation to man and the world is absolutely His own. Here God is the overwhelmingly high and distant One, the strange One, the totally Other, who veils Himself at the very

---

40. G. C. Berkouwer, *op. cit.*, pp. 23-51.
41. *Ibid.*, p. 37.
42. Published in English translation by James Strathearn McNab in "God, Grace and Gospel," *Scott. Journal of Theology Occasional Papers*, No. 8, 1959.

moment when He unveils Himself to man. All this was nothing less than a revolution, and in its critical-polemical character it was an absolute necessity. Things could not go on as they were. All theology, both liberal and evangelical, had become anthropocentric and, in this sense, humanistic. Therefore, Barth says, we had to speak of God's Godness. It was the only possibility. "Were we right or wrong? Undoubtedly we were right."[43] And there is no reason to deny the revolution now, or to cancel it out. Of course it was one-sided. Barth gives a rather crushing criticism of the early terminology:

> What mighty formulations were there partly taken over, partly newly fabricated! In the forefront of all — "and as they warbled, a thousand voices struck up and echoed them in the field" — the famous *totaliter aliter* breaking in "vertically from above" and the no less famous "infinite qualitative difference" between God and man; the vacuum; the mathematical point and the tangent, in which alone they were supposed to touch each other; the bold assertion that there is generally only one theological interest in the Bible, namely God, that there is visible in it only one way, namely, that from above downwards, that there is audible only one message, namely that of forgiveness of sins — immediate, without before or after — while the problem of ethics as such is identical with man's sickness unto death; the view of redemption which consists in the cancellation of the creatureliness of the creature, in the swallowing up of this world by the world beyond; correspondingly the summons to faith as a leap into the abyss, and the like.[44]

Yes, this was one-sided, it was cruelly inhuman, even running to some extent in a heretical direction. And yet there is no need to be ashamed of it. There is indeed a "retractation," but

> a genuine retractation . . . does not by any means consist in a retrospective withdrawal, but in a new start and attack in which what was said before has now to be said properly — in a better way. If what we then thought we had discovered and what we brought forward was no final word, but one that needed retractation, it was none the less a true word, which as such must keep its ground, which still today cannot be passed by, which rather forms the basis of what we have today to reflect further upon. Assuredly he who did not share in that earlier revolution, or who still does not find it impressive that God is God, would

---

43. *Ibid.*, p. 34.
44. *Ibid.*, p. 35.

not get a sight of what has now to be said further as true word about His humanity.[45]

These words are of great importance for the understanding of Barth's theology. Barth himself clearly points out that there is a fundamental continuity in his theological thinking. True, the emphases shift, but that never means a complete rejection of the old emphases. It only means that new accents and aspects are added, and that the old ones, with their original function, are now integrated into a more balanced whole. What, then, was the one-sidedness of the first period? It was the self-conscious contrast with Schleiermacher and his followers: God was made great at the expense of man. Almost the only concept then employed was *diastasis*, while the complementary concept of *analogy* was seldom used. God was seen as the "completely Other" and as such He was identified with the Yahweh-Kurios of the Bible. But now, afterwards, we must say that in its one-sidedness this concept of the "completely other" still had "greater similarity to the Godness of the God of the philosophers than to that of the God of Abraham, Isaac, and Jacob."[46] The great mistake was that the other aspect of God, i.e., God's humanity, His togetherness with man, was almost completely neglected. "God shows and reveals who He is and what He is in His Godness not in the vacuum of a divine self-sufficiency, but genuinely just in this fact, that He exists, speaks and acts as partner (without doubt the absolutely superior partner) of man. He who does that is the living God."[47]

Barth then asks: Where do we learn this? How is this statement justified? The answer is: it is a *christological statement*. With these words we have again come to the heart of Barth's theology. All changes that are found in Barth's thinking are related to the *increasing concentration* of all his theology *upon christology*. More and more he has realized that we cannot speak of God or of man, even for one single moment, apart from Christ. Only in Christ we find God as He is: the God who in sovereign freedom decides to be man's partner. Likewise only in Christ we find man as he is: the being for whom Christ was born, suffered, died, and rose again. All

45. *Ibid.*
46. *Ibid.*, p. 37.
47. *Ibid.*

this does mean that a *new aspect* did enter into Barth's theology. It is an aspect of a strongly objective nature. We even can speak here of an "objectivism of grace."[48]

The whole *creation* from its very beginning, yes from all eternity, stands in the light of God's grace in Jesus Christ, for the covenant of God's grace in Jesus Christ is behind the creation:

> Creation comes first in the series of works of the triune God and is thus the beginning of all the things distinct from God Himself. . . . According to the biblical witness the purpose and therefore the meaning of creation is to make possible the history of God's covenant with man, which has its beginning, its centre and its culmination in Jesus Christ. The history of this covenant is as much the goal of creation as creation itself is the beginning of this history.[49]

The joyful light of Christ falls over this creation and therefore it is good, even very good, for it is justified before God.[50]

The same holds true of *man*. From the very first beginning man stands in the light of Jesus Christ. Man was created for Jesus' sake. Barth goes even so far as to say that Jesus was the first and original man. "We are partakers of human nature, as and because Jesus is first partaker of it."[51] In the eternity of the divine counsel God decided to become man in Jesus Christ. And in this decision it was determined what man's nature would be. "There his constitution was fixed and

---

48. Cf. my book: *De Theologische Tijd bij Karl Barth*, 1955, 128f., 143f., 150f., 168f.

49. *C.D.*, III, 1, 42. Cf. 50/51: "In respect of His Son who was to become man and the Bearer of human sin, God loved man and man's whole world from all eternity, even before it was created, and in spite of its absolute lowliness and non-godliness, indeed its anti-godliness. He created it because He loved it in His Son who because of its transgressions stood before Him eternally as the Rejected and Crucified." Cf. also Barth, *Dogmatics in Outline*, 1958, p. 58: "The world came into being, it was created and sustained by the little child that was born in Bethlehem, by the Man who died on the Cross of Golgotha, and the third day rose again. *This* is the Word of creation, by which all things were brought into being."

50. Cf. *C.D.*, III, 1, 366f. It has this goodness not in itself. In itself the creation is "something on the edge of nothing, bordering it and menaced by it, and having no power of itself to overcome the danger" (p. 376). But in Jesus Christ for whose sake this world was created, in whom the Creator becomes a creature, we learn that the divine good pleasure rests upon it (i.e., justification) and therefore it is right as it is, it is good in its totality, indeed, it is the best (p. 378).

51. *C.D.*, III, 2, 50.

sealed once and for all. For this reason it cannot be different in any other man. No man can elude this prototype. We derive wholly from Jesus not merely our potential and actual relation to God, but even our human nature as such."[52] Particularly important for our discussion are the words: "No man can elude this prototype." No man, not even the most awful and persistent sinner, can cancel or annihilate this particular nature, which was derived from Jesus' nature.

> In his relation to God a man may become a sinner and thus distort and corrupt his own nature, but he cannot revoke what was decided in Jesus apart from him concerning the true nature of man. By his fall he can deny his Creator and his own creaturely nature. But he cannot make it a lie. What he is, is decided elsewhere in such a way that he cannot affect the decision.[53]

Barth even says that in the creaturely nature of man there is "a continuum unbroken by sin, an essence which even sin does not and cannot change."[54] He even takes yet another step and admits that even the man who does not know Jesus is able to discover "phenomena" of man's real nature. In connection with "fellow-humanity" as the basic form of humanity he writes:

> It is to be expressly noted that we do not have here a gracious gift of the Holy Ghost for the possession of which he must be a Christian, or an operation of the Word of God directly proclaimed to man and directly received and believed by him. What we have called humanity can be present and known in varying degrees of perfection or imperfection even where there can be no question of a direct revelation and knowledge of Jesus Christ.[55]

* * *

It cannot be denied that there are here *considerable* differences from Barth's writings of the earlier period. We are not going too far when we speak of an "objectivism of grace." It

---

52. *Ibid.* Cf. p. 59: "It is not the case that He must partake of humanity. On the contrary, humanity must partake of Him."
53. *Ibid.*
54. *Ibid.*, p. 43, Cf. p. 206: "Something constant and persistent, an inviolable particularity of his creaturely form, which cannot be effaced or lost or changed or made unrecognizable even in sinful man." Cf. also p. 285.
55. *Ibid.*, p. 276. On p. 277 Barth mentions as example the pagan Confucius, the atheist Feuerbach and the Jew Buber. Cf. also E. J. Beker, *Libertas, Een onderzoek naar de leer der vrijheid bij Reinhold Niebuhr en bij Karl Barth*, 1958, pp. 193f.

is all much more objective now. Barth does not hesitate even to speak of an objective state of affairs or to use ontological categories.[56] But at the same time, this objectivism is one of grace! It is not a neutral state of affairs, but the triumphant state which is due to the great victory of Jesus Christ. There is, as we noted above, an increasing emphasis in Barth's work upon christology, and no doubt all the "changes" are due to an increasingly more consistent application of the christological starting point. In the preface of *C.D.*, III, 4 (1951) Barth himself mentions the fact that many are searching for the real mystery behind the changes in his thinking. Barth's own answer is, "From my own point of view it is rather simply this, that gradually (though still full of joy in the battle!) I more and more got a taste for affirmations, positive answers, from which and by which man can live and die." That means a theology consistently based on christology. And that again means a theology in which the "triumph of grace" is the dominant feature. The light of Christ shines over everything. This becomes particularly clear in the anthropology:

> A decision has been made concerning the being and nature of every man by the mere fact that with him and among all other men He too has been a man. No matter who, or what, or where he may be, he cannot alter the fact that this One is also man. And because this One is also man, every man in his place and time is changed, i.e. he is something other than what he would have been if this One had not been man too. It belongs to his human essence that Jesus too is man, and that in Him he has a human Neighbour, Companion and Brother. Hence he has no choice in the matter. The question whether and to what extent he knows this Neighbour, and what attitude he adopts to Him, is no doubt important, but it is secondary to that which has already been decided, namely, whether he can be a man at all without this Neighbour. Once for all this question has been decided in the negative for every man. We cannot break free from this Neighbour. He is definitely our Neighbour. And we as men are those among whom Jesus is also a man, like us for all His unlikeness.[57]

In his lecture on "The Humanity of God" Barth goes even so far as to take up the old saying: "Anima humana naturaliter

---

56. Cf. *op. cit.* 132: "The ontological determination of humanity is grounded in the fact that one man among all others is the man Jesus."
57. *Ibid.*, pp. 133/34.

BASIC MOTIFS 213

christiana"![58] Of course this is not a statement on man in the abstract. It is a statement within the two watchwords of Blumhardt: "Jesus is Victor" and "You men are of God." In other words, it is an entirely christological-theological statement. Yet the statement is made, and that by the same man who once wrote the *Römerbrief!*

We find similar emphases throughout Barth's doctrine of reconciliation. In Jesus Christ the reconciliation between God and man has taken place once and for all. His death and resurrection have definitely changed the human situation. Yes, the *human* situation. For this does not hold true of believers only, but of every man. Says Barth:

> Note that it is not dependent on whether it is proclaimed well or badly or even at all. It is not dependent upon the way in which it is regarded, upon whether it is realized and fulfilled in faith or unbelief. The coming of the Kingdom of God has its truth in itself, not in that which does or does not correspond to it on earth.[59]

He then goes on to compare God with a king who has been pleased to confer an order on someone. Usually the man who has been singled out for such an honor will be in the happy position of being able to receive the distinction. But if this is not so, does it mean that the order has not been granted? The answer is quite clear. The same is true of the reconciliation in Jesus Christ. The conversion of all men to God has taken place in Him. That is the pure and acceptable word which is spoken in every age: all men are in Him the One and He the One is in them. True, "Not all hear this voice. Not all are obedient to Him. But it comes to all, it is relevant to all, it is said for all and to all, it is said clearly and acceptably enough for all."[60]

* * *

Once again we must ask whether this so-called shift of emphasis is sufficiently fundamental to change the *basic motifs* of Barth's doctrine of revelation and Holy Scripture. Is there now a place for an objective revelation, fixed in a written document? Would not such a "revealed-ness" correspond to the once-and-for-all-ness of the atonement?

---

58. *God, Grace and Gospel*, p. 48.
59. *C.D.*, IV, 1, 312.
60. *Ibid.*, p. 317.

Or does Barth's emphasis on the objective character of God's work in Jesus Christ mean no elimination at all of the original emphases? Is the so-called "objectivism of grace" entirely consistent with the former idea of divine freedom? May not this new objectivism be of an entirely different kind, so that it in no way endangers God's freedom? To use Barth's own terminology, is not God still the subject in spite of the once-and-for-all character of the reconciliation?

As we have already stated, we believe that the truth is found in the second series of questions. We do not believe that Barth's original doctrine would undergo a really fundamental change if he had to write it again today.[61] Of course we cannot deal here with the whole of his dogmatics. It must suffice to point to some aspects only. Yet we are of the opinion that the aspects to be mentioned are sufficient proof for our thesis.

* * *

In the first place there is the general fact that *traces* of the "objectivism of grace" are already found in the *first* volumes of the *Church Dogmatics*. True, they are not dominant there. Yet the mere fact of their presence is already a clear evidence that, at least for Barth himself, there is no fundamental change. So, for example, in his discussion of the phenomenon of religion and the problem of general revelation in *C.D.*, I, 2 he states: "When Christ appeared and died and rose again, the grace of God became event for all men, and all men are made liable for their being and activity, for their being and activity as it is revealed in the light of this event."[62] At first sight this seems to speak only of a noetic relation between Christ and man, for a few lines later Barth says that "this event is the self-revelation of the Truth, and therefore of the truth about man." In reality, however, these words have a much more ontological significance, as appears from the following quotation, taken from the conclusion of the discussion:

> The status of the Gentiles, like that of the Jews, is objectively quite different after the death and the resurrection of Christ.

---

61. Cf. also Henri Brouillard, *Karl Barth, Genèse et Evolution de la Theologie Dialectique*, 1957, I, 230ff. Especially 234/5: "sans renoncer a l'actualisme, Barth y ajoute une vue complémentaire. Il relie plus expressement l' acte divin de la révélation a ses organes humaines. Il explicite davantage l' idee d'incarnation: Verbum caro factum est . . . La Theologie de la Parole, sans cessar d'etre telle, s'elargit en une christologie conséquente."

62. *C.D.*, I, 2, 305.

By Christ the Gentiles as well as the Jews are placed under the heavens which declare the glory of God and the firmament which telleth his handiwork (Ps. 19:2). They are therefore to be claimed as "knowing God" (Rom. 1:21); but only to the extent that, like the Jews, they have not remained such (Rom. 1:28).[63]

Although the noetic aspect is still primary, yet the ontological aspect is becoming increasingly prominent. Already there is mention of an objective status of both Gentiles and Jews, i.e., of every man!

This is worked out in the following volumes, when Barth speaks of the man in the cosmos, "who confronted with God's revelation (long before he is aware of the fact, long before he has to make a decision, and whatever this decision may be) becomes, as the man confronted by God's revelation, objectively another man."[64] So this man is another man then, not only when he is actually confronted with the revelation. Barth explicitly says: "long before he is aware of the fact, long before he has to make a decision, and whatever this decision may be"! The fact that the revelation took place has objectively changed man, and the biblical witnesses, "as they proclaim God's revelation to man . . . claim man himself as the man already objectively changed by the event of revelation."[65]

It is not necessary to continue this line of the argument at great length. We find it everywhere, in particular also in the volume on Predestination. In this volume the aspect of the "objectivism of grace" has come increasingly to the fore, and to every careful reader it will be more than obvious that the anthropology, with its strongly ontological aspects, is nothing else than a very consistent outworking of lines drawn already in the doctrine of predestination. The paragraph on "The Election of Jesus Christ" opens with these words:

> Between God and man there stands the person of Jesus Christ, Himself God and Himself man, and so mediating between the two. In Him God reveals Himself to man. In Him man sees and knows God. In Him God stands before man and man stands before God, as is the eternal will of God, and the eternal ordination of man in accordance with this will. In Him God's plan for man is disclosed, God's judgment on man fulfilled, God's deliverance of man accomplished, God's gift to man present in

---

63. *Ibid.*, p. 307.
64. *C.D.*, II, 1, 110.
65. *Ibid.*, p. 111.

fullness, God's claim and promise to man declared. In Him God has joined Himself to man. And so man exists for His sake. It is by Him, Jesus Christ, and for Him and to Him, that the universe is created as a theatre for God's dealings with man and man's dealings with God. The being of God is His being, and similarly the being of man is originally His being.[66]

* * *

As we have seen in our brief discussion of Barth's anthropology, he goes so far as to say that even the unbeliever can discover *phenomena* of man's real nature. Does this not mean that, at least at this point, man does not need a new act of revelation, or, to say it in another way, that he can "have" revelation and actually has it in his anthropological knowledge? There can be no doubt that such an interpretation of Barth's words would mean a serious misunderstanding. However much he may stress the objective determination of man's nature by Christ's nature, yet he fully rejects all natural theology here. Emphatically he declares that when a man who does not know the man Jesus discovers phenomena, he has not yet discovered the real man. On the contrary, he only finds the "phantom man,"[67] for all these phenomena are in themselves and as such "neutral, relative and ambiguous."[68] Only he who knows man already, i.e., who knows him from revelation, can see in these phenomena "symptoms" of real man. But then it is clear that this anthropology is not built on knowledge of the phenomena, i.e., on philosophy, but on revelation! Here too it remains true that God first has to reveal to us who man is, before we can really recognize this man in the phenomena discovered and disclosed by philosophy or any other science.

* * *

But what about the former emphasis on God's *freedom* and *sovereignty*? Is that not partly neutralized by the new emphasis on the objective state of affairs which is due to Christ's death and resurrection? Is there sufficient place left for the element of sovereign freedom?

It is striking that even in the latest publications Barth still very strongly emphasizes the freedom of God. In his recent

66. *C.D.*, II, 2, 94. Cf. my *De Theologische Tijd bij Karl Barth*, 1955, pp. 100f.
67. *C.D.*, III, 2, 75.
68. *Ibid.*, p. 76; cf. pp. 78f.

Basic Motifs 217

defense of the "humanity of God" he explicitly declares that this never may be done at the expense of His Godness. God's humanity is His togetherness with men, but it is "a sovereign togetherness with man, based on Himself, and determined, delimited, arranged only by Himself."[69] A little further on he declares:

> And no doubt it is God's Godness which is the first and the fundamental thing that meets the eye as we view the existence of Jesus Christ attested in Holy Scripture. And God's Godness in Jesus Christ consists in God's being in Him sovereign subject, who speaks and acts: He is the One who is free, in whom all freedom has its ground, its meaning, its prototype.[70]

Of course "freedom" is not the only word. It is not an abstract freedom. That would mean some kind of *potentia absoluta*. "God's deep freedom is in Jesus Christ His freedom for love." God does not want to be and *is* not without man. That is the judgment God has once and for all given in Jesus Christ. Yet it is fully freedom. Therefore we can neither affirm nor reject *universalism*. As is well known, Barth has often been charged with an open or hidden doctrine of universalism. And indeed, we must admit that in the light of his "objectivism of grace" it seems impossible to avoid such a conclusion. Yet Barth has never committed himself here. Sometimes he seems to approach dangerously near it,[71] but he always keeps clear of any definite statement. Undoubtedly he does this because such a statement would destroy God's sovereign freedom. We have to leave this to Him. Only "one thing is sure, that there is no theological justification for setting any limits on our side to the friendliness of God towards man which appears in Jesus Christ."[72]

Moreover, the stress on the once-for-all character of the act of *reconciliation* in no way derogates from the freedom of God in Christ. Especially in this connection Barth has strongly emphasized that Jesus Christ *is* the subject of the reconciliation, today just as much as on Good Friday and Easter. That is actually the mystery which the event of Easterday revealed

---

69. *God, Grace and Gospel*, p. 37.
70. *Ibid.*, p. 39.
71. Cf. the three observations in *op. cit.*, pp. 49f.
72. *Ibid.*, p. 50. Cf. G. C. Berkouwer, *op. cit.*, pp. 262ff. (Chapter X, "The Universality of the Triumph").

and confirmed and brought into effect. On Easterday it appeared:

> Jesus not only did represent us (past), but he does represent us (present). He not only did bear the sin of the world. He does bear it. He not only has reconciled the world with God, but as the One who has done this He is its eternal reconciler, active and at work once and for all. He not only went the way from Jordan to Golgotha, but He still goes it, again and again. His history did not become dead history. It was history in His time to become as such eternal history — the history of God with the men of all times, and therefore taking place here and now as it did then. He is the living Saviour.[73]

One may not agree with Barth's view here, one may judge it to be a real confusion of the act or fact of the atonement and its eternal significance and effect, yet it is perfectly clear that here, too, Barth wants fully to maintain the freedom of God.[74]

* * *

It should not be forgotten that the *objectivism of grace* as found in the doctrines of anthropology and reconciliation and the *objectivism of a written revelation,* which would be revelation in the sense of revealed-ness, are not exactly of the same nature. The first objectivism is that of a *divine verdict* on man, apart from man's own subjective attitude. It is an entirely *forensic statement* which can never be grasped in unbelief, so that God cannot be "caught" by man. A written revelation, however, is an *objective concrete thing.* "Something" of God would be there, present for everyone, to be grasped by everyone apart from faith. God Himself would then be grasped, even in unbelief. But such is impossible. For this very reason the one objectivism is, according to Barth, fully compatible with God's freedom, yes fully presupposes it and bears it out, while the other objectivism violates and actually destroys it. Or to say it in Beker's words: "For Barth revelation rests too much in God's wide and sovereign good pleasure for man to

---

73. *C.D.,* IV, 1, 313/14.
74. Cf. *ibid.,* p. 317: "In Jesus Christ the alteration of the human situation did take place, and does take place today, the situation of Christians and of all men, the reconciliation of the world with God in Him who is the living Mediator between God and man in the power of His resurrection. What remains for them is high and appropriate and joyful and stringent enough — to welcome the divine verdict, to take it seriously with full responsibility."

dispose of it as *his* Truth. But at the same time this revelation is so widely triumphant that even people, without knowing or believing it, point to the 'Heilsgeschichte' and praise the triumph of God's grace."[75]

* * *

Here we come to the end of this study. Many important subjects have been touched upon, and some were dealt with extensively. In many cases no definite solution could be offered. Yet certain lines have become increasingly clear, and also the direction in which the solution has to be sought.

Of course, here too Reformed theology is surrounded by dangers. As Dr. Sasse says: We must traverse the narrow path "between the Monophysitism of Fundamentalists who failed to understand the human nature of the Bible, and the Nestorianism of modern Protestant and Anglican Theology, which sees the two natures but fails to find the unity of Scripture as a book at the same time fully human and fully divine."[76] The path is very narrow indeed. Sometimes it seems to be like the edge of a razor. And yet we should go on and never lose heart or slow down. However great our difficulties may be, one thing is sure: the Bible does not stand or fall with our difficulties. It is and remains the ever-living Word of the ever-living God. He will take care of His own Word.

And as for us, in all our theological study we should never forget to follow the advice of that great student of Scripture, John Calvin, who in his Geneva Catechism taught the children of his church the following answer to the question: How are we to use God's Word in order to profit by it?

> By receiving it with the full consent of our conscience, as truth come down from heaven, submitting ourselves to it in right obedience, loving it with a true affection, by having it imprinted in our hearts, we may follow it entirely and conform ourselves to it.[77]

---

75. E. J. Beker, *op. cit.*, p. 301; cf. also p. 98.
76. H. Sasse, "Inspiration and Inerrancy," *Reformed Theol. Review*, XIX, 47.
77. *The School of Faith*, The Catechisms of the Reformed Church, Translated and edited by Thomas F. Torrance, 1959, pp. 52/53.

INDEX OF AUTHORS

Aalders. G. Ch., 82, 83, 83n, 84, 90
Abba, R., 106n
Aesop, 91
Albright, W. F., 8, 9,
Alford, D., 37, 135n, 155n
Anderson, F. I., 91, 160n, 202n
Anselm, 13n
Athanasius, 110
Athenagoras, 117
Augustine, 68n, 110, 157, 170

Baillie, J., 67, 122n
Bannerman, D., 11
Barr, J., 206n
Barth, Peter, 40, 41
Bartmann, 193n
Bavinck, H., 10, 14n, 71n, 72n, 77, 83n, 85n, 110, 111, 112n, 141n, 142, 143, 145, 146, 147n, 148, 149, 152n, 154, 156, 156n, 162n, 163, 184, 187, 188
Beck, J. T., 63
Beker, E. J., 211n, 219n
Bengel, 141n
Berkhof, 1, 11, 13, 35, 65n, 130n, 151, 182n
Berkouwer, G. C., 50, 51, 74n, 82n, 90n, 103, 107n, 202n, 207, 217n
Bonaventura, 110
Bromiley, G. W., 161, 206
Brookes, J. H., 8
Broomhall, M., 143n
Brouillard, H., 214n
Bruce, F. F., 35, 36n, 106n
Brunner, Emil, 2, 43n, 47n, 52n, 101n, 105n, 119n, 124, 125n
Buber, M., 211n
Bultmann, R., 64, 89n, 90n, 119, 201n
Burmannus, F., 65n

Bijlsma, R., 118n, 141n, 156n, 159, 160n, 183, 184, 185

Calixt, G., 171
Calvin, J., 7, 8, 14n, 15-17, 38-47, 55, 63, 69, 70, 74, 77n, 97, 104, 110, 119, 138, 143, 144, 146, 147n, 148, 151, 166, 171, 176, 181, 188, 190, 202, 203, 205n, 219
Carnell, E. J., 115
Chrysostom, 147
Clavier, 45n
Cole, A., 167
Confucius, 211n
Cramer, J. A., 46n

Dankbaar, W. F., 143n
De Groot, D. J., 46n, 147n
de la Fontaine, 91
de Lerins, V., 171
de Santillana, G., 88n
Diem, H., 106n, 107n, 122n, 138n
Dillenberger, J., 90n
Dodd, C. H., 43n, 106n, 118n
Dooyeweerd, H., 86
Doumergue, E., 42, 45n
Dyk, K., 114n

Eck, J., 193n
Eichrodt, W., 99n
Ellis, Earle, 186n
Ellison, H. L., 99n

Feinberg, C. L., 8
Feuerbach, 211n
Fuller, R. H., 72n, 89n

Geelkerken, J. G., 101n
Gerrish, B. A., 44, 46n, 55n
Godet, 63

Gogarten, F., 2
Grosheide, F. W., 51, 53, 76n, 82-84, 90, 139n
Grotius, H., 171
Grimm, 91
Grunewald, 21

Haitjema, Th. L., 127
Hamer, J., 200n
Harrison, E. F., 98, 99n, 158n
Hebert, G., 43n, 72n, 96, 97, 101n, 118n, 122n
Henderson, I., 89n
Henry, C. F. H., 14, 98n, 158, 165n
Hepp, V., 83n
Heppe, H., 45n, 166, 182n
Herodotus, 9
Herrmann, W., 2
Hippolytus, 117
Hodge, C., 53n, 65n, 114n, 153
Hofmann, 63
Hollaz, 142
Hoskyns, E. C., 63n
Hunter, A. M., 106n

Irenaeus, 70, 170

Jacobs, D., 54n
Jerome, 157
Jewett, P. K., 119n
Johannine, 37

Kahler, M., 24, 25
Kantzer, K. S., 82n, 148n
Keller, W., 10n
Kleinknecht, 65n
Kohlbrugge, F., 202
Kooiman, W. J., 152n
Korff, F. W. A., 69n
Kuyper, A., 68, 69n, 71n, 143, 153n
Kuyper, F., 86, 87, 90n, 101

Lecerf, A., 67n, 98n, 181n
Lenski, R. C. H., 150n, 151n
Lipsius, R. A., 142n
Luther, 63, 104, 110, 144, 150, 151n, 171, 173, 190, 193

McConachie, J., 2n, 22n
McIntyre, J., 32
McNab, J. S., 207n

Mackay, J., 164
Manley, G. T., 100n
Marston, C., 10n
Meeter, H., 17n
Morris, L., 53n, 66, 150n
Murray, J., 35n, 124n

Newman, J. H., 119n
Niesel, W., 40, 41, 42, 145n

Orr, J., 75, 76, 99n, 100n, 111, 112n
Overduin, J., 164, 165n

Packer, J. I., 67n, 74n, 77n, 90n, 100n, 109n
Pannier, 45n
Parker, T. H. L., 17n
Patton, F., 11
Peter, J. F., 32
Polman, A. D. R., 90n
Pope Pius XII, 72n
Parrot, Andre, 10n
Preiss, Theo., 183n
Pringle, 40n

Quenstedt, 142, 157

Rahtmann, H., 141
Ramm, B., 201n
Ramsay, A. M., 107
Reid, J. S. K., 4n, 42, 43, 44, 45n, 46n, 72n, 141n, 144n, 157n, 160, 166, 175, 177, 178, 179, 183n, 205n, 206n
Richardson, A., 91, 92n
Ridderbos, H. N., 29, 30, 37, 68, 83n, 85, 89n, 184n, 185n, 186, 187n, 197, 198
Ridderbos, N. H., 83n, 92n, 93n, 100n, 101n, 182n
Ritschl, A., 2
Rolston, 130n
Rowley, H. H., 104n, 106n, 119n
Runia, K., 101n, 210n, 216n
Rusk, R. D., 90n

Sadolet, 145
Sasse, H., 65, 119n, 150n, 187, 219
Schaff, P., 65n, 162n
Schilder, K., 69n
Schippers, R., 26n, 34, 165n

Schlatter, A., 63
Schleiermacher, F., 2, 5, 123, 130
Schouten, W. J., 81, 82
Sevenster, G., 105, 106n
Spier, J. M., 86
Stibbs, A. M., 14n
Stonehouse, N., 35n, 100n
Strathmann, R., 26, 29

Tasker, R. V. G., 76n, 147n, 150n
Taylor, H., 143n
Tenney, M. C., 14n
Tertullian, 170
Thomas, Aquinas, 110
Thucydides, 8
Thurneysen, E., 1, 2
Toornvliet, G., 90n
Torrance, T. F., 219n

Unger, M., 104n, 119n

Vander Leeuw, G., 202n
Van Dyk, M. P., 83n, 200n, 202n
Van Leeuwen, J. A. C., 54n

Van Niftrik, G. C., 127n, 179
Van Oosterzee, 11
Voetius G., 182
Vogel, H., 95n
Vollenhoven, D. H. Th., 86
Von Harnack, A., 64n
Vriezen, Th. C., 106

Wallace, R. S., 40n, 43n, 69n, 74n, 205n
Walvoord, J. F., 82n, 104n, 119n, 148n
Wand, 43n
Warfield, B. B., 11, 30n, 32, 43n, 67n, 71n, 73n, 77n, 111n, 112, 113, 114, 115n, 152n, 153n, 157, 185, 197n
Watson, P. S., 144n
Westcott, B. F., 52, 197n
Wilkinson, B. G., 158
Wingren, G., 190n
Woolley, P., 35n

Zwingli, 181

INDEX OF SCRIPTURE

Genesis
1 — 100n, 102, 103
1:3 — 188
1:31 — 92, 102, 103
2 — 100, 102
2:2 — 197n
2:5-25 — 102
3 — 100, 101, 102
11:5 — 188

Exodus
12:37 — 166
20:4 — 83
24:10 — 69
25:22 — 194
33:10 — 203
33:18 — 203, 204

Deuteronomy
4:18 — 82
25 — 196
28:4 — 147n

I Samuel
4 — 194, 195, 204
5 — 204

II Samuel
23:2 — 56n

II Chronicles
4:2 — 84n

Job
37:18 — 87

Psalms
19:2 — 215
68 — 178
68:21-23 — 176
82 — 185
90 — 151n
97 — 197n
104:2 — 87

136:6 — 82
137 — 106n

Proverbs
8:27 — 82

Isaiah
1:11-14 — 204n
13:31 — 85n
34:14 — 85n
40:22 — 87
61:1 — 56n

Jeremiah
7:21-23 — 204n
17:9 — 195
31:12 — 70n

Hosea
6:6 — 204n
11:1 — 104n

Amos
5:21-25 — 204n
9:6 — 82

Micah
6:8 — 204n

Matthew
1:22 — 197n
2:15 — 197n
4:4 — 110, 197
4:6 — 110
4:7 — 110, 197
4:10 — 197
5:18 — 197
10:19, 20 — 36
10:40 — 19, 34, 38, 205
11:27 — 55
12:1-8 — 185
12:27 — 145
12:43 — 85

Luke
15:4 — 85
15:4 — 197n
19:5 — 197n
22 — 195
28:18 — 26

Mark
3:14 — 19
1:2 — 27
1:14 — 65
1:70 — 197n
4:4 — 110
4:8 — 110
4:12 — 110
4:21 — 20
10:16 — 19, 34, 38, 47, 205
10:22 — 145
18:31 — 20
24 — 25
24:27 — 20, 186
24:44ff. — 186
24:48 — 25, 33

John
1:1 — 68n
1:9 — 147n
1:14 — 27, 70, 74, 163
1:16 — 159
1:34 — 28
1:45 — 20
3:5 — 147n
3:16 — 162
4 — 143n
5 — 22
5:36 — 28
5:39 — 20
5:46 — 20
6:10 — 19
7:8-20 — 19

INDEX

7:18 — 181n
8:13ff. — 13
8:25, 26 — 14
8:46 — 80
8:58 — 80
10 — 185
10:35 — 109
11 — 78
14:26 — 30, 36, 154
15:26 — 30
15:27 — 27, 30
16:12-14 — 154
16:13 — 30
16:14 — 30
17:8 — 38
19:35 — 27n, 28, 96
20:21 — 19, 34, 38, 155n
20:30 — 33
20:31 — 28
21:24 — 27n, 28
21:25 — 33

Acts

1:8 — 25, 33
1:16 — 38, 197n
1:21, 22 — 27
1:22 — 28
2:32 — 28
3:15 — 28
3:18 — 197n
3:21 — 52n
4:24, 25 — 52n
4:25 — 38, 197n
4:33 — 28
5:30ff. — 28
5:32 — 30, 35
7:14 — 166
10:39 — 27
10:41ff. — 28
10:42, 43 — 31
13:31 — 29
13:34, 35 — 52n
15:28 — 35
17:18 — 28n
22:14 — 29
22:15 — 29
26:16 — 29
28:25 — 38, 197n

Romans

1:4 — 28
1:21 — 215
1:28 — 215
3:2 — 52n
10 — 54
10:8 — 197

I Corinthians

2:1-5 — 156n
2:6-16 — 140
2:10-14 — 150
2:12f. — 122n
2:13 — 161
2:14-15 — 149, 150
3:16-18 — 150
4:7 — 71
7:9 — 176
7:25 — 53n
12:3 — 145
13:12 — 41
15:8f — 29
15:14 — 28
16:14 — 66n
16:16 — 66n

II Corinthians

3 — 139
3:4-18 — 139
3:16-18 — 149
3:17 — 140
4:6 — 147
5:1 — 47
5:7 — 40, 41, 47
5:16 — 76
5:20 — 20, 53

Galatians

1:8 — 53

Ephesians

3:18, 19 — 37
4:11 — 19

Philippians

2:10 — 85

Colossians

1:19 — 159
2:9 — 159

I Thessalonians

2:13 — 156n, 162, 198

II Timothy

3 — 131, 135, 138, 155, 190

3:14-17 — 131
3:15-17 — 112, 197, 205
3:16 — 78, 141n, 154

Hebrews

1:1-2 — 51
1:5f. — 197n
1:6 — 52n, 197n
2:3 — 27n
2:13 — 197n
2:14 — 73
2:17 — 73
3:7 — 38, 197n
4:3 — 197n
4:4 — 197n
4:12 — 80
4:15 — 74
5:5-6 — 197n
6:4 — 147n
7:26 — 75
9:26 — 51
9:28 — 51
10:15 — 27n
10:30 — 197n

I Peter

1:10, 11 — 31
1:10-12 — 155
1:11 — 51, 52n, 56
1:21 — 70n
5:1 — 27n

II Peter

1 — 135, 138, 154, 190
1:2 — 154
1:8 — 154
1:16 — 27n, 148n
1:16-18 — 155
1:19-21 — 131
1:19-21 — 197
1:21 — 37, 66, 78, 113, 138, 154
3:16 — 54

I John

1:1ff. — 27
4:2, 3 — 145
5:8 — 148n

Revelation

18:2 — 85n
22:18, 19 — 56

www.ingramcontent.com/pod-product-compliance
Lightning Source LLC
Chambersburg PA
CBHW070312230426
43663CB00011B/2094